WILFRED BION, THINKING, AND EMOTIONAL EXPERIENCE WITH MOVING IMAGES

Being Embedded

Kelli Fuery

LONDON AND NEW YORK

First published 2019
by Routledge
2 Park Square, Milton Park, Abingdon, Oxon OX14 4RN

and by Routledge
711 Third Avenue, New York, NY 10017

Routledge is an imprint of the Taylor & Francis Group, an informa business

© 2019 Kelli Fuery

The right of Kelli Fuery to be identified as author of this work has been asserted by her in accordance with sections 77 and 78 of the Copyright, Designs and Patents Act 1988.

All rights reserved. No part of this book may be reprinted or reproduced or utilised in any form or by any electronic, mechanical, or other means, now known or hereafter invented, including photocopying and recording, or in any information storage or retrieval system, without permission in writing from the publishers.

Trademark notice: Product or corporate names may be trademarks or registered trademarks, and are used only for identification and explanation without intent to infringe.

British Library Cataloguing-in-Publication Data
A catalogue record for this book is available from the British Library

Library of Congress Cataloging-in-Publication Data
Names: Fuery, Kelli, author.
Title: Wilfred Bion, thinking, and emotional experience with moving images : being embedded / Kelli Fuery.
Description: Abingdon, Oxon ; New York, NY : Routledge, 2019. | Includes bibliographical references and index.
Identifiers: LCCN 2018004494 (print) | LCCN 2018005989 (ebook) | ISBN 9780429490811 (Master) | ISBN 9780429956034 (Web PDF) | ISBN 9780429956027 (ePub) | ISBN 9780429956010 (Mobipocket/Kindle) | ISBN 9781138590809 (hardback : alk. paper) | ISBN 9781138590816 (pbk. : alk. paper)
Subjects: LCSH: Psychoanalysis and motion pictures. | Motion pictures—Psychological aspects. | Bion, Wilfred R. (Wilfred Ruprecht), 1897–1979.
Classification: LCC PN1995.9.P783 (ebook) | LCC PN1995.9.P783 F837 2019 (print) | DDC 791.43019—dc23
LC record available at https://lccn.loc.gov/2018004494

ISBN: 978-1-138-59080-9 (hbk)
ISBN: 978-1-138-59081-6 (pbk)
ISBN: 978-0-429-49081-1 (ebk)

Typeset in Bembo
by Apex CoVantage, LLC

Printed and bound by CPI Group (UK) Ltd, Croydon, CR0 4YY

*For my partner in everything, Patrick;
And my very special sons, Morgan, Noah and Joshua.
With all my love*

CONTENTS

Acknowledgments *viii*

1 Introduction 1

2 A theory of thinking for moving image experience 24

3 Wandering reverie and the aesthetic experience of being adrift 48

4 Metaphor, the analytic field and the embedded spectator 69

5 Group experience, collective memory and dreaming 90

6 Linking, intentionality and the container-contained 112

7 Transformation: the idiomatic encounter and use of moving image as object 136

8 Being embedded: rhizome, decalcomania and containment 159

Index *178*

ACKNOWLEDGMENTS

Throughout the writing of this book, there were many moments where other minds helped me think through the complexities of Bion's work and facilitated the playful spaces that made the book possible. For helpful feedback on chapters, thanks to Carla Ambrósio Garcia, Ian Barnard and William Brown who have been gracious with their time, and critical friends in their comments. I would also like to thank the three reviewers whose support for this project was very motivating and, in particular, helped to identify the more diverse potential connections between Bion and Tomkins. In particular, I would like to thank all the authors whose writings on Bion I have had the joy to follow and read, as each has written with such enthusiasm and love for his work. Thanks to Charles Bath and Kate Hawes for their support and congeniality throughout this project.

In the early stages of this project, emerging ideas found their way into various conferences papers that were presented at the Association of Psychoanalysis, Culture and Society conference and Society for Cinema and Media Studies conference. My thanks go to the comments I received from colleagues that helped to make this book stronger. For embracing and pursuing Bion's ideas in the world of television, I thank my Dodge College students, whose own research has taken Bionian and Bollasian ideas into interesting areas of cultural identity politics.

I thank the following publisher for their permissions:

> Ogden, Thomas H. (2008). *Rediscovering Psychoanalysis: Thinking and Dreaming, Learning and Forgetting*. New Library of Psychoanalysis. pp. 90, 91, 93, 95, 97, 98, 100–3, 113. Routledge Publishers. Reproduced by permission of Taylor & Francis, LLC.

Finally, thanks to my Patrick who has always been the best container; and to Morgan, Noah and Joshua who have been so supportive of this work and the time and attention it has required.

1
INTRODUCTION

In "The Psycho-Analytic Study of Thinking", Wilfred Bion argues that his theory of thinking, whilst sharing similarities with other philosophies of thought, is different because "it is intended, like all psycho-analytical theories, for use" (Bion 1962b: 306). Similarly, in *Learning from Experience*, he writes "danger lies in being cramped by a theoretical system that is frustrating not because it is inadequate but because it is not being properly used" (Bion 1962a: 88). In that spirit, and ideally what will also come to be seen as a particularly Bionian approach, this book seeks to counter the frustrations a classical application of psychoanalysis has engendered within film and media studies. I explore the ways in which Bion's theory of thinking might work as a thematic frame of 'being embedded' that investigates different contexts for aesthetic and emotional experience with moving images, one that foregrounds the question of affect through a specific psychoanalytic point of view. This very specific frame is to explore the validity of Bion's 'theory of thinking' by examining in detail its varying components, so that a different application of psychoanalysis for the study of moving image experience might emerge. It also looks closely at the vital correlation Bion emphasizes between thinking as a psychic apparatus and the sensoria of lived emotional experience by discussing some of his core concepts together with other thinkers whose works are relevant for his theory of thinking.

Bion, an object-relations psychoanalyst, offered an approach that set out to examine our reactions to different and new experiences in everyday life by developing a theory of thinking that observed and analyzed affective, emotional experience. It was essential for Bion that his theoretical model was to be used in practice, because as noted above, there is the invitation to question previous uses and inadequacies of psychoanalytic theory and to determine which model can be used better, particularly for film and media studies. In terms of what counts as 'better', Bion offers a warning, stating that whilst all 'helpful endeavors' have a wish to improve things, he does not "imply that it is 'nicer' or 'pleasanter'. Whether it is 'better' is a matter of opinion which each individual has to arrive at for himself: his opinion and *only his* [or hers]" (1962a: ii, italics original). Bion's invitation is to present the usefulness of psychoanalysis in a new light, one that investigated the importance of emotional turbulence, to identify difference within its approaches and models. This book takes up such an invitation and presents a study of moving image experience through the context of a Bionian psychoanalytic frame.

In the clinical psychoanalytic world, Bion's life work is well known, as are his departures from Freudian and Lacanian approaches (see Civitarese 2012, 2014; Ferro 2009, 2015; Grotstein 2007, 2009, 2014; Ogden 2008, 2009). Antonino Ferro and Giovanni Foresti have noted that "[a] major change in psychoanalytic thinking in the last few years has been the transition from a concentration on mental contents to an attention to the development of instruments that permit weighing, feeling and dreaming" (2013: 380). Bion's theories differ from classical approaches on key psychoanalytic points, including dreaming as unconscious waking dream thought, of the intersubjective analytic situation (also referred to as the analytic field), of reality and everyday life, and even of the contact between body and mind, each offering very different and highly fruitful perspectives on lived experience. Yet very little of his work has entered into the field of visual culture, which is surprising given the high degree of promise Bionian psychoanalysis contains for the analysis of moving images, as an art form and as aesthetic experience. Psychoanalysis and visual culture have a long, formative history together, particularly with regard to theories of spectatorship and gender identification, so it is even more surprising when one notes that he remains one of the ten most popular and most cited authors in his field,[1] yet he remains relatively unheard of within film, television or wider screen studies.[2]

Bion's many works formulated a comprehensive theory of thinking as an outcome of processing the experience of emotion, or sensory data through the development of significant concepts, or models. At the start of his *Learning from Experience*, he comments that his focus rests "with emotional experiences that are directly related both to theories of knowledge and to clinical psychoanalysis, and that in the most practical manner" (1962a: n.p.) demonstrating that the integral relationship between psychical and physical experience was to form the foundation of his methodology. Ferro and Foresti further observe, with regard to Bion's theory of thinking, that it is a notion which is "addressed in greater or lesser depth, in almost all his writings" (2013: 361), and Thomas Ogden echoes this observation, referring to Bion's theory of thinking as his lifework, spanning over 40 years and all involving "an effort to develop one aspect or another of that theory of thinking" (Ogden 2009: 90). Bion's contributions to psychoanalysis mark a shift from the classical emphasis on pleasure and drive gratification and one's ability to conform to social reality, by emphasizing the activity and structure of thinking as a necessary response to feeling and dreaming everyday lived experience. Yet both models explore relationships with sensations of satisfaction and frustration. Bion similarly shares interest with Sigmund Freud on the importance of one's relationship to and perception of reality, where each psychoanalyst viewed mental functioning as key to the development of the human psyche. As Ogden (2009: 91) notes, their respective viewpoints on the formation of this relationship were quite different.

> Freud's principles begin with the search for pleasure in the discharge of instinctual tension (the pleasure principle) and end with the perception of, and the capacity to adapt to, reality (the reality principle).... [Bion's theory of thinking] begins not with instinctual pressure but with lived emotional experience in the real world, and ends with thinking and feeling that experience.

The differences between Freud and Bion go even further, deviating on the theory of dreams and on the conception of the unconscious. "[F]or Freud (1911), the unconscious is characterized by an 'entire disregard for reality-testing" while, for Bion (1967), "without [unconscious] phantasies and without dreams you have not the means to think out your problems" (Ogden 2008: 12). Bion foregrounded the confusing, challenging and painful emotional experiences we have with other people and new situations within his models, believing that only through an increased "capacity for suffering" can there be a hope "to decrease pain itself" (Bion 1963: 62).

As the reader will no doubt have experienced, or come to experience in the reading of Bion's work, his terms are perplexing because, as Gérard Bléandonu has noted, they run "the risk of being reduced to a meaningless jargon of catchphrases" (1994: 2). These terms – intersubjectivity, alpha function, unconscious waking thought, container-contained, reverie, concept of O, attacks on linking – are the significant models that work as the cumulative instruments which form his theory of thinking, and also come together to offer a framework for how thinking works as an affective psychic apparatus, why it is necessary, and what happens when it works and doesn't work effectively. Bion intended such concepts to act as models to help people use them for their own purposes; Bléandonu notes, "[Bion] always maintained that his writing should be forgotten in order that each reader might discover its meaning within themselves" (1994: 2). As such, I discuss these key Bionian terms in separate chapters within the wider contexts of moving image criticism in order to locate his ideas as broadly as possible for considerations of spectatorship and use of moving images within cultural experience. At key points, I use close textual analysis of cinema, television and other visual examples to show how his psychoanalytic notions offer the reader the opportunity to "discover meaning within themselves". Each concept is introduced theoretically and at length in order to highlight the relevance of different aspects of Bion's theory of thinking, not just in themselves but how they might relate in broader terms to different, yet relevant areas of scholarship. This is to place Bion in context with non-psychoanalytic work, and within reach of relevant issues pertaining to film and media studies.

Ferro and Foresti refer to Bion's theory of thinking as "the successful outcome of two mental processes: *the formation of thoughts* and *the evolution of the apparatus required to cope with them*" (italics original, 2013: 365). Ogden has organized these key elements of Bion's theory of thinking into four principles of thinking, which he terms as 'mental functioning', which I discuss in greater depth in Chapter 2. Briefly these themes are:

1) thinking is driven by the human need to know the truth – the reality of who one is and what is occurring in one's life;
2) it requires two minds to think a person's most disturbing thoughts;
3) the capacity for thinking is developed in order to come to terms with thoughts derived from one's disturbing emotional experience; and
4) there is an inherent psychoanalytic function of the personality, and dreaming is the principal process through which that function is performed.

(Ogden 2008: 11)

In response to these principles identified by Ogden, the following chapters discuss in detail the different elements that come together to form Bion's theory of thinking in an attempt to similarly organize these Bionian themes within the context of moving image experience. The aim is to show how these principles of thinking relate to other relevant, interdisciplinary works that already have links and presence as conceptual frameworks within moving-image studies. Therefore, whilst Bionian theory is the primary focus of this book, I have also included key writings from other scholars to show how Bion's ideas connect with well-known and well-studied themes (such as memory, affect, perception, aesthetics and embodiment) within moving-image studies. This embraces Ogden's second principle of Bion's theory of thinking – that thoughts need another mind (thinker) in order for thinking (and growth) to occur. This principle is returned to throughout the book again and again, as in a very ambitious way, I have tried to embed Bion's ideas within related concerns of other writers' work with the hope that other, more fruitful links, might evolve through the other minds that read, think and dream this book.

On 'Being Embedded'

The term 'being embedded' is intentionally abstract, yet used to immediately invoke an awareness of social relationships with other people and other environments. It is used here to both denote and acknowledge the link between thinking and emotional experience within the lived reception of visual culture, specifically here with moving images. To embed, as defined in the *Oxford English Dictionary*, is to perform an action that fixes something "firmly in a surrounding solid mass of some solid material". Within linguistic contexts, 'to embed' refers to meaning which is "contained within a larger sentence; subordinate" via a clause or word equivalent. In both definitions, the action of embedding is concerned with a negotiating relationship. It requires an interaction (or at the very least, an awareness) between the inside and outside of material, the practices involved in location of meaning – a word within a sentence, or an object within a more comprehensive amount of matter, similar to being a member of a family. Regarding the noun 'embeddedness', the *OED* draws on a 1937 reference emphasizing a more conceptual recognition of relativity between matter and of ourselves, "when we know how to deal with the erst-while novelty, when we have 'got it taped', it falls into embeddedness and becomes, or engenders, a part of ourselves". There is a strong sensibility to the word 'embeddedness' that connects the psychical element of awareness of one's own mind and the physical, biological element of one's own bodily activity, or put another way, the potential receptivity between one's inner and outer worlds, present in these *OED* definitions.

'Being embedded' is a concept that encapsulates Bion's idea of ambiguity – another significant aspect in his writing. As Bion advises in the introduction to *Learning from Experience* (1962a: n.p.), he deliberately uses ambiguous terms "because of the association" they invoke and that he wishes "the ambiguity to remain" so that the plurality of a word's meaning can be carried into whichever way it is used and conceived. It is due to the ambiguous quality of the term 'embedded', that the experience of 'being embedded' within a place, a relationship, a feeling, a memory is widely shared. People are able to speak to what 'being embedded' might mean for themselves, as individuals, without it being prescriptive or duplicitous for another person. I use the concept of 'being embedded' to illuminate the sensory and perceptive aspects of aesthetic interpretation that rest at the core of lived, thinking and feeling experience. It incorporates Ogden's four principles of mental functioning and identifies the self-reflexive sensation of emotional experience that results through psychic growth.

The overarching premise of the book is to present the difference of a Bionian psychoanalytic approach, one that foregrounds emotional experience over classical agencies of pleasure, to return to the field of psychoanalysis as a productive and rewarding method for the study and analysis of moving image experience. I argue that moving images are tools which we use to help us think our emotional experience, which reflects a more focused attention on the intersubjective aesthetic experience present in contemporary psychoanalytic theory (Ferro and Civitarese 2015; Civitarese 2010, 2012, 2014; Ferro 2011; Kohon 2015; Hagman 2005). I explore this in further depth in Chapter 4, discussing the difference and developments since 1970s film theory. By way of context, the central premise of examining intersubjective aesthetic experience within the specificity of Bionian psychoanalysis is to emphasize how his theory of thinking offers a more phenomenological psychoanalytic model that discusses affect in ways classical psychoanalytic film theory has not. In very broad strokes, this echoes Alain de Botton's and John Armstrong's claim in *Art as Therapy* (2016: 5):

> Like other tools, art has the power to extend our capacities beyond those that nature has originally endowed us with. Art compensates us for certain inborn weaknesses, in this case of the mind rather than the body, weaknesses that we can refer to as psychological frailties . . . art (a category that includes words of design, architecture and craft) is a therapeutic medium that can help guide, exhort and console its viewers, enabling them to become better versions of themselves. A tool is an extension of the body that allows a wish

to be carried out, and that is required because of a drawback in our physical make-up. A knife is a response to our need, yet inability to cut. A bottle is a response to need, yet inability, to carry water. To discover the purpose of art, we must ask what kind of things we need to do with our minds and emotions, but have trouble with.

This project is not capable of (nor interested in) making the grand theoretical claim that Bion's ideas apply to all art, or all aesthetic experience. Rather the intention here is to think where Bion's ideas might permit a rethinking of moving image experience, specifically to readdress the older, more traditional psychoanalytic models that were used to consider cinematic spectatorship. 'Cinema' has become a word that is so increasingly varied in what it includes in terms of aesthetic experience, that I use de Botton and Armstrong's statement to underscore my intention throughout this book, which is to explore how a Bionian approach might allow us to look more closely at our aesthetic experience *with* moving images, and specifically move away from a focus on pleasure to thinking about a moving image experience that is difficult and challenging.

Moving images, as time-based art, offer templates, spaces, times, methods and practices, affect – that change over time and across cultures, yet all of which are utilized as structuring presences to enable us to think through our lived emotional experiences. They are external tools that create and engender affect for our inner worlds, and as such have immense power to bring about transformative self-experience. The pull or seduction of cinema, television and gaming is to realize an outcome (one that is either desired or attained) which is this transformative self-experience – satisfaction or modification of inner frustrations. Even though within Bion's psychoanalytic models we cannot know these inner thoughts directly, we can speculate that our use (rather than just our watching) of moving images helps to facilitate inner change within our external environments. Christopher Bollas writes, "[i]n a way, the experience of the aesthetic moment is neither social nor moral; it is curiously impersonal and even ruthless, as the object is sought out as deliverer of an experience" (Bollas 2011: 11). I discuss Bollas's theory of the transformational object and transformative experience in greater depth in Chapter 7, but note here the strong echo of Bion's own theory of thinking, which as Ogden puts it, "we are throughout our lives in need of other people with whom to think" (2008: 21). Of these 'other people' and 'objects' that are sought out as deliverers of experience, we might include the stories offered in the moving images of cinema and television.

Being Embedded contributes to what Agnieszka Piotrowska has referred to as "different psychoanalytical thinking" (2015: 5), and to the recent works that have explored object relations psychoanalysis within visual culture (specifically through the writings of Melanie Klein and D. W. Winnicott), but it differs in its reference and examination of previously overlooked, but highly pivotal, thinkers such as Bion, Bollas, Civitarese, Ferro and Ogden. The consequences of this is that many fruitful pathways with other writers attentive to similar terrain are equally passed over. To this end, Chapter 2 incorporates the ideas of Silvan Tomkins and the more contemporary works of Adam Frank, Elizabeth Wilson and Teresa Brennan – where relevant – so that not only are Bionian concepts introduced and explored within moving image culture, but that they are shown to have connections with sister subjects and modes of inquiry. Given that much of Bion's own writing has concentrated on emotional experience (1962a, 1965, 1967, 1970), a theorization of thinking as an affective structure within moving image experience provides a fresh avenue for psychoanalytic theory within visual culture. The goal is to diversify what is included within the reference to 'psychoanalytic' film theory through presenting Bion's ideas in conjunction with other relevant and related theorists on affect in moving-image studies. It responds to Piotrowska's question, "what makes a spectator feel touched by a film in such a physical way without an actual embodied touch taking place?" (2015: 6), by placing a specific emphasis on Bionian approaches.

Different psychoanalytic thinking and cognitive film studies

Another reason for writing this book was a growing desire to create a bridge, a link, between 'psychoanalytic film theory' and the cognitive studies approach for the examination of emotional experience and affect within moving images. To me, there didn't seem to be as large a gap as cognitive studies theorists suggested between psychoanalytic and cognitive perspectives, particularly within the models offered by the object-relations school (inclusive of Bion, Winnicott, and later Bollas, Ogden, Ferro and Civitarese, amongst others). Yet, I found myself in agreement with assessments that noted the problems of a psychoanalytic approach that predominantly focused on drive gratification, or agencies of pleasure (equally an issue for Tomkins (1962) between motivation and drive discussed in his four-volume *Affect, Imagery, Consciousness*) in the study of moving image experience. In my reading of Bion, and other object relations psychoanalysts, however, there appeared to be many points of convergence between cognitive studies and object-relations psychoanalytic approaches rather than the widely identified differences.

Carl Plantinga's and Greg M. Smith's *Passionate Views: Film, Cognition and Emotion* (1999) was a key work that ushered in fresh attention regarding the impact of cinema on the individual viewer and collective audiences through a specific and structured examination of emotion within cognitive studies approaches, to discuss "some of the ways films cue emotional responses" (1999: 1). Plantinga and Smith articulate what I regard as a very strong and readily apparent connection between cognitive and contemporary psychoanalytic perspectives, with each area of study both agreeing on the fact that "cinema offers complex and varied experiences; for most people . . . it is a place to feel something" (1999: 1). Throughout their introduction, a key connection for the cognitive film scholar is made very clear – "a cognitive perspective on emotions asserts that cognitions and emotions work together" (1999: 3), and this founded the examination of the processes involved with emotional experience and emotional expression. This assertion reads very much like a Bionian (and therefore psychoanalytic) claim. Bion (1962b: 302) put forward his revolutionary 'theory of thinking' wherein he makes plain the very same connection between cognitions and emotions:

> It is convenient to regard thinking as dependent on the successful outcome of two main mental developments. The first is the development of thoughts. They require an apparatus to cope with them. The second development, therefore, is of this apparatus that I shall provisionally call thinking. I repeat – thinking has to be called into existence to cope with thoughts.

I discuss this further in Chapter 2, but it is immediately apparent that Bion's reversal of the normative way of considering the flow between thoughts and thinking echoes the position of cognitive film scholars who view cognitions and emotions as working together. Bion further writes that a "central part is played by alpha-function[3] in transforming an emotional experience" (Bion 1962a: 42). The term 'alpha function' is Bion's phrase for the 'mental structure' or 'psychic apparatus' that he believes is necessary for processing sensory data into thoughts. Put simply, 'alpha function' refers to the process of 'thinking', or we could use Plantinga's and Smith's term 'cognitions', which is the mechanism for processing emotional experience. Ogden has also observed this connection, "[w]hen Bion speaks of thinking, he is always referring to thinking and feeling, which he views as inseparable aspects of a single psychological event" (2008: 13). As such, *Being Embedded* examines 'emotional experience' as 'thinking and feeling', both psychic and physical, through cinema, television and documentary web-based work, and considers its role in establishing and determining what it is to feel or to think oneself as 'embedded'. I draw attention to the importance of Bion's key psychoanalytic ideas (reverie, aesthetic experience, group experience, container/contained and transformation) to the aesthetic and emotional experience of moving images, that is, what it is to know and reflect on experience of thinking and feeling images. This concentration on the interrelationship between lived experience, and the necessity for thinking it, is where I see strong connections rather than divisions existing between cognitive studies and contemporary psychoanalytic film studies.

Plantinga and Smith further discuss the purpose and function of emotions as they result from formal elements of cinema (through genre, narrative and other aspects of film style), as well as how they work within and between moving images (rather than look specifically at the representations of emotions themselves – similar to what Katrin Pahl (2015: 2) has referred to as 'the logic of emotionality'). This logic belongs to cognitive processes that, through a series of underlying structures, "help us to evaluate our world and react to it more quickly". The experiences that occur with moving images are argued to offer profound meaning, echoing the social aspect of emotionality that acknowledges the interrelationship between cultural mythologies, ritualistic practices and ideological forces that both shape and regulate mind and body behaviors. Bion (1962a: 8) claims,

> [t]o learn from experience alpha-function [thoughts that are able to be processed as thoughts through thinking] must operate on the awareness of the

emotional experience; alpha-elements are produced from the impressions of the experience; these are thus made storeable and available for dream thoughts and for unconscious waking thinking.

Again, this is a Bionian statement on the link between thinking and emotional experience.

It is through his guiding principle of 'experience' where Bion clearly differs from Freud, particularly with regard to the purpose of emotions. For Bion, emotional experience is how we learn, how we process our world and the happenings that occur within it. The word 'experience' also appears in another of his seminal works, *Experiences in Groups* (1961), making clear that the affective power of thought and emotion is dependent on 'experience' either through learning or interaction with another mind, person, or object. It is very different from the Freudian view, which Plantinga and Smith note "[f]or Freud, the emotions are a discharge phenomenon" (1999: 12). There is even further agreement between the cognitive scholars/philosophers and Bionian psychoanalysis – that the emotions that one experiences within cinematic contexts are the same as those one experiences in other everyday life situations. Within this context, while there is room to agree with Smith and Plantinga that Freud may be "a poor choice for a theory of emotions" (1999: 13), the same cannot be said for the psychoanalytic writings of Bion and other relational psychoanalysts. Not in the least because Bion's work is "centrally concerned with emotions", much like cognitive philosophers and cognitive psychologists. Bion's treatment of many psychoanalytic terms and concepts (emotional and aesthetic experience, dreaming, projective identification, for example) are ambiguous and divergent from Freud's, and therefore have a history of prior meaning and large body of scholarship to work against. However, as Joan and Neville Symington write, "psychoanalysis seen through Bion's eyes is a radical departure from all conceptualizations which preceded him. We have not the slightest hesitation in saying that he is the deepest thinker within psychoanalysis – and this statement does not exclude Freud" (2008: xii), and in this way once more finding some agreement with the cognitive scholarship of Plantinga, Smith and their contemporaries.

Indeed, psychoanalysis has had a volatile past within cinema and media studies, often dismissed as a foundational component of 'Grand Theory' (Bordwell and Carroll 1996) within other cognitivist studies of cinema. If I place an emphasis on the resistance from cognitive film scholars, it is perhaps because theirs has been the loudest, most dismissive of voices regarding the potential and promise psychoanalysis as a discipline holds for the study of the moving image. Even in the works of Wilson, Sedgwick (2003), Frank (2015) and Tomkins (1962) (discussed further in Chapter 2), psychoanalysis is still recognized as possessing potentiality and opportunity for divergent thought. Indeed, particularly in Wilson's *Psychosomatic: Feminism and the Neurological Body* (2004), there is a return to the very early works of Freud in order to reorient and reorganize contemporary emphases and perspective on the interrelationship between biology and psychology of lived experience. My aim with *Being Embedded* is to challenge the presupposition that psychoanalysis no longer holds promise for film or media theory, and to argue that its validity for the examination of affect remains strong. The conceptualization of 'being embedded' acts as a watchword to contain the different emphases relational psychoanalysis places on affective emotional experience. I would like to take a moment, a slight digression as it were, to illustrate via brief example, the complexities of histories and theories of psychoanalysis in and on film. My example comes from an oft-cited author, but not often in a pro-psychoanalysis context, or one that supports such theoretical approaches regarding film. However, the manner in which Bordwell utilizes the concept of 'embedding' below illustrates the relevance of the term as identified in my own project, even if ultimately, this is not how I conceive of the term 'being embedded' throughout the book.

Bordwell has noted the important 'principle' of embedding within cinema as a narrative device, which I see as also reflective of the sharing of emotional experience involving two minds, both within and between the screen and the viewer (further discussed in Chapters 3 and 4 as the intersubjective field). Bordwell, in an analysis of the structure of the dream writes of the embedded story:

> The principle of embedding has been found in cinema too, of course. *Citizen Kane* is the classic example, since it embeds recounted stories (most of the flashbacks), a written text (Thatcher's memoirs), and even a film-within-a-film (*News on the March*). Many of the embedded stories we find in films are presented as flashbacks, and those are usually motivated by a character recalling or telling another character about past events.[4]

What Bordwell identifies is undeniably psychoanalytic when read through Bionian terms regarding the practice of embedding – Kane's flashbacks, being motivated by a need to share a story – these are indicators of Bion's concept of "thoughts in search of a thinker" (1970: 117), a phrase that short-handedly encapsulates the relational psychoanalytic approach, and which Ogden's four principles treat to varying degrees. Ferro and Foresti discuss the purpose of '*visual flashes*' (2013: 368, italics original) in terms of Bion's theory of '*waking dream thought*' (2013: 366, italics original). The authors note that for Bion, we dream all the time, while awake, while asleep, and that the "dream is the result of the operations carried out by the *alpha function* on all the perceptual and sensory data in which we are normally immersed" (2013: 366, italics original).

Bordwell writes further:

> we have all experienced dreams, so the film [Christopher Nolan's *Inception*] can appeal to folk wisdom about them. I suggest, though, that the purpose of the film is not to explore the dream life but rather to use the *idea* of exploring the dream life to justify creating a complex narrative experience for the viewer. *That* is the purpose of the film; the dreams operate as alibis.

Ferro and Foresti point out that it is not possible to have conscious, direct access with waking dream thought and that it is precisely such things as visual flashes – we can include Bordwell's reference to Kane's flashbacks here – that occur when we are not able to effectively 'think' (or process) lived sensory data into emotional experience. In *Elements of Psychoanalysis* (1963), Bion speaks of dream thoughts and their importance within the analytic situation. He maintains, as per Freud, that a dream is formed of manifest and latent content, and that through psychoanalysis one can achieve more sophisticated interpretation. However, Bion continues to shift importance to the *presence* of the dream thoughts rather than the recounting of the dream narrative.

> The statement that a patient has had a dream is ordinarily sufficient evidence to allow work to proceed, but not if we need to know what has occurred when the patient says he has dreamt. For example, if a patient complains that he had a pain in his leg are we to suppose, in the appropriate setting, that he *dreamt* he had a pain in his leg or ought we to consider that sometimes the manifest content of a dream is a series of pains rather than a series of visual images that have been verbalized and linked by narrative?
>
> *(1963: 23)*

Bordwell's position on the embedded story within *Inception* – using dreams as alibis for complex viewer experience – is remarkably similar to Bion's view of dream narratives as alibis for dream thoughts. In both instances, the alpha elements of the dream thoughts, the 'pictograms' (or visual images) that are eventually expressed, appear to be more concerned with relating physical, that is biological, sensation and emotional experience rather than offering 'grand theory', and that each rely on the notion of embeddedness (as being a smaller, yet meaningful part of a larger structure) in order to form a meaningful narrative. Similarly, Wilson makes the point that as psychoanalysis and its theory grew more technical and sophisticated, its attention to biology attenuated. Bion's model offers the opportunity to return to an attentive state for the role and significance of the corporeal in the study of moving image experience.

In *Film Structure and the Emotion System* (2003), Smith writes, "[i]n psychoanalytic film criticism's discussion, there is a conspicuous absence of the word 'emotion' in favor of the terms 'pleasure' and 'desire' (2003: 174) and that "[p]sychoanalytic film theory fails to encourage specific explanations of filmic emotion in particular films" (2003: 194), which echoes much of the frustration with the psychoanalytic film theory that emerged from 1970s and 1980s Christian Metz and Laura Mulvey schools of criticism. The primary difficulty with Smith's position (and that of other cognitive studies scholars) however, is that it homogenizes psychoanalytic theory as belonging only to drive-gratification and psychosexual development – that is, the fulfillment of instinct and drives. Smith notes that his analysis "examines the foundations of those writings in the Freudian-Lacanian assumptions about emotion" (2003: 174), but there are other areas of psychoanalytic theory, such as Bion's, which have yet to find widespread influence within moving-image studies that share much in common with phenomenological approaches and emphases on lived experience, as well as the affective resonances of cognitivism (Grodal 2009; Plantinga and Smith 1999; Plantinga 2006, 2009) and film-philosophy (Sorfa 2014, 2016; Laine 2007, 2013, 2017; Sinnerbrink 2011; Sobchack 1992, 2004). This confluence is noted by other recent scholars, such as Piotrowska, who have spoken on the critical need for "the validity of different psychoanalytic thinking in the academy and elsewhere and on the belief that the notion of embodiment and the unconscious can be held together in one space" (Piotrowska 2015: 5). Piotrowska speaks to the sticky legacy of classical psychoanalysis as a rationale for why newer and more divergent theories of psychoanalysis have not been included in the recent turn toward studying emotion, embodiment and affect within moving-image studies. She looks to the historical influence of the post-1968 French film theory canon and the emergence of critique against Freudian–Lacanian methodology in tandem with the critical resistance to patriarchy in the mid-1970s, which "made psychoanalysis immediately sound like a reactionary and conservative system" (2015: 2); and yet, it is noted that there has always been a 'political dimension' to the applications of psychoanalysis within cultural (and culturally related) studies. Carla Ambrósio Garcia also counters the traditional psychoanalytic placement and interpretation of pleasure in her Bionian analysis of film as retreat, for "Bion, the retreat can be conceived as a space and time where the pleasure and the reality principles coexist, where neither is precedent nor necessarily dominant" (Ambrósio Garcia 2017: x). It is evident that a challenge to the traditional, classical models of psychoanalysis to examine emotional experience within moving image culture is not simply emerging but burgeoning.

Lisa Cartwright, in *Moral Spectatorship: Technologies of Voice and Affect in Postwar Representations of the Child* echoes this challenge of difference within psychoanalytic thinking, asking, "[w]hich psychoanalysis was taken up in feminist film theory, and what can we learn from revisiting some psychoanalytic notions and practices that were not?" (2008: 11). She indirectly responds to Smith's point that it is *film theory itself* that has not explored a wide enough range of psychoanalytic approaches that provides diversity in what becomes referred to as 'psychoanalytic film theory'. Cartwright accounts for the trends and attentions to the subject via Lacanian theory and its emphasis on the structuring of language and "construction of theories of femininity and representation in the late 1970s" (2008: 12). Cartwright provides a clear revisionist analysis of why classical psychoanalytic models – again privileging Freud and Lacan – were adopted and prevailed over more contemporary object relations approaches. The result is an alternative map for a film theory that has the potential to introduce and develop a psychoanalytic emphasis which does not rest on drive-gratification but looks to incorporate the significance of object relations and emotional experience, "[f]ilm theory's writing off of object relations theory and self psychology . . . left us without a variety of useful concepts and tools that object relations theory offered" (2008: 13). Cartwright discusses the work of Melanie Klein, René Spitz, André Green and Silvan Tomkins, foregrounding the much-overlooked concepts of splitting, projective identification, affect, and intersubjectivity. *Being Embedded* continues to discuss overlooked areas of relational psychoanalysis to continue to further film theory's attention and use of psychoanalysis as a diverse area of thought that addresses and contributes to the intersubjective value of moving images and their potential for the study of emotional and transformative self-experience through Bion's theory of thinking.

Relational psychoanalysis, with its concern and emphasis on affect and emotional experience, is a pertinent methodology for the recent interest in sensation and emotions within cinematic experience. In *Film Theory: An Introduction through the Senses* (2015), Thomas Elsaesser and Malte Hagener write, "[f]rom the very beginning, inventors, manufacturers, artists, intellectuals, educators, and scientists asked themselves questions about the essence of cinema: Was it movement or was it interval? Was it single image or series? Was it capturing place or was it storing time?" (2015: 1), recognizing in their work that the questions of cinema have now moved away from what cinema *is* to what cinema *does*. Indeed Elsaesser and Hagener's book concentrates on the sensory potentiality and affect within cinematic experience, but it neglects to include any reference to or discussion of Tomkins or Bion on the question of affect. In their historical survey, and specifically in the chapter "Cinema as Eye – Look and Gaze", the emphasis rests on traditional rather than contemporary models of psychoanalysis. We might ask, if the same classical psychoanalytic models from Freud and Lacan are being used to offer a history of the theorizing of the cinematic look and gaze, rather than turning more toward relational psychoanalytic considerations of the practices and affects involved in watching, looking and more significantly feeling, as found in Bion's, Tomkins's and other relational psychoanalytic scholarship, how different can the discussion become, how much can it develop? By using Bionian and other relational psychoanalytic theory to consider cinematic experience, I outline how an object-relational approach provides new conversations about the emotional and lived experience that results from the relationships between cinematic spectatorship, aesthetic experience and affect.

Bion's psychoanalytic models are important for film analysis and the theorization of emotional experience as his work offers a very different psychoanalytic perspective to that of Freud and Lacan, and therefore demands that we rethink and reorganize the psychoanalytic foundations that were used by writers such as Smith in their theorization of emotional experience. At the same time, my aim is to incorporate Bion's work within the larger context of debates that are already at work within the discipline, such as the frames of memory, affect, emotion, phenomenology and embodiment. This is to highlight the growing prevalence of Bion's work, and to indicate its validity for current issues and concerns. The additional methods and approaches will be drawn from scholarship in the areas of continental critical theory, visual culture theory and phenomenology, to support and converse with Bion, predominantly the work of Klein, Winnicott, Tomkins, Bollas, Ogden, Ferro and Civitarese, Maurice Halbwachs (1992), Hannah Arendt, Vivian Sobchack, Lacan, Gilles Deleuze and Felix Guattari (2014). These particular thinkers are appropriate for two main reasons. The first is that any discussion of 'being embedded' is about how we relate to objects, the sociality of the relationships, how they are received and shared through thought and taken into our inner worlds, resulting in emotional and transformative experiences. Moving images invariably excel in this form of relating, not simply because we all use them and talk about them, but because, as tools they work as vehicles which contain thoughts and feelings that we might not be in a position to do so ourselves, yet in connection with them, may have the opportunity to do so. Linking Bion to the work of the theorists listed above echoes this agenda of relating, linking and embedding. To use the most influential object relations theorists shifts the usual focus of psychoanalysis away from drive gratification and sexuality to that of affect and emotional experience. To make sure such ideas are not discussed within a disciplinary vacuum, it is necessary to include other well-known scholars in related fields of critical film and visual studies to show the shift in approach and to develop their own positions regarding 'thinking and feeling' experience.

Secondly, Bion in particular has not been given the same amount of attention in the humanities, especially film studies, despite his suitability for any study of affect via the moving image and cinematic experience. His work is significantly influenced by the ideas of Klein, notably her theory of projective identification which was particularly influential on his theory of thinking as involving two minds, "[t]he activity we know as 'thinking' was in origin a procedure for unburdening the psyche of accretions of stimuli [sensory data] and the mechanism is that which has been described by Melanie Klein as projective identification" (1962a: 31). Her inclusion in the book is apposite for this reason. Winnicott's ideas, the most popular and most cited author in object-relations psychoanalysis,[5] and also the most well-known within film theory (see Lebeau 2008; Kuhn 2013), are often aligned with Bion's, particularly on the issues of transitional phenomena and transitional objects, the holding environment (Winnicott's term) and the container/contained (Bion's term). These are not equivalent terms or experiences and, as with 'being embedded', need to be carefully worked through to distinguish their relativity between insides and outsides, inclusions and exclusions. I discuss this turn to object-relations approaches that privilege Winnicott's work within film studies in Chapter 2.

Embedded and embodied – a relational distinction

'Being embedded' is used therefore to refer what Tarja Laine has called "a carnal understanding of cinema" (Laine 2017: 1), that is to the concurrent experience of being both psychically and physically engaged with our immediate environments, which speaks to the resonance of experience that belongs to both the mind and the body when we are embedded within and between moving images. Her work on emotions, aesthetics and carnality speaks to the complexity of the types of emotional experience that occur in the reception of film, television and visual media. 'Being embedded' is different from cinematic immersion and distinct from the interpellation of ideologies involved with identification, which I discuss further in Chapter 4, referencing Daniel Yacavone's *Film Worlds: A Philosophical Aesthetics of Cinema* (2015). The notion of 'being embedded' nevertheless draws on both immersive and identifying experiences in order to be understood as a meaningful and shared affective happening. We might say that being embedded is a convergent process that involves attachment and relating, echoing much of the recent writing and interest within cinema and media studies which considers the role of thinking and its relationship to the perceptive and expressive elements involved in moving image experience. The concept of embeddedness that I develop throughout this book involves equal attention toward the aesthetics of our physical lived experience of the artistic and imaged worlds on screen, as much as it involves the sensuous and psychical responses to them. In this way it is indebted to Luke Hockley's 'third way' of watching cinema, which "involves becoming aware of the ways in which viewing a film is a whole-body experience; in other words, that it is both a conscious and unconscious process . . . entering into a cinematic experience where meaning does not reside in the narrative of the film, nor its audio-visual structure, but instead rests in the experience of the film" (2014: 81). Whilst there are elements of embodiment that 'being embedded' aligns with, there are also important points on which it differs, specifically the intersubjective field of cinematic experience, which is discussed at length and in more Bionian (rather than Jungian) terms in Chapters 2 and 3.

The examples referred to throughout this book have been chosen to work through and develop my own conceptualization of 'being embedded' as a model through which to situate the relevance of Bion's theory of thinking as an instrument to evaluate emotional experience regarding the reception of moving images. In doing so, I aim to challenge fixed notions of what 'being embedded' might mean and accept Bion's implicit invitation to modify the frustrations of psychoanalysis as "a theoretical system that is frustrating not because it is inadequate but because it is not being properly used". The different and relevant aspects of relational psychoanalytic ideas, such as Bion's theory of thinking, place vision and the practice of looking within displaced contexts in order to create resistance in the normative applications of psychoanalytic approaches to readings of film and theorization of film spectatorship. In some places, I make a lengthier analysis of moving image experience in order to challenge traditional positions within film theory, or to make clear the relevance of complex psychoanalytic concepts, such as the key components of Bion's theory of thinking.

In Chapter 2 I present a more detailed overview of Bion's theory of thinking to what has been discussed so far, paying attention to the definition of key terms that come together to form Bion's overall model. I show why Bion's theory of thinking is revolutionary for the study of emotional experience with moving images, and demonstrate how object-relations theory has begun to adopt a more prominent place within moving image scholarship. This book and its emphasis on the significance of Bion's (and other object-relations psychoanalysis) for moving image analysis is made possible by earlier works that have ventured into similar terrain. As such, I address key works within film studies that have engaged with other object-relations psychoanalysts (predominantly Winnicott and Klein), which emphasize sensory experience with moving images, and which have indirectly laid the foundations for the more mystical and abstract thinking found in Bion's work.

Terms such as 'emotional experience', 'aesthetic experience' and 'intersubjective field', are defined and within the context of the overall notion of 'being embedded'. These terms form the basis of the following chapters and are examined separately, supported by close study of moving image experience and within the context of other relevant non-psychoanalytic scholarship.

Chapter 3 explores Bion's concept of reverie, which he claims is the foundation of mental functioning and which makes possible psychic growth. Reverie, if it occurs in an open manner, represents the capacity for two minds to receive each other and think together in fruitful ways that permit psychological development. I use Bion's concept of reverie to discuss the spectator's "intersubjective aesthetic experience" within the cinematic encounter, which is one of the most important differences between a classical and relational psychoanalytic approach. As mentioned above, one of the most significant changes that has occurred within the field of psychoanalysis is that there has been a shift from examining content (of a dream – but we can also say of the text) to a stronger consideration of what occurs through the formal aspects of a given situation "that permit weighing, feeling and dreaming". I look at formal elements in Nicolas Roeg's *Walkabout* (1973) and *Don't Look Now* (1978) to discuss the function and existence of reverie within moving images, and to identify how formal aspects (such as soundscapes) serve to facilitate intersubjective experience.

Intersubjective aesthetic experience is a phrase that responds to this shift, focusing on what happens in the in-between conversing and constructing of sensory experience, and it is one of Bion's key notions in his theory of thinking. It is also a phrase that looks at dreams in terms of a process, where dreaming can be said to occur as "unconscious waking dream thought", meaning that dreams are not simply left to nighttime experience, but they are always occurring within our minds, awake as well as asleep (Bion 1962a). Bion viewed dreaming as the essential process through which one's psychoanalytic function of the personality is performed. Freud, who viewed dreams as central to the formation of the scientific method of psychoanalysis, also placed dreams and their analysis as the key to access unconscious thoughts, feelings and wishes and make them conscious. This Freudian approach formed the basis of traditional film theory's theorization of the spectator, where the film's images, its narrative structure and politics of representation were said to facilitate unconscious identification (Mulvey 1975; Metz 1982). This chapter discusses Bion's alternative theory of the dream, and the subsequent activity of dreaming as being more indicative of how external (conscious) sensory data is used for the processing, or the (unconscious) dreaming, of emotional experience. As Ogden (2009: 113) puts it:

> Dreaming – whether on our own or with another person – is our profound form of thinking: it is the principal medium in which we do the psychological work of being and becoming human in the process of attempting to face the reality of, and come to terms with, our emotional problems.

It is a claim of this chapter that such a modality of dreaming works similarly within cinematic spectatorship. These three terms, reverie, spacing and dreaming, are fundamental to Bion's theory of thinking and are introduced and discussed within the context of the theorizing of film spectatorship in order to reignite the significance of psychoanalysis for the examination of lived, visual and emotional experience.

Chapter 4 discusses the function of metaphor within the analytic field. It was through a range of metaphors that Bion established his theory of thinking and this chapter takes up the particular revision put forward by Ferro and Civitarese (2015) in order to show how Bion both connects to and departs from classical psychoanalytic approaches, advancing the use and function of metaphor. This includes both the metaphors of 'being embedded' and the metaphors used to create Bion's theory of thinking (what I have referred to as the 'key elements' of his theory above). The chapter retains the Bionian relational approach, but considers the historical use of metaphor as it was used within Metz's Lacanian film theory. This is done in part to acknowledge the significant and lasting contribution to the development of Lacanian psychoanalytic approaches regarding metaphor, as well as the history and evolution of psychoanalytic film theory, and to note the contributions from other interpretative, relational models. To reorganize psychoanalytic film theory so that it includes and foregrounds Bion is not to throw the baby out with the Lacanian bathwater.

Chapter 5 takes up the emphasis present in the *OED*'s definition: "when we know how to deal with the erst-while novelty, when we have 'got it taped', *it falls into embeddedness and becomes, or engenders, a part of ourselves*" (italics added). I compare Maurice Halbwachs's theory of collective memory (1992) and Bion's theory on group experience, to examine 'being embedded' as a collective and individual experience. As previously mentioned, experience was an important word for Bion, who viewed it as something dependent on and demanding of sensory life, which is pivotal to the formation of thoughts and the apparatus of thinking. His book *Experiences in Groups* (1961) laid down the foundation for the later development of his theory of thinking, and was concerned with the observation of group life and interpretations of behavior that group life gave rise to. He wrote, "[t]he group is essential to the fulfillment of man's [*sic*] essential life" (Bion 1961: 53), placing the group as a lived experience for all participants. The experience that is moving image spectatorship and reception shares many elements of group life as outlined by Bion and, in different but related ways, by Halbwachs. Despite these two authors' works offering different disciplinary approaches (sociology and psychoanalysis), each author evaluates the role and structure of society in determining the experience of belonging in group scenarios and circumstances.

I refer to two examples that reflect different elements of group experience. *Force Majeure* (Östlund 2014) is a Swedish film which presents the tensions within groups and their expectations through Halbwachs's social framework of the family unit; and the web-based documentary work, *Prisons Memory Archive* (McLaughlin 2010), which represents the potential of Bion's theory of the work group "refer[ing] not to the people who constitute the group but to the mental activity in which they are engaged" (Symington and Symington 2008: 126) – a particular quality of documentary practice as an observational and archival form. I have chosen these examples from different media because each embodies the thinking of Bion's and Halbwachs' study of groups, in that they observe and resist interpretation of the group, whilst at the same time offer analysis of what the function of groups and memory is within group experience. I include Annette Kuhn's (2010) conceptualization of visual media as memory work and memory texts, situating the examples as individual and collective practices of experience (and being embedded) because Kuhn's treatment of memory parallels Freud's notion of the 'dream work'. Through this Freudian echo of 'dream work', I connect Bion's and Halbwachs's study of groups to their respective perspectives of dreaming and return the discussion to how a relational model of psychoanalysis – which foregrounds thinking and sensory experience – disrupts previous frustrations of classical psychoanalytic approaches.

In Chapter 6 I draw on the phenomenological concepts of intentionality, appearance and lived experience as they relate to the current consideration of 'thought' within Bionian theory. Perception and expression are two recent key phenomenological issues in film theory and cultural studies, that have considered embodied (that is, lived physical experience) cinematic spectatorship, overturning the dominance of ocular-centrism as a theory of spectatorship. Informed by the work of prominent film scholars Allan Casebier (1991), Sobchack and Laura Marks, I discuss the corporeal sensorium of cinematic experience alongside a Bionian interpretation of the body's role in emotional experience. Bion viewed the connections we have with other human beings as emotional 'links' and I continue to examine 'emotional experience' as a psychical activity. This is so that emotional 'links' are seen as also referring to knowledge that is not just of the psyche but also of the soma. Emotional experience is not limited to ideational contexts – a position that draws on the work of Marks, but also connects with the affect theory of Tomkins, Sedgwick and Frank, and the neurology studies of Wilson. Symington and Symington (2008: 30) note the importance of perception regarding sensory data, which they argue engenders emotional experience: "[perception of sensory data] is the link between one human being and another. It is out of this emotional experience that either a thought process or a discharge will take place". Marks, in her discussion of intercultural cinema and the memory of senses, makes reference to the disruptive power of film and its capacity to craft new "patterns of sense experience" and "new cultural organizations of perception" (2000: 195). I view Marks's claim, that "senses are a source of social knowledge" (2000: 195), as reflecting Bion's understanding of 'links' constituting emotional experience, "emotional experience cannot be conceived of in isolation from a relationship" (Bion 1962a: 42), here highlighting his intention to interpret 'relationship' as not simply being a psychical connection to another person, but also involving physical sensoria of sight, touch, taste, smell and sound. Our interactions with each other and with the world around us, inclusive of sense encounters, shape and establish emotional experience, and

I discuss the phenomenological concept of intentionality through the writings of Edmund Husserl, Maurice Merleau-Ponty and Hannah Arendt to explore points of similarity between theories of lived experience that involve physical and psychical sensory responses to cinema. Bion's container-contained model is outlined here, responding to the interrelationship between linking, emotion and thought.

Chapter 7 introduces Bion's pivotal concept of O, which encapsulated his ideas of transformation. It is a term that Bion developed toward the end of his career, where he grew more interested in the relationships between experience and interpretation. In *Transformations* (1965: 4), his first discussion and outline of the concept of O, he writes: "[a]n interpretation is a transformation", and through this simple statement established the importance of interrelationship for his idea of O. For Bion, O is not able to be known directly: "it is useful to regard it as a thing-in-itself and unknowable (in Kant's sense) it is denoted by the sign O" (1965: 13). He goes on to equate his concept of O with a theory of transformations, which forms a series of interpretations that indicate the processing of emotional experience. Put in the context of moving image experience, we might think of this in terms of our desire to share our experience of a film that has moved us to tears, or scared us senseless, made us feel good or, even more interestingly, compelled us to share our boredoms with equal fervor. Our experiences, in order to *become* (to become meaningful, to become realized) require thinking. We recount parts of the film's story, or we might discuss the quality of performance given by the actors, and we may even cross-analyze previous films of the same director or writer. In any case, the experience of film is shared via interpretation, through conversation, through comparison of physical responses (I cried/laughed/was moved by this film, not by that one, etc.), perhaps through writing, or even in the watching of other films. Bion states his theory of transformations as follows, "the total analytical experience is being interpreted as belonging to the group of transformations, denoted by the sign T [for total]. The experience (thing-in-itself) [cinema, for example] I denote by sign O" (1965: 13). In this chapter, I discuss Bion's concept of O and his theory of transformations alongside Bollas's concepts of idiom and the 'Transformational Object' to consider the potential of the moving image to work as an object that triggers transformational self-experience.

The term 'object' is used within the psychoanalytic context of being both a material and immaterial thing-in-itself. Cinema, as a medium and as phenomena, is referred to here as 'object' (and all is parts), equally acknowledging its materiality and immateriality that we consciously and unconsciously 'use' – all the while knowing it has a variable purpose (artistic, entertaining, revolutionary, technical), a timeframe, and reason for existing. I also use 'object' to refer to sensory data (more specifically the audio-visual unity of moving images) as is used within the Bionian frame of 'realizations', that is things that incur meaning or value through our thinking of them. Chapter 7 continues by exploring Michelangelo Antonioni's *Blow-Up* (1966) as a case study to consider both Bion's and Bollas's theory of transformation within the context of moving image experience. I argue that moving images, as external objects, require interpretation in order for transformational self-experience (and perception of it) to occur. Thomas's (David Hemmings) enlarged photographs adopt a specific meaning for him because of how he perceives them and thinks them. *Blow-Up* follows Thomas's journey of incertitude regarding the dead body he believes he sees in the photographs, mirroring the spectator's journey from interpretation to transformation. What becomes important is much less about the veracity of the dead body, than it is about the transformative self-experience Thomas's belief about the body brings about. Through a close analysis of *Blow-Up*, I discuss the 'use' of cinema, placing films as 'external objects' that are then used to engender transformative self-experience within the spectator, unconsciously and consciously. This echoes the emphasis of object-relating psychoanalytic theory, privileging what it means "to 'live a life in the world of objects'" (Winnicott in Bollas 1989: 26). I argue that cinema is used as a transformational object as per Bollas and outline how such 'use' of the moving image reflects our capacity to "articulate and elaborate [our] personality idiom(s)" (Bollas 1989: 8).

Continuing on from Bion's more mystical idea of O (as an unknowable but felt, or embodied and affective, 'truth'), the final chapter examines 'being embedded' within the Deleuzian and Guattarian concepts of rhizome, decalcomania (tracing) and affect. I interpret 'being embedded' as a 'becoming', that is as a never-completed action, which sees 'being embedded' as possessing rhizomatic qualities. 'Being embedded', or becoming embedded, can be observed through projective identifications (as sharings and as splittings), transference, or a set of transferences, as cartographies and decalcomanias that are governed by a range of variables including time, territory and surfaces. Rhizomes are about connection and utility, about life and object value. Their intricate composition, '*the tracing should always be put back on the map*' (Deleuze and Guattari 2014: 13), mirrors Bion's placing of thoughts as transfers or tracings that need to be 'put back into' thinking. I conclude with a return to the initial presentation of Bion's theory of thinking as offering a new method within psychoanalytic film theory, one that considers emotional experience as a central preoccupation in relational psychoanalysis.

Notes

1 This statistic, first noted by Ferro and Foresti (2013), remains true. Also significant is that it is the work of object relations psychoanalysts who hold the majority of top ten citations in the electronic database *Psychoanalytic Electronic Publishing* – for most popular and most cited.
2 Carla Ambrósio Garcia's recently published *Bion in Film Theory and Analysis* (2017) is the notable exception, which I discuss throughout this book.
3 See Chapter 2 where I write in greater depth on Bion's theory of thinking. For further reading within a clinical practitioner context, see Symington and Symington (2008) who dedicated a chapter to the alpha function.
4 Bordwell, David. "*INCEPTION; or, Dream a Little Dream within a Dream with Me*", Observations on Film Art. August 6th, 2010.
5 As of January 2016, Winnicott was the second most cited author in the *Psychoanalytic Electronic Database* (with over 1000 citations). His article 'Transitional Objects and Transitional Phenomena' is listed as the most popular by viewing (listed as having 2953 views in 2015).

References

Ambrósio Garcia, C. (2017). *Bion in Film Theory: The Retreat in Film*. Abingdon, UK: Routledge.
Bion, W.R. (1961). *Experiences in Groups and Other Papers*. New York: Basic Books.
Bion, W.R. (1962a). *Learning From Experience*. London: Tavistock.
Bion, W.R. (1962b). The Psycho-Analytic Study of Thinking. *International Journal of Psycho-Analysis*, 43, pp. 306–310.
Bion, W.R. (1963). *Elements of Psycho-Analysis*. London: William Heinemann Medical Books.
Bion, W.R. (1965). *Transformations: Change From Learning to Growth*. London: William Heinemann Medical Books.
Bion, W.R. (1967). *Second Thoughts*. London: William Heinemann Medical Books.
Bion, W.R. (1970). *Attention and Interpretation: A Scientific Approach to Insight in Psycho-Analysis and Groups*. London: Karnac Books.
Bléandonu, G. (1994). *Wilfred Bion: His Life and Works, 1897–1979*. Translated by C. Pajaczkowska. New York: Other Press.
Bollas, C. (1989). *Forces of Destiny: Psychoanalysis and Human Idiom*. London: Free Association Books.
Bollas, C. (2011). *The Christopher Bollas Reader*. Hove, East Sussex: Routledge.
Bordwell, D. and Carroll, N. (eds.) (1996). *Post-Theory: Reconstructing Film Studies*. Wisconsin: The University of Wisconsin Press.
Cartwright, L. (2008). *Moral Spectatorship: Technologies of Voice and Affect in Postwar Representations of the Child*. Durham: Duke University Press.
Casebier, A. (1991). *Film and Phenomenology: Toward a Realist Theory of Cinematic Representation*. Cambridge: Cambridge University Press.
Civitarese, G. (2010). *The Intimate Room: Theory and Technique of the Analytic Field*. London and New York: Routledge.
Civitarese, G. (2012). *The Violence of Emotions: Bion and Post-Bionian Psychoanalysis*. London and New York: Routledge.
Civitarese, G. (2014). *The Necessary Dream: New Theories and Techniques of Interpretation in Psychoanalysis*. Translated by Ian Harvey. London: Karnac Books.
de Botton, A. and Armstrong, J. (2016). *Art as Therapy*. London: Phaidon Press.
Deleuze, G. and Guattari, F. (2014). *A Thousand Plateaus: Capitalism and Schizophrenia*. Translated by B. Massumi. Minneapolis: University of Minnesota Press, 1987.
Elsaesser, T. and Hagener, M. (2015). *Film Theory: An Introduction Through the Senses*. 2nd edition. London and New York: Routledge.
Ferro, A. (2009). *Mind Works: Technique and Creativity in Psychoanalysis*. Translated by P. Slotkin. London and New York: Routledge.
Ferro, A. (2011). *Avoiding Emotions, Living Emotions*. Translated by I. Harvey. Hove, East Sussex: Routledge.
Ferro, A. (2015). *Torments of the Soul: Psychoanalytic Transformations in Dreaming and Narration*. Translated by I. Harvey. Hove, East Sussex: Routledge.
Ferro, A. and Civitarese, G. (2015). *The Analytic Field and Its Transformations*. London: Karnac Books.
Ferro, A. and Foresti, G. (2013). Bion and Thinking. *The Psychoanalytic Quarterly*, 82 (2), pp. 361–391.
Frank, A. (2015). *Transferential Poetics, From Poe to Warhol*. New York: Fordham University Press.
Freud, S. (1911). Formulations on the two principles of mental functioning. In J. Strachey (ed. and trans.) *The Standard Edition of the Complete Psychological Works of Sigmund Freud* (vol. 12). London: Hogarth Press.

Grodal, T. (2009). *Embodied Visions: Evolution, Emotion, Culture and Film.* Oxford: Oxford University Press.
Grotstein, J. (2007). *A Beam of Intense Darkness: Wilfred Bion's Legacy to Psychoanalysis.* London: Karnac Books.
Grotstein, J. (2009). *But at the Same Time and on Another Level: Psychoanalytic Theory and Technique in the Kleinian/Bionian Mode.* London: Karnac Books.
Grotstein, J. (2014). *Who Is the Dreamer, Who Dreams the Dream? A Study of Psychic Presences.* Abingdon, UK: Routledge.
Hagman, G. (2005). *Aesthetic Experience: Beauty, Creativity, and the Search for the Ideal.* Amsterdam, NY: Rodopi Editions.
Halbwachs, M. (1992). *On Collective Memory.* Translated by L.A. Coser. Chicago: The University of Chicago Press. Original work published 1925.
Hockley, L. (2014). *Somatic Cinema: The Relationship Between Body and Screen – a Jungian Perspective.* Abingdon, UK: Routledge.
Kohon, G. (2015). *Reflections on the Aesthetic Experience: Psychoanalysis and the Uncanny.* London and New York: Routledge.
Kuhn, A. (2010). Memory Texts and Memory Work: Performances of Memory in and With Visual Media. *Memory Studies*, 3 (4), pp. 298–313.
Kuhn, A. (ed.) (2013). *Little Madnesses: Winnicott, Transitional Phenomena and Cultural Experience.* London: I.B. Tauris.
Laine, T. (2007). *Shame and Desire: Emotion, Intersubjectivity, Cinema.* Oxford: Peter Lang Publishers.
Laine, T. (2013). *Feeling Cinema: Emotional Dynamics in Film Studies.* London: Bloomsbury Academic.
Laine, T. (2017). *Bodies in Pain: Emotion and the Cinema of Darren Aronofsky.* New York and Oxford: Berghahn Books.
Lebeau, V. (2008). *Childhood and Cinema.* London: Reaktion Books.
Marks, L. (2000). *The Skin of the Film: Intercultural Cinema, Embodiment, and the Senses.* Durham: Duke University Press.
McLaughlin, C. (2010). *Recording Memories From Political Violence: A Film-Maker's Journey.* Bristol: Intellect Books.
Metz, C. (1982). *The Imaginary Signifier: Psychoanalysis and the Cinema.* Translated by C. Britton, A. Williams, B. Brewster and A. Guzzetti. Bloomington and Indianapolis: Indiana University Press.
Mulvey, L. (1975). Visual Pleasure and Narrative Cinema. *Screen*, 16 (3), pp. 6–18.
Ogden, T. (2008). Bion's Four Principles of Mental Functioning. *Fort Da*, 14, pp. 11–35.
Ogden, T. (2009). *Rediscovering Psychoanalysis: Thinking and Dreaming, Learning and Forgetting.* London and New York: Routledge.
Pahl, K. (2015). The Logic of Emotionality. *PMLA*, 130 (6), pp. 1457–1466.
Piotrowska, A. (2015). *Embodied Encounters: New Approaches to Psychoanalysis and Cinema.* London and New York: Routledge.
Plantinga, C. (2006). Disgusted at the Movies. *Film Studies*, 8, pp. 81–92.
Plantinga, C. (2009). *Moving Viewers: American Film and the Spectatorship Experience.* Berkeley: The University of California Press.
Plantinga, C. and Smith, G.M. (1999). *Passionate Views: Film, Cognition and Emotion.* Baltimore, MD: Johns Hopkins University Press.
Sedgwick, Eve Kosofsky. (2003). *Touching Feeling: Affect, Pedagogy, Performativity.* Durham: Duke University Press.
Sinnerbrink, R. (2011). *New Philosophies of Film: Thinking Images.* London: Continuum Press.

Smith, G.M. (2003). *Film Structure and the Emotion System*. Cambridge, UK: Cambridge University Press.
Sobchack, V. (1992). *The Address of the Eye: A Phenomenology of Film Experience*. Princeton, NJ: Princeton University Press.
Sobchack, V. (2004). *Carnal Thoughts: Embodiment and Moving Image Culture*. Berkeley: University of California Press.
Sorfa, D. (2014). Phenomenology and Film. In Branigan, E. and Buckland, W. (eds.) *The Routledge Encyclopedia of Film Theory*. London and New York: Routledge.
Sorfa, D. (2016). What Is Film-Philosophy? *Film-Philosophy*, 20 (1), pp. 1–5.
Symington, N. and Symington, J. (2008). *The Clinical Work of Wilfred Bion*. London and New York: Routledge.
Tomkins, S. (1962). *Affect, Imagery, Consciousness, Volume 1, The Positive Affects*. New York: Springer.
Wilson, E. (2004). *Psychosomatic: Feminism and the Neurological Body*. Durham: Duke University Press.
Yacavone, D. (2015). *Film Worlds: A Philosophical Aesthetics of Cinema*. New York: Columbia University Press.

Filmography

Blow-Up (1966). Directed by Michelangelo Antonioni.
Force Majeure (2014). Directed by Ruben Östlund.

2
A THEORY OF THINKING FOR MOVING IMAGE EXPERIENCE

Bion's theory of thinking infuses every aspect of his psychoanalytic approach and is instrumental for the reorientation of psychoanalysis for film theory, one that emphasizes affect and emotional experience. This chapter outlines its specific aspects, positioning it as a meta-structure for the book within relevant historical developments particular to object-relations psychoanalysis, highlighting the influence of Melanie Klein. The phrase 'moving image experience' has been chosen over 'film or cinema spectatorship' for the reason that in the constantly evolving digital mediascape of the 21st century, it is not constructive for my project to privilege film over television, or establish hierarchies between technologies and how they are used (even though I do draw most of my examples from cinema). Post-cinematic media is the closest term I see as identifying an inclusive aesthetic and receptive experience across visual media, but it does not foreground the primary reason we watch – which is to experience images and stories that affect us in their respective and specific ways. Further, the term 'post-cinematic media' asks that we attend to an awareness of the technology itself and the teleology of its emergence, which is not my intention here. In keeping with the Bionian frame which focuses on learning from experience, I prefer the phrase 'moving images' so that a discussion of aesthetic experience may emerge, that is how it might adumbrate one's awareness of, and orientation to reality. As I stated in Chapter 1, my aim is to introduce Bion's theory of thinking as a divergent psychoanalytic model as it applies to film theory, and to suggest that the inclusion of a Bionian psychoanalytic approach moves us more toward considering how moving images are used to transform inner psychic life, how we physically respond to the impact and affect of such aesthetics. Of course, this is a much larger project than the scope of this chapter, even this book; nevertheless, it is the start of a conversation in considering the application of Bion more broadly in film and media studies.

Using Ogden's four principles of mental functioning (set out in Chapter 1), I discuss how Bion's interrelated conceptualizations of thinking and lived experience move away from the cathectic emphasis within Freudian psychoanalysis, that is the motivation of libidinal energy, toward an attention on the motivation of feelings about the people and environments we relate to and associate with. Ogden's (2008) principles highlight the rationale behind Bion's theory of thinking as a cohesive model that concentrates on affect and emotional experience, which I argue, presents a core challenge to the dominance of classical psychoanalysis within theories of spectatorship and moving image experience. Following Adam Frank's work (2015), I discuss how object-relations psychoanalysis, specifically the Bionian model of emotional experience, links with Silvan Tomkins's study of affect. I acknowledge the growing body of work both within and outside film and media scholarship that has already broken ground for new psychoanalytic thinking, so that attention to object-relating and theories of 'being embedded' with moving images is possible.

Toward a (meta)theory of thinking

The origins of Bion's more comprehensive meta-theory of thinking are evident in his first major contribution to psychoanalytic theory, *Experiences in Groups and Other Papers* (1961). This book includes his clinical work on groups, wherein he develops a general theory of thinking by observing different types of group experience.[1] It was in this work that Bion began to associate thinking with experience, by observing a group's behavior and their capacity to work effectively. The more nuanced and detailed theory of thinking appears later in his journal article, "The Psycho-Analytic Study of Thinking" (1962b), which is repeated again (though with a different numerical layout) in *Second Thoughts* (1967). Here Bion writes more directly about the apparatus for thinking as a necessary development in order to cope with the (intra-psychic) pressure of thoughts that evolve into emotional experience of either satisfaction or frustration. Bion's method for group analysis was largely influenced by the work of Melanie Klein. Specifically, it was Klein's concentration on the psychotic defenses within mental functioning that Bion followed with great interest and saw as the foundation for all group life, observing that the psychotic parts of personality are more readily manifested within group experience than within individual analysis. Groups, more specifically group experiences, are so central to Bion's work – particularly with regard to how we learn from experience – that it is worth noting their role in the development of Bion's theory of thinking and how it illuminates our moving image experience.

To recall, Ogden's four principles of mental functioning are: 1) "the human need to know the truth"; 2) "it takes two minds to think one's disturbing thoughts"; 3) "thinking develops in order to cope with thoughts"; and 4) "dreaming and the psychoanalytic function of the personality" (2009: 91), which he uses to thread together the relevance and complexity of the metaphors constitutive of Bion's theory of thinking. Psychoanalytic theory has been criticized for lacking efficacy in its application in film and media studies due to its neglectful attention on how we use the aesthetic objects in our external worlds to create inner change, but as I show, Bionian psychoanalysis can be used to refute this argument. Ogden's four principles move beyond a cold-categorization of Bion's concepts and communicate a 'transferential poetics' (Frank 2015) that uncover the essence within thinking and emotional experience. Frank qualifies his use of poetics as being indicative of "compositional force, as consisting of powerful wishes about and images of how an audience will respond to a work; in this way *poetics always embed ideas* about emotional connection and disconnection" (2015: 2, italics added). Frank writes that feelings are key to how "we perceive things, people, ideas, other feelings" (2015: 24), and although he is referring to "*the compositional aspect of affect in perception*", he is inadvertently referring to Bion's theory of thinking. Bion, like Klein and Tomkins, "departed from Freud's writings . . . [and] emphasized the phenomenological qualities of affective or emotional experience and the place of phantasy and everyday theory in moment-to-moment living and thinking" (Frank 2015: 24). Ogden's principles, then, structure and navigate *the compositional aspect of affect in* [Bion's theory of] *thinking*, or if we are to combine Frank and Ogden, *the compositional aspect of affect in 'being embedded'*, which includes the intersubjective field of thinking, emotion, perceptions, embodiment and biological responses to such affective transmissions, all which I discuss below.

Bion does not see psychoanalysis as a specifically separate individual experience (an important political intervention in classical psychoanalytic theory); rather it is constitutive of the analyst and the environment itself, that evolves into the intersubjective field (Ogden 1994; Ferro and Civitarese 2015).[2] The intersubjective analytic field (discussed further in Chapter 4) denotes the area and experience regarding the transmission of affect as much as it notes a relationship and a context. It is not simply the physical or geographical location of two people (such as the analyst's office – although it includes this); it includes 'atmosphere' – a transmission of affect (Brennan 2004). Transmission itself is an intersubjective activity – incorporating physical responses to another's behavior, language or movement – a biological and neurological transferential poetics. Bion saw thinking and its function in terms of inter- and intra-subjective experience, which I discuss later. Brennan argues that despite the psychosocial origins in the transmission of affect, our feelings of hate, love, anxiety and grief (emotions that are thought and felt concurrently) are "also responsible for bodily changes . . . the transmission of affect, if only for an instant, alters the biochemistry and neurology of the subject. The 'atmosphere' or the environment literally gets into the individual" (2004: 1). Frank also notes that affect theory, specifically Tomkins's approach, connects well with more recent works that have returned to the questions of biology and psychology and their interaction within "technological and media landscapes" (Frank 2015: 4).

In "Like-Minded" (2012), Frank and Elizabeth Wilson (2012) argue that the affective realm has been discussed in various contexts and for differing purposes, but that overall, such works, particularly those that engage with emotion and affect within cultural and political contexts, share a glaring neglect of Tomkins's four volume *Affect, Imagery, Consciousness* (1962–1963, 1991–1992). The same criticism can be made regarding Bion's work in the context of psychoanalytic film theory, and media affect theory more generally. I see Tomkins's work on the interrelatedness of cognition and affect holding many similarities with Bionian psychoanalysis for the examination of thought, emotion and affect. In particular, they share a similar perspective on the notion of motivation which differs from the classical Freudian model of drive gratification, emphasizing "a motivational system of great freedom" (Tomkins 1962a: 108) and to learn from experience (Bion 1962a), both positions involving varying systems of feedback and structures of affect. My intent is not to fully explicate the degrees of interconnectivity between Tomkins and Bion, rather I wish to bring these two thinkers closer together so that a question of 'being embedded' might begin to be seen as having greater relevance and association with the topic of affect as it reaches beyond theories of cinematic spectatorship and the specificity of moving image experience. In what follows, I view my close reading of Bion's theory of thinking as illuminating a different psychoanalytic feedback system to that of Freud's, one that echoes Tomkins's motivation of affects as a 'freedom of the will' (*AIC* 1: 109), which I see as functioning similar to Bion's desire to know.

An example of such association is found in Frank and Wilson's contestation of Ruth Leys's interpretation of Tomkins, wherein they claimed that "emotions do not involve cognitions or beliefs about the objects in our world" (2012: 871). They assert that Tomkins "argues that cognitions combine with affects" and this aligns with Bion's theory of thinking, which is premised on the reversal of how thinking and thoughts are usually conceived. For Bion, thinking is a secondary act – required to process (his word is cope) with thoughts. This formulation echoes Tomkins's position, for Bion's reversal on thought and thinking reverberates with Tomkins's claim that Freud "belittled the significance of consciousness" (*AIC* 1: 3). More specifically Tomkins writes:

> we must determine, empirically, *the conditions under which messages become conscious* [for Bion – how thoughts require an apparatus for thinking], and the role of consciousness as part of a feedback mechanism.
> (*AIC 1: 4, italics added*).

Outside the context of film theory, but completely within the concerns of feedback mechanisms that include thought and affect, Wilson's *Psychosomatic: Feminism and the Neurological Body* (2004) explores the topic of conversion hysteria and Freud's early writings to re-explore the roles biology and neurology played in the determinism of "the nature of the body and the character of the psyche" (Wilson 2004: 3). Wilson's main argument is that, specifically within feminist theories of the body, investigation of biological and neurological aspects have been sidelined in favor of socio-cultural, political and historical analyses. Whilst Wilson is not directly speaking of transmission of affect or the intersubjective field of emotional experience, there are many echoes between her approach and that of Brennan's work that explores similar questions that involve biological and neurological mechanisms in

28 A theory of thinking for moving image experience

affect transmission, particularly along lines that are relevant to audience theory, such as the notion of contagion. Aware of criticisms of essentialism here, I note the attention on biology and neurology to highlight how such scholarship is examining the phenomenological implications within traditional psychoanalytic theories (Wilson) and within contemporary psychoanalytically influenced theories of affect (Brennan).

Brennan asks, "If contagion exists, (and the study of crowds says it does), how is it effected?" (2004: 68), arguing that transmission of affect within crowds, and therefore intersubjective fields (much like the in-between spaces of screens across present and absent, but nevertheless connected audiences) is made possible through entrainment. Entrainment is a term used to refer to the consequence of affective transmission – "the form of transmission where people become alike . . . whereby one person's or one group's nervous and hormonal systems are brought into alignment with another's" (2004: 9). Brennan argues that smell is the primary unconscious communication involved with entrainment, which might account for transmission of affect within audience groups (the exchange of pheromones of fear or arousal for example) but not for the transmission of affect between the screen and audience, or even of transmission between virtual groups (such as online communities). Tomkins writes that the primary site of affect is the face (*AIC* 1: 204), a counter to Brennan's neurological entrainment-transmission model, as it privileges the outer-over-inner empirics of the body, "affect is primarily facial behavior. Secondly it is bodily behavior, outer skeletal and inner visceral behavior" (205–206). Tomkins's position is ocular-centric; we must be able to see a face in order to respond to it. In this light, Tomkins views the intersubjective field as dependent on sight even if future affect can work mnemonically.

Frank notes this works as a 'hinge-mechanism', where affect is "both outward and inward, which acts both on and between bodies and operates at the interface of physiology and psychology" (2015: 9), and because affect, as Tomkins claims, emanates from the face, its transmission is continuously shared "to the self and to others, sometimes to the self as an other, serving as a hinge-mechanism between individual and group" (Frank 2015: 9). The way in which Frank positions this concept of hinge as the means through which transferential experience evolves offers a solution to the transmission of affect that Brennan's concept of entrainment overlooks within moving image experience. Such experience necessarily involves the intersubjective transmission of the compositional aspects of affect both for perception and for thinking, as we engage with moving images via screened others (psychical and virtual) and within the atmosphere of other physically present people.

I briefly include this discussion on the biological emphasis of affect in order to acknowledge that despite Bion's theory of thinking including phenomenological attention within his examination of emotional experience, the word 'thinking' itself lies too firmly in the favor of the psyche over soma. It is hard to see how a 'theory of thinking' works as a transmission of affect on face value, particularly as thinking is often ascribed to the inner world of the individual rather than shared and observable group experience (as with audiences virtual or actual). However if we follow that Bion's theory developed through his clinical group therapy, and pay attention to Brennan's claim that any theory of affect is also a theory of groups, we can begin to move closer to how Bion's term 'emotional experience' – that is thinking and feeling – might be more balanced between psyche and soma than first appears. Let us return to Bion and his theory of thinking.

Within the context of the intersubjective field, Bion viewed individual personality working similar to group function, formed of disparate parts that are often in conflict with other parts of the self. Some parts of the self wish to think and work through lived experience, whilst other parts do anything they can to avoid it because of their fear of thinking (psychotic parts). This in itself offers a template for how groups function – there are parts of a group that work and are capable of thinking, and others that are not and are full of hatred for the working, thinking parts. Bion's term for these psychical parts is 'mentalities' and identifies the respective "unanimous expression of the will of the group, an expression of will to which individuals contribute anonymously" via their types – "basic assumption group mentality" and "work group mentality" (Bion 1961: 59). Such emphasis on groups and their mentalities is critical for the study of moving image experience and film theory, particularly if we are to concentrate on the examination of emotional experience. Bion's theory of thinking accounts for the transmission of affect and emotional experience within the audience-group, offering a psychoanalytic model that accounts for both psychic and biological experience as divergent from classical psychoanalysis. By exploring the key principles (as per Ogden) in Bion's theory of thinking, and discussing in detail their relevance for the study of aesthetic and lived emotional experience, the presumption is that theories of spectatorship will need reorganization to include rather than ignore Bion's contribution to psychoanalysis, offering new perspectives on emotion and lived experience with respect to the study of the moving image. In this way, we can begin to diversify 'psychoanalytic theory' by pluralizing its influences within film and media affect studies. Some brief points worth accentuating: although Bion wrote about his observations of group experience *in situ*, he held it to be a constant that a group does not have to meet in order for the various group mentalities to exist. The individual's role in the group continues whether or not the group is together. Additionally, whilst Bion identifies two different mentalities of groups, he saw them as co-existing within the same group, with different mentalities dominating at any given time. A group can be concurrently a work group that functions within the limits of their shared purpose or goal, and also be a group that is connected together through the negative affects present in basic assumption mentalities.

Basic assumption refers to the shared unconscious beliefs within a group that equally shape and drive its behaviors and subsequently establish the group experience.[3] These basic assumption mentalities are divided into three different types – all of which are what Ogden phrases as "fearful orientations to reality", and which we can view as being fueled by affect. They are not conscious, rather proto-mental – referring to thinking that is both physical and mental activity (Bion 1961). This is why, for Bion, such thinking is also feeling – the two cannot be separated. Brennan notes, "basic assumptions are about the affects Bion groups together 'anxiety, fear, hate, love'" (2004: 63). For Brennan, any theory of the group is also a theory about the transmission of affect, but in addition "it is also a theory of the group based on what is produced by 'group', as well as the individuals within it: the emotions of two are not the same as the emotions of one plus one" (2004: 51).[4] Inasmuch as Bion discusses group experience through different assumptions, he does not focus on how affect evolves or transmits within or across groups in the way Brennan or Tomkins do. This is of particular significance for the study of moving image experience, especially regarding audiences and theories of spectatorship. As a group, the idea of the audience begins with the assumption that group assembly occurs through shared interests (going to see a specific film with friends – literally or with the assumption that other friends are also viewing new releases within similar time-frames; participating in an online game; watching television programs that you can discuss with others), but also (and I would argue more importantly) through the embeddedness that results from the transmission of affect.

Ogden states that a group's evasion of thinking is "to evade the task of coming to terms with, and making efforts to modify, what is actually occurring both within and outside of the group" (2009: 93). The three basic assumption groups identify three ways of evading thinking; that is the group does not have the capacity to tolerate frustration and elects to evade thinking and growing. Whilst all three types can exist in any one group at a time, one specific type will dominate the experience of the group. Of the three basic assumptions, the 'dependent' group depends on a leader to think for the group (so that the group does not have to do thinking work itself), but at the same time, refuses to listen to what the leader has to say. The fight-flight group believes resolution and growth will result from fighting with or fleeing from a common enemy to the group; and the pairing group believes that two members of the group will produce a savior who will solve all the group's problems and deliver them from unhappiness. This savior assumption (phantasy) of the group, once more, excuses the whole group from having to think for itself.[5]

Bion uses these three basic assumption mentalities to show how group thinking, as a proto-mental activity (we might say a method of embedding ourselves in experience), is often evaded. Through this model, he sets up the groundwork for his later book *Learning from Experience* (1962a) – where thinking is discussed in greater detail and within the context of knowing as emotional experience. His theory of group experience reorients the emphasis of psychoanalytic theory to focus not on the fulfillment of instincts and drive gratification, but more on the working through of negative, fearful emotions and subsequent lived experience. Even further, Bion emphasizes the emotions of fear and hatred the group (and parts of our personality) has for those parts which are incapable of thinking, of not knowing, of being powerless (Ogden 2009). In Ogden's view, basic assumption groups invest in what he calls 'magical thinking', a term that he creates to identify the wish embedded in the evasion of thought, where groups will do anything to avoid the hard graft of thinking for themselves. At the same time, they desperately want to feel the maturity and emotional growth that comes with learning from experience. The attraction of lifestyle television programs that offer home renovations from trash to treasure in sixty minutes; or cooking programs that broadcast false journeys of growth through culinary skills; or extreme makeover programs that suggest inner transformation comes from external alteration (see Whitehouse-Hart 2014) are all examples of such 'magical thinking', where instead of questioning the draw and popularity of such programs, they remain 'magical worlds' that are idealized and act as inhibitors of real growth in audiences.

Bion argues that the wish to learn from experience is our "need for truth" – what Ogden's lists as his first principle of mental functioning, which sees the non-thinking (the evasion of thinking) and thinking (effort to work through frustrations in order to grow) as inseparable from each other (Bion 1961; Ogden 2009). The affects that lead to emotional experience within group phenomena are intricately tied to the formation of thoughts and their potential for satisfaction or frustration, and it is this point in particular where Bion's psychoanalysis departs stridently from Freud's. Here Bion is arguing that we are overwhelmingly seduced by experience that results in the evasion of thinking, yet he also says that we continuously seek ways to engage with genuine thinking, from which emotional growth results. Where Freud argued that we seek to avoid unpleasure and pain, Bion claims that we have a need for truth that places us squarely in the paradox of developmental conflict (Bion 1961). Further, Bion argues that we must also tolerate our incapacity or inability to know within our efforts to face developmental conflict. Ogden phrases it as, "*the human need to know the truth of one's experience is the most fundamental impetus for thinking*" (2009: 95); 'know the truth' is better explained within the specifics of Bion's vocabulary. To 'know' is not the same as possessing information or acquiring facts about a topic, or person. Knowing in a Bionian sense is an emotion, knowledge *is* emotional experience, "The question 'How can x know anything?' expresses a feeling; it appears to be painful and to inhere in the emotional experience that I represent by x K y [analyst/Knowing/analysand]" (Bion 1962a: 48). Truth also has a different inflection for Bion. Truth is not something that can be known directly; it is something one becomes: "I shall use the sign O to denote that which is the ultimate reality represented by terms such as ultimate reality, absolute truth, the godhead, the infinite, the thing-in-itself. O does not fall in the domain of knowledge or learning save incidentally; it can 'become', but it cannot be 'known'" (Bion 1965: 26). In Chapter 7 I write on Bion's concept of O in greater detail with regard to Bion's and Bollas's theory of transformation, but briefly, when Ogden writes "to know the truth of one's experience", he is speaking about a goal, an aim, a process – not a concrete, final or fixed outcome. To 'know the truth' therefore is much more about having emotional experience that results in inner transformation from self-awareness, which includes (or rather depends on) tolerance of frustration and acceptance of open endings. It is a constant flux within adult lived emotional experience. Is this why non-narrative film or open-ended stories appear as frustrating in comparison to their dominant narrative counterparts that privilege linearity and closure? Frustrating moving image experience has greater potential to 'stick' to us for quite some time afterwards, progressing more toward what Bion termed 'learning from experience'.

There is a third element that Ogden views as relative to Bion's need for truth – the concept of 'binocular vision', a term that Bion uses to link thinking (and growth in mental functioning) with a capacity to perceive, most specifically from multiple points of view. On the face of it, and certainly at the start of *Experiences in Groups*, 'binocular vision' suggests a dual perspective, which is an ability to consider another's point of view or think the orientation to reality from another position. In reflecting on the ability to perceive the same phenomena from two different approaches, individual and group, Bion states "[t]he two methods provide the practitioner with a rudimentary binocular vision" (1961: 8). Rafael López-Corvo adds to this, noting that there "is also binocular vision between the *presence* and the *absence* of an object" (López-Corvo 2005: 47, italics original). Within the mention of binocular vision in *Experiences in Groups*, it is possible to see the beginnings of Bion's ideas on intersubjective experience, which emerged more fully in "A Theory of Thinking" and later in "The Imaginary Twin" (included in *Second Thoughts* 1967). It is also possible to interweave Tomkins's concept of the hinge mechanism (Frank 2015: 9) as method to study the transmission of affect in moving image experience. Binocular vision, like group mentalities, is not wedded to time or space, and links with Tomkins's view that from memory we generate affect from recollected images that previously incurred "facial, skeletal or visceral responses" (*AIC* 1: 206). As López-Corvo states, binocular vision can occur after an experience (absence) or in the midst of it (presence), and in this way becomes much more about one's capacity to think realistically across points of view[6] as they exist within the individual or group, and over past, present or future experience. Ogden puts it as eloquently as ever:

> [t]hinking, so conceived, is a process in which ideas and feelings live in continual conversation with one another, a conversation in which thoughts are forever in the process of being transformed (de-integrated) and formed anew as a consequence of shifting organizations of meaning.
>
> *(2009: 97)*

I want to separate and emphasize Bion's concept of binocular vision from the other ideas that Ogden includes in his first principle of mental functioning – the need for truth – and position it as a 'compositional aspect' vis-á-vis Frank, because it connects quite clearly and directly with Tomkins's affect theory. Bion's concept of binocular vision argues that for mature mental functioning to occur, a person (or group) must be able to hold multiple perspectives of reality in their psyche across time, or as Robert Hinshelwood phrases it, "to integrate the psychological and social sides of people" (2013: 46). Tomkins, in discussing the relativity of the transmuting response and the image, writes on our ability to learn perceptually and the necessity of conflict or error within the process, a very similar position to Bion's learning from experience and the capacity for mental and emotional growth through developmental conflict, "the possibility of error is the inherent pride of any mechanism capable of learning" (*AIC* 1: 13). For Tomkins, binocular vision (his specific term is 'binocular information') refers to the overabundance of sensory data that is perceived, and whilst used more literally than Bion, the similarity of the two concepts share a significant amount of affect-ground. Where Tomkins states (in terms of perceptual feedback) we "see one world, though we receive two worlds" (*AIC* 1: 14), we can induce Bion's presence/absence of binocular vision as viewing reality from multiple vertices. We can further associate Tomkins's claim – "the world changes over time and so, therefore, does the information it transmits" (*AIC* 1: 14) – with Bionian binocular vision as possessing the capacity to incur thinking as a means to know and experience affect and emotion.

Not much has been written on the affect and emotional experience of binocular vision relative to theories of spectatorship, which is a lacuna given that what Bion's concept offers is a rethinking of the affective relationship between time and reality, as well as the tools to consider the usefulness of moving image experience to bring about inner transformation – that is mental and emotional growth. Ambrósio Garcia writes of binocular vision in Pier Paolo Pasolini's *Porcile* (*Pigsty*, 1969), wherein she argues that the camera point-of-view can be read as aligning with protagonist Julian's (Jean-Pierre Léaud) own binocular vision: "the camera alternates between an observation of Julian's present in his parent's mansion and . . . Julian's phantasy of his imaginary twin personified by the nameless character roaming the volcanic landscape" (2017: 93). Her choice to interpret the camera as effecting a type of binocular vision shows how the concept works within the limits of diegesis, and even further to analyze the genesis for Julian's actions within the film as reflective of the epistemophilic thrust (need for truth) of Bion's psychoanalysis. Whilst Ambrósio Garcia's use of Bion's binocular vision offers a rich textual analysis of *Pigsty*, my interests are more focused on the emotional experience that is central to both Bion and Tomkins's conceptualization of binocularity,[7] which enables audiences to use the presentation of another's (albeit screened and fictional) binocular vision as a hinge to loosen the seduction of magical thinking, that is the evasion of thinking for oneself. Films such as *Pigsty* (one could argue all of Pasolini films!) are intentionally complex and alienating. In style, Pasolini refuses to explain the disruptive shifts in time, geography and character storylines; but also in story, Pasolini never explains or resolves theme or direction. Put another way, Pasolini refuses to think the film for the audience, instead *Pigsty* is 'hinge-worthy'; the audience must find the transferential poetics within the film through their own lived emotional experience of it. This is why aesthetic experience conceived on the basis of pleasure (I liked the film; I didn't like the film) only serves to maintain magical thinking. What is more pertinent aesthetically is if the film worked as a hinge, enabling the audience to "loosen [their] reliance on the illusion or delusion of safety that is provided by magical thinking, and to attempt to engage in genuine thinking" (Ogden 2009: 95). It is also a further means to identify how the intersubjective field within moving image experience requires "two minds to think one's disturbing thoughts", Ogden's second principle of mental functioning in Bion's theory of thinking.

I have discussed the intersubjective field above, and how it relates to the transmission of affect as argued via Brennan, Tomkins and Wilson, and I have referred to Frank's emphasis of transferential poetics in the 'hinge-mechanism' that belongs to such transmission. In the second principle of Ogden's fashioning, Bion's theory of thinking revises Melanie Klein's formative theory of projective identification, a concept that offers a very different interpretation of what happens within audiences' moving image experience, especially with regard to affect theory. Before I examine the purchase of Bion's revision of Klein's theory of projective identification, and how it relates to a theory of 'being embedded' which involves affective and emotional experience, it is necessary to contextualize Bion's ideas more broadly via the influence of Klein with regard to the good and bad object. This is due to the shift in Klein's own psychoanalytic approach, which was the first to emphasize feelings over drives. I then show how Bion's interpretation of Klein's theory of projective identification continues to further connect with Tomkins's hinge-mechanism as an outside-inside transmission model of affect that leads to a process of 'being embedded'.

From drive to feeling: Melanie Klein and projective identification

Kuhn has noted that the negotiation and interplay of our inner and outer worlds is a "lifelong process that is formed through early object-relating and in playing" (2013: 6) and that such relating and playing continues into adulthood constituting much of our cultural experience. Kuhn interprets this specific concept of cultural experience, taken to represent the intermediate or intersubjective area that negotiates inner and external worlds, from the writings of D.W. Winnicott (1991),[8] whose object-relations psychoanalysis was also influenced by the writings of Klein. I see Klein as offering the formative theory of affect within object-relations psychoanalysis as it relates to a theory of thinking and becoming embedded. I discuss the emergence of object-relations psychoanalysis as a method in film and media studies later in the chapter, but for now I wish to highlight the critical role of Kleinian psychoanalysis not for the identification of play as a negotiation of inner and external worlds, but how such observance of child play was the empirical manifestation of working through the affects in mental functioning which became a formative element in Bion's theory of thinking. Kleinian psychoanalysis highlighted the importance of viewing destructive impulses as feelings in psychoanalytic theory, and this in turn paved the way for a 'school' of object-relations psychoanalysis, which is highly relevant for the current discussion of Bionian thinking and emotional experience.

In *The Ego and the Id* (1923), Freud revised his conceptualization of the psyche and its functions. His original view of the ego was that it opposed and managed the libidinal forces of the unconscious through mechanisms of repression; however, this structural model became problematic when trying to locate consciousness as a descriptive component within it. As such, Freud introduces his preferred term

'Id', clarifying the previous confusion with the use of 'unconscious'[9] and, as Klein states, "made it clear that these parts of the self [ego and id] are not sharply separated from one another and that the id is the foundation of all mental functioning" (1958: 236).[10] Klein herself outlines the trajectory and development of her work in *On the Theory of Anxiety and Guilt* (1948), where she states that even though Freud's (1920) discovery of the death instinct and Karl Abraham's (1924) exploration of sadism noted the destructive impulses of aggression, psychoanalysis continued to foreground libidinal impulses and "correspondingly underrated the importance of aggression and its implications" (1948: 41). What Klein gains from Freud and Abraham's revision of the life and death instincts operative in the ego and the id, is a greater awareness and concentration on the affect and interrelationship of aggression and anxiety. It was due to Klein's interest in anxiety and its causes in young children that she developed the play technique through which she observed the manifestation of aggression and anxiety of a child's inner world through the external world of play. This is what Winnicott (1991) would come to term the intermediate area of experience, and what we can regard as the origin of 'object relations' as relevant to Kuhn's discussion of cultural experience being of the "interplay of inner and outer worlds", and the intersubjective field.

The consequence of Klein's shift within psychoanalytic thought was the de-emphasizing of conflict between sexual instincts and their gratification, and the censorship of the outside world, as well as a reorientation which viewed inner conflict resulting from opposing parts of one's inner self (what were to become good and bad objects). This is where Kleinian psychoanalysis took up the investigation of feelings, specifically the love-hate conflict (Klein 1935, 1952a, 1957) over sexual drives. In "The Origins of Transference" (1952a), Klein writes of the tension between the life and death instincts, demonstrated as love-hate feelings that were attached to objects. Klein believed that inner conflict was a consequence of such opposing feelings that exist constantly within oneself and which are also directed to internal and external objects, and it is here that we can locate the beginnings of Bion's "psychotic parts of the personality". In infancy, such overwhelming feelings are unable to be defended against and subsequently, in order to cope with such inner emotional turmoil, the infant must maneuver parts of their personality (through projective identification and splitting) in order to reach the two different Kleinian emotional 'positions': paranoid-schizoid and depressive, which occur not just in infancy but all throughout adult emotional life. The paranoid-schizoid position was initially presented by Klein as a coherent theory in 1946, and later summarized in "Some theoretical conclusions regarding the emotional life of the infant" (1952b). This is the initial position the infant occupies intra-psychically to cope with anxiety and marks the first capacity to distinguish between good and bad, inside and outside the self. As Klein calls it a 'position', it is helpful to foreground 'paranoid-schizoid' as a state that we move in and out of throughout life as we respond to various affective and emotional experiences, and it is also a formative element that leads Bion to conceive of thinking in terms of intersubjective functioning between personalities.

Early on, Klein used the paranoid-schizoid position to identify the early months of infant life as negotiating the immense anxiety that resulted from inner hateful, hostile and fearful feelings that are directed to the mother and the self simultaneously. The infant, who loves her/his mother, introjects her as a loved (good) object in order to nourish and protect their ego against any sense of persecution (perceived both within and outside of the infant self). At the same time, the infant splits the bad internal parts of the self (hate, envy and fear) off from the good, and projects these into the mother. It is important to note that for Klein, this is an intrapsychic phenomenon and she notes the failure of language to adequately convey the unconscious projection (Klein 1946: 8*fn*1). Ogden sees Bion's extension of Klein's theory as emphasizing the intersubjective dynamics over the intrapsychic and that this distinction is what eventuates in his theory of container-contained. The good and bad objects are then returned to the infant (introjected) and the pattern continues.

> The development of the infant is governed by the mechanisms of introjection and projection. From the beginning the ego introjects objects 'good' and 'bad', for both of which the mother's breast is the prototype – for good objects when the child obtains it, for bad ones when it fails him.
> *(Klein 1935: 262)*

The infant uses the splitting processes involved in the paranoid-schizoid position as a means to maneuver the parts of their personality that create anxiety in order to ward off feelings of hate and fear. This pattern, if healthy, facilitates mental development that is able to cope and deal with paranoia and feelings of anxiety. Klein's object-relations theory – that divided objects into good and bad; where good internal objects serve to nourish the ego and deflect the perniciousness of the superego, and bad objects are those parts of the self that are hated and expelled (such as envy and anxiety) – was the critical move away from the classical psychoanalytic frame of infantile impulses and drives and toward an inner world that concentrates on object-relating on the basis of affect and emotion. Klein saw aggression and anxiety as feelings that results from object-relating, not as secondary responses to negative external world experiences (such as abandonment trauma or interpersonal abuse).

The depressive position, first outlined in Klein's 1935 paper "A contribution to the psychogenesis of manic-depressive states", and elaborated on subsequently in 1940 and 1945, and placed in context in 1946 with the paranoid-schizoid position, is seen as occurring in the "second quarter of the first year" (Klein 1952b: 71) of life, commensurate with the development of the infant's ego and range of emotional experience witnessed in the intersubjective relating with the Mother and, to a lesser degree, other people. As the infant's ego has gradually developed, there is a greater awareness of the Mother as a whole person. The infant realizes its love for the Mother (good object), who is now seen as a whole person with the capacity to have real feelings herself. With this awareness comes guilt for the previous hateful feelings that were projected toward her. The depressive position brings awareness of the self and of the object, and that

> goes hand in hand with anxiety for it (of its disintegration), with guilt and remorse, with a sense of responsibility for preserving it intact against persecutors and the id, with sadness relating to the impending loss of it. These emotions, whether conscious or unconscious, are in my view among the essential and fundamental elements of the feelings we call love.
>
> *(Klein 1935: 270)*

The benefit of reaching the depressive position, and feeling the emotional experience of guilt, is that the infant attempts to repair the love link with the good object (the Mother). This mental, emotional growth is born from a sense of (real or perceived) loss, and also what I see as the theoretical origins of Bion's binocular vision – which to recall, is the awareness of another's feelings, or put another way, the capacity to perceive reality from the potentiality of another's emotional experience.

Klein saw aggression and anxiety as being the primary affects that are negotiated in our inner worlds, which goes some way to illuminating Bion's theory of basic assumption groups. In each of the basic assumption mentalities lies a destructive (or negative) affect – hate, envy, fear – all directed toward thinking and facing one's own capacity to cope with frustrating emotional experience. It is worth reminding ourselves that for Bion, thinking and feeling are proto-mental – a concurrent embodied psychical experience. Where Klein adheres to love and hate conflict as it pertains to objects, Bion's extension of her theory of projective identification is better viewed as a further consideration of the function of personality that is, how we are to regard the capacity to think thoughts in the different parts of ourselves, and to think thoughts with other people. Klein (1946) writes that the negative affects present in the infant's early mental functioning are directed outward toward the mother (that is whomever occupies the socio-cultural role of mothering), where the paranoid-schizoid and depressive positions include her analysis of the affect of envy within the infant's early mental life. The infant, deeply envious of the mother's creative life and capacity to experience creativity, projects hate and envy into the mother's breast. Klein clarifies her use of the term envy later in her work:

> A distinction should be drawn between envy, jealousy, and greed. Envy is the angry feeling that another person possesses and enjoys something desirable – the envious impulse being to take it away or to spoilt it. Moreover, envy implies the subject's relation to one person only and goes back to the earliest exclusive relation with the mother . . . [envy] seeks to rob in this way [forcing high selfish demands on the mother that exceed the infant's needs and the mother's capacity to give], but also to put badness, primarily bad excrements and bad parts of the self, into the mother, and first all into her breast

in order to spoil and destroy her. In the deepest sense this means destroying her creativeness.

(Klein 1957: 181)

In order for the infant to cope with their envy directed toward the mother – who is also loved by the infant – the good breast must be split from the bad breast: "object-relations exist from the beginning of life, the first object being the mother's breast which to the child becomes split into a good (gratifying) and bad (frustrating) breast; this splitting results in a severance of love and hate" (Klein 1948: 2). This splitting incurs anxiety within the infant, who fears that a vengeful reaction from the mother will result from their own envious and destructive attack. In terms of group experience, this anxiety (consequential from envy) arises in the belief (reality or phantasy) that other members are pairing off and excluding the individual.

Projective identification is often interpreted as the expulsion of only the bad, hated parts of the self. While this may be a predominant manifestation, projective identification is to be understood as the expulsion of any part of the self that is split off from other parts and projected to another object in order to identify with it. Aggressive projective identification is often a reaction to feelings of persecution (Klein 1946). As a mechanism that aims to expel those parts of the self that are hated and feared, projective identification also incurs attachment, meaning that the infant also seeks these hated and feared parts to be returned to them for re-introjection. "The processes of splitting of parts of the self and projecting them into objects are thus of vital importance for normal development as well as for abnormal object-relations" (Klein 1946: 9). Positive projective identification incurs the same mechanism of expulsion, projection and desire for re-introjection, and is the basis for good object relations. (This is an essential element of reverie that I explore within the context of intersubjective experience in Chapter 3 and consider in terms of Deleuze and Guattari's rhizome in Chapter 8).

Klein's projective identification is the key concept that Bion profoundly extends to develop his theory of thinking as it informs the functioning of our personality and lived emotional experience. Ogden notes that within basic assumption group mentality, the group leader and the group are drawn to think each other – not always in productive ways, but in ways that are necessary for the group leader to properly understand the group experience. Binocular vision further operates via the group leader's participation in basic assumption mentality, as even though the experience involves negative affect or "the numbing feeling of reality" (Bion 1961: 149), it nevertheless still facilitates the capacity to view reality from multiple perspectives. Bion's revision of Klein's projective identification highlights the necessity for intersubjective experience in the development of mental and emotional growth. This use of projective identification is the foundation of Bion's sense of the *intersubjective* field that results in the emotional experience of thinking. It moves beyond the mechanism of expulsion (per Klein) as it informs the thinking of reality and emotional experience between two people, where thinking as the psychic activity that occurs between separate people enables emotional growth that is not able to occur within the individual alone. The transmission of affect, as it happens in moving image experience, involves such intersubjective projective identification, particularly when, as Ogden puts it, "facing emotional experience for which one feels unprepared [whatever is foreign, new or unknown], we are throughout our lives in need of other people with whom to think" (2009: 100).

Cartwright locates projective identification within Tomkins's affect theory, noting that

> the object of affect (which may be a person, an image, a material artifact) is always subject to projection, and can be subject to projective identifications that may animate and anthropomorphize the object in the narrow sense by giving it power to 'make me' feel
>
> *(Cartwright 2008: 47)*

In this way, Cartwright highlights the demand that is involved with the affect that is transmitted through projective identification; that asks for more than is able to be given, for example, watching scenes that make us feel physically and psychically uncomfortable. Used in this way, the theory of projective identification becomes the basis (physical and psychical) for a psychoanalytic theory of affect within moving image experience. It places theories of pleasure to the side and moves the demands of affect and potential for painful experience to the center.

Satisfaction and frustration: Bion's apparatus for thinking

The historical psychoanalytic context from which Bion's theory of thinking unfolds began with Freud's revision of the ego and Klein's concentration on the conflict between love and hate feelings, and arrived at the application of her theory of projective identification as the basis for his conception of thinking as an intersubjective activity. For Bion, thinking and emotional experience are two sides of the same coin. His innovative theory of thinking was to establish an approach that examined the psychoanalytic process itself, which is the transition from knowing to becoming. Thinking is Bion's term for the 'experience' of 'emotions', that is emotional experience: "Thinking is a development forced on the psyche by the pressure of thoughts and not the other way round" (Bion 1967: 111). This model differs from Freud's model, which viewed thought as a biological response that negotiated drives and their gratification via sensory experience with the world around us (Stein 1991). This is Bion's third principle of mental functioning as Ogden puts it – Bion's reversal of thoughts leading to thinking and not thinking producing thoughts. Thinking is the mental apparatus that Bion sees as necessary for the negotiation of raw sensory data (denoting aesthetic experience) which create thoughts.

Ferro and Foresti summarize it as "[t]houghts are classified as *ideas* (what [Bion] calls *pre-conceptions*), conceptions or *thoughts*, and *concepts*" (Ferro and Foresti 2013: 365, italics original). In order for a conception or thought to emerge, it must be first a preconception that is then married to a realization. Bion's example is "the infant has an inborn disposition corresponding to an expectation of a breast" (Bion 1967: 111); we might see this as the sensation of hunger and the expectation of being fed, or the wish to be nurtured and the expectation of mother's attention, more broadly. In either case, the idea is not based on lived experience to begin with. When this expectation is met with reality, that is, when the breast appears and the hunger is satisfied through the infant being fed or nurtured, a realization occurs which links the expectation (preconception) with realization (presence of the breast). Bion calls this a conception, and this becomes the model he bases his theory of satisfaction on, wherein the event that a conception occurs (through the satisfaction of a preconception with its realization) – a satisfactory emotional experience occurs. We get what we think we want. A thought, and this distinction becomes a key difference between Freud and Bion that I discuss below, occurs when a preconception *does not* meet its realization, where frustration occurs because the expectation has not been met with its realization.[11]

This model, where a preconception + realization = conception marks the basis for satisfaction in emotional experience; and preconception + no realization = thought, marks the basis for frustrating emotional experience, presents a reorganizing of emotion and its significance with psychoanalytic theory. More importantly, it is Bion's first move toward associating emotion with sensory knowledge, or knowing, and in this manner further links with Tomkins who has vociferously argued for the study of consciousness to not only be concerned with what a human thinks but also what a human being feels. Indeed Tomkins (*AIC* 1: 5) writes that it was unclear why psychoanalysis, 'slighted the role' of affects given that much of Freud's early work was very much engaged with questions concerning the interrelationship between biological and psychical affect.[12] Tomkins was unlikely to have been familiar with the work of Bion when he published the first and second *AIC* volumes, the same year Bion publishes "A Theory of Thinking", which means that Bion was not included in Tomkins's assessment of psychoanalysis' treatment of affect, emotion and consciousness. However by volume 3, which Tomkins published in 1991, Bion has still not been incorporated into Tomkins's research (or vice versa), which is unfortunate given the many fruitful links regarding memory, dreams and thinking they share.[13]

On the capacity to tolerate frustration

Adam Phillips writes "[t]ragedies are stories about people not getting what they want, but not all stories about people not getting what they want seem tragic" (Phillips 2012: 1). Here Phillips subtly speaks to the layers involved with frustration and emotion derivative of Bion's theory of thinking, very cleverly noting that the tolerance of frustration is a configuration of another type of satisfaction. The central tenet of Freud's pleasure principle is the avoidance of unpleasure and pain, achieved through the release of instinctual tension or the gratification of drives. The pleasure principle is, in theory, disciplined by the reality principle, or put another way, external reality is brought to bear on the working of our inner world so that we are able to adapt to society. Bion views the relationship to reality somewhat differently, in that he prioritizes emotional experience with the external world, and then views a relationship to reality being dependent on our capacities to think and feel such experience. For Bion, the capacity to tolerate frustration in reality is what leads to mental growth, whereas "the denial of reality is a function of the psychotic part of the personality" (Ambrósio Garcia 2017: 42). His model of frustration outlined above, where the infant's expectation is met with no realization, that is the no-breast (and therefore no satisfaction) is pivotal for the development of the infant's thinking apparatus (or lack thereof).

Does the infant tolerate or avoid the frustration, or elect to modify it? If frustration is tolerated, if the infant has the capacity to deal with there being no breast, then Bion argues this becomes a 'thought', that is the expectation + lack of its realization = thought (no-breast) and this psychical model establishes an apparatus for thinking. Alternative realizations might occur and the option of there being one satisfaction has now diversified. Bion viewed this development in mental functioning as equivalent to Freud's reality principle, where the ability to think was the act of mental functioning that ameliorated desire and oriented us to adapt to reality. For Bion, the apparatus for thinking is tied to the infant's capacity to cope with frustrating emotional experience, both in the event of specific frustration – but more broadly, to lay down the psychical framework for dealing with frustrating emotional experience in future life: "A capacity for tolerating frustration thus enables the psyche to develop thought as a means by which the frustration that is tolerated is itself made more tolerable" (Bion 1967: 112). Bion is stating that facing frustration (or displeasure) leads to mental growth, which is a significant departure from the Freudian emphasis. If this infrastructure is not possible, that is if the infant is not able to tolerate frustration, then there are two choices; to modify or avoid the frustration altogether. If modified, the frustration is not completely tolerated but also not evacuated through excessive projective identification, and "omnipotence will develop" (Ferro and Foresti 2013: 365).

The alpha function is Bion's term that identifies the transformation of raw, sensory data into emotional experience. López-Corvo defines it as "the product of an adequate relationship between the baby and the mother, which permits the existence of normal projective identifications", which to recall is essential in order to relate to the external world. Gérard Bléandonu calls the alpha function "the cornerstone of the knowledge process" (1994: 151), echoing its importance as the psychical mechanism that transforms the pressure of 'sense data' into dream thoughts. I see it as having a similar function to Tomkins's hinge-mechanism in his 'inverse archaeology' that Frank argues is a 'transferential moment' (2015: 7). The alpha function is also a transferential moment that takes the 'outer' sense data in and transforms it into the 'inner' apparatus to form dream thoughts, what make thinking possible. "Dream-thoughts are the symbolic representation of the disturbing experience that was originally registered primarily in sensory terms" (Ogden 2009: 101). Ferro and Foresti see the alpha function as the critical basis for what they regard as "Bion's most important contribution" which is the re-imagination of dreaming as "*waking dream thought*" (2013: 366, italics original). They argue that there is no direct access to waking dream thought save through reverie phenomena, explored in greater detail in the following chapter.

These technical terms within Bion's theory of thinking, whilst complex to follow, are essential as they eventuate into his more sophisticated theory of container-contained. Drawing on Klein's theory of projective identification, Bion creates a model – "the idea of a container into which an object is projected and the object that can be projected into the container: the latter I shall designate by the term contained" (1962a: 90) – which briefly outlines the mechanism and movement of emotional experience in the thinking apparatus. Ogden summarizes the 'container' as a 'process' that effects dreaming as unconscious waking thought and 'conscious secondary process thinking'; the 'contained' are feelings and thoughts that require thinking to process 'lived emotional experience' (2009: 102). As the apex of Bion's meta-theory of thinking, container-contained is the process that engenders emotional growth by creating the capacity for thinking (Sandler 2009). It is productive to view the container-contained model as a dynamic process, and to focus on it as a mechanism that involves the transmission and reception of affect that derives from lived experience. In Chapter 6, I explore cinema via Bion's container-contained model, arguing that moving image experience has the capacity to work as a mechanism that facilitates similar transformation via waking dream thought.

Ambrósio Garcia locates the transformative/transferential nature of container-contained within the context of retreat in cinema, and discusses the capacity to suffer pain. She writes "Bion is trying to formulate a theory that can account for the difficulties of tolerating pain, and this includes a situation in which the subject experiences pain but is not *suffering* it" (2017: 46, italics original). As a model to reorganize psychoanalysis for the study of moving image experience, Bion's container-contained is useful if we interpret it loosely along the lines that López-Corvo suggests, that is "when to 'include' or 'exclude' something, and related to questions like 'what?', 'where', 'when?', or why something is included or excluded?" (López-Corvo 2005: 70). If we consider that multiple instances of moving image experience include versions of pain envy, anxiety, aggression, shame, fright, joy, arousal, love, then we can use Bion's container-contained model to further explore the transmission of affect in emotional experience as "subject and cinema can be seen as a growing entity in which each party is able to retain knowledge and yet be receptive to new ideas" (Ambrósio Garcia 2017: 48). Put simply, container-contained involves the expulsion of a thought/emotion (bad object) that is perceived as having the capacity to destroy the self. This bad, expelled object seeks another mind – container – to receive and respond to this awful and disturbing part of the other's self so that such annihilating emotions can be absorbed and returned by another mind. This function of container-contained, when it works adequately, is what Bion saw as establishing the basic capacity for one's self-awareness and ability to perceive reality, meaning lived experience with other people. This is why the container-contained is regarded as the pinnacle of Bion's theory of thinking.

As a holistic process, container-contained is about the mother's capacity to receive and respond to the very worst and most feared and hated parts of the infant's self. If this is possible, if the mother has the capacity to contain the hostile fragments of the infant's mind, then a foundation is laid down that facilitates their "intuitive understanding of [the self] and others" (Bion 1967: 47). In terms of how container-contained works as a model within moving image experience, or indeed as elements within cinema positively, I view the container as offering the audience the capacity to use moving image experience to dream their own lived experience. The contained (thoughts and feelings that result from lived experience) is informed by moving images that present simulated 'lived' experience that the audience cannot contain inside of them. Moving image experience makes possible a range of emotions that the audience is able to introject in order to make meaning (or dream) their own lived experience. Bion's container-contained model offers an opportunity to consider how moving images are worked with for very real psychological work, beyond previous psychoanalytic models that have rested on identification as it related to various cultural politics, such as gender, race, sexuality and class. It is a model where we can position the moving image as the 'other thinker' through which we can think (via choices of inclusion and exclusion) our most disturbing thoughts. In this way, it contributes to the work that has been done on cinema as therapy (Izod and Dovalis 2015). A potential of Bion's container-contained model lies in its function, which allows a consideration of the moving image experience as a dynamic relationship between image and audience, one equitable to the hinge-mechanics of Tomkins's 'inverse archaeology', where cinematic experience (and its like) becomes more about receptivity and "being absorbed in [one's] task of observation . . . absorbed in the facts" (Bion 1962a: 95).

The final principle of mental functioning that Ogden identifies within Bion's theory of thinking is the "inherent psychoanalytic function of the personality, and dreaming is the principal process for performing that function" (2009: 103). Dreaming, as Bion uses the term, refers to "unconscious psychological work that one does with one's emotional experience" (Ogden 2009: 5). This happens as different parts of the personality link together. As has been discussed, dreaming for Bion is another way of recognizing thinking as an emotional experience. Ogden's four principles of mental functioning are instructive in contextualizing Bion's meta-theory of thinking because they highlight the key functions involved. Bionian dreaming can be viewed as another reversal, similar to his approach of thoughts requiring thinking rather than thinking producing thoughts; a reversal of Freud's model, where the unconscious precedes the conscious, the aim being to make manifest infantile wishes and desires to the conscious mind (latent to manifest). Instead, Bion sees it as conscious-unconscious where the raw sensory data gained via lived experience can be turned into material that can then be dreamed by the unconscious. When Ogden writes that this is how we "dream ourselves into existence", he is noting Bion's emphasis on the unconscious as being the core part of our personality that contains all parts able to think and not think, and the paradoxes that are involved therein.

To use Bion's concept of dreaming as a new psychoanalytic model for the study of moving image experience is to foreground 'experience' in the consideration of how images and audio-visual experience overall facilitate a capacity for dreaming. In many ways, Bion's theory of dreaming allows us to look more closely at how we use moving images to enrich lived aesthetic experience by centering the experience of transference and its potential for transformation. By claiming dreaming is unconscious waking thought as well as night time sleep thought, Bion extends psychoanalytic theory to include thinking/dreaming as a way to achieve self-awareness. In the case where this does not occur, where dreaming or the capacity to dream is absent or avoided, the psychotic parts of the personality are at their strongest. Ferro's and Foresti's description of dreaming as waking dream thought highlight the dynamic, unconscious creativity that uses beta elements (raw sensory data from lived experience) which "are transformed by the alpha function into *alpha elements*, or emotional pictograms, which syncretize instant by instant all the beta elements present, regardless of their origin in the soma, our own mind, others' minds, or the environment" (2013: 366). Even though deconstructing the structure of a dream feels quite like deconstructing a joke – a little of the magic gets lost – Ferro and Foresti show that Bion's waking dream thought works processurally like montage. They argue that the pictograms "which form continuously without our knowledge, *when linked together*, make up the waking dream thought" (2013: 367, italics added). From this, Ferro and Foresti link dreaming to narration which are echoed in external "plots and literary genres" (367) and are "as good as another; what matters are the alpha elements they convey" (368). Put another way, what matters is how such image-sense narrations enable the dreaming of one self. In the following chapter, I discuss the role of reverie in waking dream thought in detail.

Throughout the writing of *Being Embedded*, my goal has been to position Bionian psychoanalysis in such a way that its models are seen as divergent from classical psychoanalysis, offering very rich pathways for the exploration of affect and emotional experience from a psychoanalytic perspective. It is not to separate and analyze specific emotions or affects via taxonomy, or even forcefully apply Bion's psychoanalytic concepts only for their own reification, but rather to argue that psychoanalysis still has something to say about the need for moving image experience and what it offers us as audiences – particularly in a time where we are seeing such a spike in the transmission of affect via social media. The concept, or indeed the experience, of 'being embedded' then is attentive to why we use moving images for emotional work and why we will continue to do so. Bion's theory of thinking, and its apex model of container-contained, is the basis for my primary concern: that there are objects that we wish to avoid or modify in our thinking of everyday life that we wish to expel and have returned to us so that we may then think them, dream them and grow. I argue that moving images are powerful 'other minds' that we seek to think through our disturbing thoughts. Spectator experiences that encourage 'magical thinking' are those which maintain and extend avoidance of genuine thought – we remain longing and lusting for the shallow and the superficial, entertaining phantasies of omnipotence; but there are also aesthetic experiences that contain, where we are embedded within, the duality of non-thinking and thinking within emotional and aesthetic experience. Moving images allow our very basest fears to be performed outside of our inner world so that they can be dreamed. Ogden writes that "[p]rimitive fears of learning by experience and of emotional development are the very experiences from which a group learns about itself and develops" (2009: 95). 'Being embedded' is not one thing or a singular experience; I see it as a form of relating that facilitates learning from experience, enabling the most transformative mode of thinking and dreaming the most feared, hostile and threatening parts of ourselves in order to grow from them.

Notes

1. I discuss Bion's theory of group experience in relation to memory and dreaming in greater depth in Chapter 5.
2. Ogden defines the intersubjective field [or analytic third]: "the intersubjectivity of the analyst – analysand coexists in dynamic tension with the analyst and the analysand as separate individuals with their own thoughts, feelings, sensations, corporal reality, psychological identity and so on. Neither the intersubjectivity of the mother – infant nor that of the analyst – analysand (as separate psychological entities) exists in pure form. The intersubjective and the individually subjective each create, negate and preserve the other" (1994: 4). Compare with Ferro and Civitarese's definition: "The field metaphor is, of course, borrowed from electromagnetic or gravitational field theory. Its essential properties are that it represents a *dynamic* totality, and that it is *inclusive, invisible* (but deducible from its effects on its constitutive elements), and *delimited* (even if constantly in the throes of contraction and expansion). The field is unstable and subjected to continuous displacements of energy. The forces concentrated at a given point in the field can have effects on other forces in locations remote from that point. Hence, all elements in a field are structured as a differential system in which each term is defined in relation to the others in a process of constant, mutual cross-reference" (2015: 7, italics original). These authors note the involvement but not the specificity of the individual, instead the dynamic between individuals as it pertains to the interrelationship and to those *not* present is emphasized.
3. Ogden emphasizes the fearful component of the basic assumption mentality and equates the term with the more widely known 'phantasy' (Ogden 2009).
4. See also Gibbs 2001 on 'contagious affects' who emphasizes the work of Tomkins in her study of media objects as amplifiers of affect.
5. The Kleinian influence in Bion's theoretical work is evident in the structuring of the three basic assumptions. Dependence comes from reliance on the parental relationship; pairing is believed to produce new life (through birthing the best parts of the pair – effectively a child); and fighting and fleeing are responses to the perceived threat to the individual's ego (mostly in that it is forcing one to confront their evasion of thinking, that is confronting the most intimate part of the self, which we are all quite happy to avoid).
6. Bion's preferred term is 'vertex' because it specifically addresses one's orientation to reality rather than their interpretation of it. He argued that 'vertex' or 'vertices' were "a 'point of view' provided by regarding an analysis as an ordinary conversation" (Bion 1970: 21).
7. See Ambrósio-Garcia's textual analysis of *Pigsty*, which offers a very erudite discussion of the key elements in Bion's concept of binocular vision, particularly on the notion of distance between parts of the self and on the Kleinian notion of symbol-formation.
8. Winnicott defines cultural experience as such: "I have used the term cultural experience as an extension of the idea of transitional phenomena and of play without being certain that I can define the word 'culture'. The accent indeed is on experience ... I am thinking of something that is in the common pool of humanity, into which individuals and groups

of people may contribute, and from which we may all draw if we have somewhere to put what we find" (1991: 99). This emphasis on the intersubjectivity of the individual with the group is another link to Bion's treatment and extension of the term 'emotional experience'.
9 As Angela Richards notes, "[the term Id] cleared up and in part replaced the ill-defined uses of the earlier terms 'the unconscious', 'the Ucs.' and 'the systematic unconscious' " (1987: 345).
10 See Ambrósio Garcia who discusses such Kleinian developments within the context of Jean-Louis Baudry and Christian Metz's apparatus theories.
11 This goes some way toward the idea that even though open ended narratives frustrate us, they enable greater potential for emotional growth than the usual happy ending in narrative closure because it is through tolerating the frustration of a lack of closure that we are able to embrace the difficulty of determining what the meaning might be for us, without it having to be thought for us.
12 See Wilson (2004), whose work on neurasthenia is exceptional with regard to the discounting of biology and its role in evaluating conversion hysteria.
13 In more contemporary works on affect and emotion, the correlation between Bion and Tomkins remains under-evaluated overall, save notable exceptions such as Frank (2015), Marilyn Charles (2011) and Ruth Stein (1991).

References

Abraham, K. (1924). A Short Study of the Development of the Libido Viewed in Light of Mental Disorders. In *Selected Papers of Karl Abraham*. Translated by D. Bryan and A. Strachey. New York: Basic Books.
Ambrósio Garcia, C. (2017). *Bion in Film Theory: The Retreat in Film*. Abingdon, UK: Routledge.
Bion, W.R. (1961). *Experiences in Groups and Other Papers*. New York: Basic Books.
Bion, W.R. (1962a). *Learning From Experience*. London: Tavistock.
Bion, W.R. (1962b). The Psycho-Analytic Study of Thinking. *International Journal of Psycho-Analysis*, 43, pp. 306–310.
Bion, W.R. (1965). *Transformations: Change From Learning to Growth*. London: William Heinemann Medical Books.
Bion, W.R. (1967). *Second Thoughts*. London: William Heinemann Medical Books.
Bion, W.R. (1970). *Attention and Interpretation: A Scientific Approach to Insight in Psycho-Analysis and Groups*. London: Karnac Books.
Bléandonu, G. (1994). *Wilfred Bion: His Life and Works, 1897–1979*. Translated by C. Pajaczkowska. New York: Other Press.
Brennan, T. (2004). *The Transmission of Affect*. Ithaca and London: Cornell University Press.
Cartwright, L. (2008). *Moral Spectatorship: Technologies of Voice and Affect in Postwar Representations of the Child*. Durham: Duke University Press.
Charles, M. (2011). *Working With Trauma: Lessons From Bion and Lacan*. Lanham, MD: Jason Aronson.
Ferro, A. and Civitarese, G. (2015). *The Analytic Field and Its Transformations*. London: Karnac Books.
Ferro, A. and Foresti, G. (2013). Bion and Thinking. *The Psychoanalytic Quarterly*, 82 (2), pp. 361–391.
Frank, A. (2015). *Transferential Poetics, From Poe to Warhol*. New York: Fordham University Press.
Frank, A. and Wilson, E. (2012). Like-Minded. *Critical Inquiry*, 38, pp. 870–877.
Freud, S. (1920). Beyond the Pleasure Principle. In *The Standard Edition of the Complete Psychological Works of Sigmund Freud*, 18. London: Hogarth Press.
Freud, S. (1923). The Ego and the Id. In *The Standard Edition of the Complete Psychological Works of Sigmund Freud*, 19. London: Hogarth Press.

Gibbs, A. (2001). Contagious Feelings: Pauline Hanson and the Epidemiology of Affect. *Australian Humanities Review*, 24. http://www.australianhumanitiesreview.org/archive/Issue-December-2001/gibbs.html.

Hinshelwood, R. (2013). The Tavistock Years. In Torres, N. and Hinshelwood, R.D. (eds.) *Bion's Sources: The Shaping of His paradigms*. Hove, East Sussex: Routledge.

Izod, J. and Dovalis, J. (2015). *Cinema as Therapy: Grief and Transformational Film*. Hove, East Sussex: Routledge.

Klein, M. (1935). A Contribution to the Psychogenesis of Manic-Depressive States. *The International Journal of Psychoanalysis*, 16, pp. 145–174.

Klein, M. (1946). Notes on Some Schizoid Mechanisms. In *Envy and Gratitude and Other Works: 1946–1963*. London: Hogarth Press and the Institute of Psychoanalysis.

Klein, M. (1948). On the Theory of Anxiety and Guilt. In *Envy and Gratitude and Other Works: 1946–1963*. London: Hogarth Press and the Institute of Psychoanalysis.

Klein, M. (1952a). The Origins of Transference. In *Envy and Gratitude and Other Works: 1946–1963*. London: Hogarth Press and the Institute of Psychoanalysis.

Klein, M. (1952b). Some Theoretical Conclusions Regarding the Emotional Life of the Infant. In *Envy and Gratitude and Other Works: 1946–1963*. London: Hogarth Press and the Institute of Psychoanalysis.

Klein, M. (1957). Envy and Gratitude. In *Envy and Gratitude and Other Works: 1946–1963*. London: Hogarth Press and the Institute of Psychoanalysis.

Klein, M. (1958). On the Development of Mental Functioning. In *Envy and Gratitude and Other Works: 1946–1963*. London: Hogarth Press and the Institute of Psychoanalysis.

Kuhn, A. (ed.) (2013). *Little Madnesses: Winnicott, Transitional Phenomena and Cultural Experience*. London: I.B. Tauris.

López-Corvo, R.E. (2005). *The Dictionary of the Work of W.R. Bion*. London: Karnac.

Ogden, T. (1994). The Analytic Third: Working With Intersubjective Clinical Facts. *International Journal of Psycho-Analysis*, 75, pp. 3–19.

Ogden, T. (2009). *Rediscovering Psychoanalysis: Thinking and Dreaming, Learning and Forgetting*. London and New York: Routledge.

Phillips, A. (2012). *Missing Out: In Praise of the Unlived Life*. New York: Farrar, Strauss ad Giroux.

Richards, A. (ed.) (1987). Editor Preface. In Freud, S. (ed.) *On Psychopathology: Inhibitions, Symptoms, and Anxiety*. Harmondsworth: Penguin.

Sandler, P.C. (2009). *A Clinical Application of Bion's Concepts: Dreaming Transformation Containment and Change, Vol. 1*. London: Karnac Books.

Stein, R. (1991). *Psychoanalytic Theories of Affect*. London: Karnac Books.

Tomkins, S. (1962a). *Affect, Imagery, Consciousness, Volume 1, The Positive Affects*. New York: Springer.

Tomkins, S. (1962b). *Affect, Imagery, Consciousness, Volume 2, The Negative Affects*. New York: Springer.

Tomkins, S. (1991). *Affect, Imagery, Consciousness, Volume 3, The Negative Affects*. New York: Springer.

Tomkins, S. (1992). *Affect, Imagery, Consciousness, Volume 4, Cognition, Duplication, and Transformation of Information*. New York: Springer.

Whitehouse-Hart, J. (2014). 'Programs for People Who Are Paranoid About the Way They Look': Thoughts on Paranoia, Recognition, and Mirrors. In Bainbridge, C. and Yates, C. (eds.) *Media and the Inner World: Psycho-Cultural Approaches to Emotion, Media and Popular Culture*. Basingstoke: Palgrave Macmillan.

Wilson, E. (2004). *Psychosomatic: Feminism and the Neurological Body*. Durham: Duke University Press.

Winnicott, D.W. (1991). *Playing and Reality*. London and New York: Routledge.

3
WANDERING REVERIE AND THE AESTHETIC EXPERIENCE OF BEING ADRIFT

Bion (1962a) writes that reverie is the foundation of mental functioning, which, if it occurs in an open manner, represents the capacity for two minds to receive each other and think together in fruitful (and emotionally turbulent) ways that permit mental growth. This chapter explores the concept of reverie to discuss the spectator's 'intersubjective aesthetic experience' within the moving image encounter, examining Bion's claim that dreaming is an action that occurs as 'unconscious waking thought'. I argue that such a modality of dreaming works similarly within moving image spectatorship through the emotional experience of wandering reverie. Three specific Bionian terms are introduced to the theorizing of moving image experience (reverie, spacing and dreaming) in order to highlight the potential of a psychoanalytic theory of affect regarding the examination of lived, visual and emotional experience. Through the formal analysis of soundscapes and montage within *Walkabout* (1971) and *Don't Look Now* (1973), I discuss the function of reverie within cinema and its potential for moving image experience.

Reverie, as it is generally used, refers to one's capacity to daydream. Less known, it has been used to refer to "senses relating to wild or uncontrolled behaviour", "wantonness", "a state of wild joy or delight" and even "a fit of fury; a state of anger or irritation" – clearly highlighting its association not just with thought but also with lived experience (*Oxford English Dictionary*). Bion extends the connotation of emotion within the term 'reverie' to describe the unspoken and unpresentable link between mother and infant, more specifically to note the mother's capacity to receive and respond to the inner emotional life of the infant. This is otherwise known as the mother's alpha function, its key purpose being receptivity and adaptation to her infant's affective states. Bion argues that the mother's capacity for reverie is "inseparable from the content for one clearly depends on the other" (1962a: 36), indicating that reverie is an intuitive response from the mother, how she shows she loves her child. This conceptualization forms the foundation for Bion's later theorization of dreaming, discussed in detail later in the chapter, where he links the function and receptivity of reverie to the capacity for unconscious waking thought (dreaming).

We can interpret Bion's concept of reverie as an affective response as it is dependent on the transmission of sensuous experience – although not necessarily via embodied means (touch, smell, etc.).[1] Avner Bergstein notes the example of anxiety which "has no shape, colour, or sound" (2013: 627) and points to Bion's proposition that reverie functions more as intuitive reception and response to sensory experience, rather than direct observation of the senses. The significance of seeing reverie as an intuitive, affective response is that it possesses a wandering quality. In this respect, it echoes Cartwright's comment on Tomkins's affect theory, that "*affect wants to be free*" (2008: 44, italics original) – yes but free how? Moreover, free from what? Bergstein cites Bion's discussion of reverie in *Taming Wild Thoughts* (1997) as a type of wandering (although Bion never uses the word 'wandering'). Bion writes,

> of this peculiar state of mind where we see things and go to places which, when our state of mind changes because we happen to do what we call 'wake up', then we ignore these facts, these journeys, these sights, on the grounds that they are only dreams.
>
> *(1997: 28)*

Wandering reverie begins to appear 'free' within the context of Cartwright's "problematic of motivation action" (2008: 49), which is not always conscious but invariably concerned with the movement of feeling between two minds. She writes "how "I" (the spectator) *respond* when I believe that I "know how you feel"; what is produced "in me" when feelings are projected through representations [inclusive of sound, light, montage]; and how I act in response to that process, whether I am cognizant of my affective response or not" (Cartwright 2008: 49, italics original). Cartwright argues that Tomkins's classifications of affect speak more clearly and specifically to emotional and aesthetic experience, although she is careful to resist the binary values within Tomkins writings, and instead applies a wandering reverie of her own in her theorizing of "attachments, historical determinations, responses of other bodies, and transitional objects such as photographs, television and film images, and computer keyboards and displays" (2008: 50) that crossover multiple screen media.

Bion (1997: 32) sees reverie working most effectively as an idle state of mind, a type of "thinking in a way one might describe as being almost thoughtless". These idling, wandering and intuitive moments are specific to reverie, and which Bion argues possess the greatest potential for mental growth, and what we can further regard as potential for Tomkins's 'affect being free'. If, as Bion claims, we seek another mind to think our most disturbing thoughts in order to grow, then reverie is the capacity that links the gaps between such minds and emotional experience, "[r]everie makes it possible to listen to what happens in the gap [between two minds]" (Bergstein 2013: 629). In this chapter I take up the wandering quality of reverie that Bion and Bergstein refer to and consider more specifically how it might work as a type of wandering (in terms of psychic thought) and as a proto-mental (thought and felt) spacing in the cinematic field via the work of Ferro and Civitarese (2015). The term 'spacings', as used here, incorporates the conception of movement in wandering as an exchange between subjectivity, space and place, and also adds to the technique of wandering as dreaming in new ways. Ferro and Civitarese write, "[s]pacing is the very means whereby the subject is constructed. Non-presence is inscribed in presence, the negative in the positive, death in life" (2015: 70). The last term I use to qualify reverie is 'dreaming', which differs significantly from its initial classical psychoanalytic configuration.

A note on wandering

Within the conceptualization of 'being embedded', it is possible to acknowledge a perception of being fixed in a place and/or in a time, a perception that appears to put the experience and sensation of embeddedness as opposite to that of wandering. The *Oxford English Dictionary* defines 'wandering' as "[t]ravelling from place to place or from country to country without settled route or destination; roaming ... sometimes denoting a protracted period of *devious journeying*" (italics added). This idea of wandering as *devious journeying* emphasizes the perception of wandering as a moveable state of being in-between one's inner world and outer reality. Following the *OED* definition, wandering doesn't appear to have many positive qualities at all, described as 'devious', 'irregular turning' or 'aimless passing' – arguably viewed as the taking of time rather than an experiencing of time between places that are viewed as having better uses and virtues, or possessing nobler intentions. Put simply, instead of wandering, the message is one ought to be doing (or at least *seen to be doing*) something else, something more direct, more regular, more aim-*full*.

This is reflected in Bion's attempt to speak of reverie working best via an idle state of mind, to have the masquerade of laziness in the hope that such wandering of thought might catch something significant "in the net of my idleness" (Bion 1997: 32). We might then say that the process of wandering, in relation to the idea of reverie and of 'being embedded', appears to be one of evasion, actively avoiding becoming embedded. I argue that nothing could be further from the truth of what the wandering of reverie is or what it is doing. Wandering is often regarded as daydreaming, as fantasy – as movements that we resist or that are ascribed to artistic and alternative ways of thinking. We do it multiple times a day in a myriad of situations. It may have some purpose, in terms of personal advantage or function (daydreams have often been viewed as indulgent and escape the classification of 'worry'), but rarely is wandering movement seen as commonly productive. Like daydreams, other people are not said to benefit from another's wandering, but how can we be sure of this? As Bion writes, the fear of being idle (a type of wandering) is similar to being asked "[w]hy on earth don't you find something to do?" (1997: 32). What importance could aimless passings and irregular turnings have for relating or embedding?

What is missing from negative qualifications of wandering is the possibility that 'to wander' has a very specific, necessary and *central* purpose that produces its own particular satisfactions and connections with others in its being unattached from punctuality; that its purpose and importance can lie in the necessity of maintaining the interstices of spaces between people, places and things, or even in a sensibility of time not framed by capitalistic means. Bion's concept of reverie offers the definition of wandering a critical quality, and speaks directly to what might also be happening when we idle with and intuit moving images. The wandering within reverie is used here as a conceptual tool, to evoke ideas of moving and movement that are both psychic (mental, thought) and corporeal (felt, sensed, embodied), so as to draw attention to the activity of participation in intersubjective interaction and where the effect of 'being embedded' might fit with the construction of 'embedded' feeling in the circumstance of moving image experience. Wandering is also something we do and are conditioned to do in certain ways, to the extent that we can call wandering an unexamined practice of how people interact and use the world of things around them. This leads us to the recent work of Ferro and Civitarese on analytic field theory (discussed in greater depth in Chapter 4), which I apply to the 'cinematic field' with the claim that the intersubjective wanderings of patient and analyst, so central and constructive to the analytic situation, are also utilized within moving image experience between spectator, audience and screen. Analytic field theory emphasizes relations between people certainly, but beyond the specific bodies of analyst and patient, there are also relations of transferring, wandering, and of sensations, sensualities, emotions, reveries, feelings – which are unspoken, unconscious in relationships (see Bollas's unthought known in *The Shadow of the Object*, 1989). I argue such wanderings and transitions are the foundation of moving image experience, which act as a potentiality of socio-cultural psychoanalysis in a non-clinical setting.

In defining the analytic field, Ferro and Civitarese acknowledge the critical influence of phenomenologist Maurice Merleau-Ponty (1964), who stressed the constant exchange and correlation between the subject and their (spatial and temporal) place in the world:

> Like Klein, Merleau-Ponty considered that identity can be thought of only in terms of difference, of the intersection between the subject's body and the world of things and other people. A person can be himself only by projecting himself outside his own self into the other, and vice versa.
> *(Ferro and Civitarese 2015: 2 fn 3)*

This projection identifies the intuitive movement of reverie. Cinema invites and nurtures the projection of the spectator so that they may wander and dream their "self into the other and vice versa". If moving image experience mirrors the intersubjective space and time of analysis, where the spectator and film (subject and object) are participants in the establishing of what is communicated and exchanged to create 'cinematic experience', then it is possible to view moving images as echoing an experience that facilitates a wandering of mind, where

> various parts of the mind incessantly carry on among themselves, while always seeking better ways of thinking about [the spectator's] current emotional problem (however, terms such as unconscious thought, dreaming, thinking, and the like must be seen as virtually equivalent).
>
> *(Ferro and Civitarese 2015: 6)*

Whilst wandering may be a conceptual way of describing what is happening in unconscious waking thought, it is also a way of identifying the technique or process of intuiting affect via reverie which is at work in spectatorship. For example, through formal aesthetics and narrative convention, which have directed such unconscious wandering thought in specific ways (through genre or other referential cultural codes – of identity, for example).

Anyone who has walked somewhere with a child will have experienced the difference between an idle wandering and a walk as a means of getting to somewhere else; such walks are about our experience with time. Children rarely take the uninteresting path; they are far more interested and invested in the experience of getting to where they are going than in the punctuality of their arrival. Can we speak of moving image experience in similar terms? Experimental, avant-garde and post-classical films are examples of moving images that formally foreground a concern with the sensuous experience of cinema, but more recently emergent media and creative productions of reality through VR (and developments in augmented reality) suggest similar invitations to the sensuous wandering of both mind and body.[2] Their direction and treatment of time deviates considerably from its narrative cinema counterparts, yet equally encourage experience *with* them. Is this 'cinema' wandering within itself? The argument here is that the imaginary of wandering determines much of our moving image experience – as broadly as can be interpreted within the post-cinematic media landscape. As adults, we may have lost the childlike ability to idly wander with purpose, lost its associated sense of child-time that wanders in-between the places we are going, but it is argued here that we still seek out the existential equivalent of wandering reveries. Reveries carve out spaces and times that allow us to escape our attachments to punctuality (indeed punctuation) and other such erosive impositions on our creativity, that is, on our capacity to dream, to experience unconscious waking thought.

As we roam away from classical psychoanalytic theories toward the more contemporary configurations found in Bion's work and that of his commentators (who concentrate on the centrality of the dream as a way of thinking and as a structure of how we process emotional experience), moving images remain as vital cultural phenomena that represent what it means to wander as well as determine both the space and time for an entertainment of psychic wandering. 'Being embedded' is therefore reasoned here to exist within the sensibility of wandering reverie and is exemplified through our moving image experience, where we become moved and affected by moving images in ways that could not have been prescribed or expected, through the intersubjective aesthetics that grow from cinema and visual media. The idea of wandering reverie is used here with the intention to disturb the association of 'being embedded' with an idealization of stability and stasis. Specifically it is the interrelationship of space, time and movement that wandering reveries are argued to disrupt, which holds particular significance for film and media studies, given that these interrelationships are the most fundamental formal aspects of the cinematic arts. The other aim interweaves lesser known psychoanalytic ideas of contemporary thinkers (Bion, Ogden, Ferro and Civitarese) within areas relevant to film and media studies so that 'cinema' is not only diversified in terms of its technological platforms and experiences, but it is also further regarded as something which we use, via dreaming, rather than solely something we watch (argued, for example, via older paradigms that emphasized visual pleasure).

The intention is to 'return' to an altogether more original interpretation of wandering, something that is perhaps more primary to the human condition. As such, the term 'wandering' is reclaimed in two main ways: 1) that 'to wander' is a necessary part of the proto-mental process, that is how it aligns with Bion's theory of thinking and his revision of dreaming; and 2) the reclamation of 'wandering' foregrounds Bion's revisionist process of thinking itself – we wander back through psychical processes and their affective resonances (which constitutes aesthetic experience). These reclamations are the foundations of reverie, spacing and dreaming. This approach readdresses wandering by retaining, as well as celebrating, the devious, irregular and aimless elements specific to it, in order to show that 'being embedded' is also an emotional experience crafted through *oscillation* between spaces and times, that is precisely outside of stable and static spaces, times and movements. This *poiesis* of 'being embedded', the making and becoming a part of reality (or even the creative production of reality), is examined through three key psychoanalytic potentialities – reverie, spacings and dreaming as the basis for a theorizing of wandering that embeds us, experience which is evoked within our uses of the moving image.

Wandering as reverie

The idea of reverie presents a curious question for the sensoria of 'being embedded' within aesthetic audio-visual experience. The primary theoretical paradigm and methodology used – Bionian psychoanalysis – one that is entirely invested in what remains hidden, unknown, unseen (such as the dream) and unshared (what is shared within dreams is never clearly (or precisely) determined, but rather worked *with* (Civitarese 2014)). Reverie is one concept found in both traditional and contemporary models of psychoanalysis – Freud called it free association,[3] where the analysand is said to be consciously unattached to the thoughts that enter their mind and are expressed through speech. Bion (1962a) wrote that reverie is used to infer and relate to the intersubjective relationship between (unconscious) knowledge and experience, specifically within the mother's adaptability to her child. Reverie identifies the transformative potential and function of thought, which is specifically aligned with the mother's ability to experience, process, transform and return the infant's emotional experience that they themselves could not bear. The mother does this without awareness or instruction. It is an unconscious process. Bion further writes,

> reverie is that state of mind which is open to the reception of any "objects" from the loved object and is therefore capable of reception of the infant's projective identifications whether they are felt by the infant to be good or bad. In short, reverie is a factor of the mother's alpha function.
> *(Bion 1962a: 36)*

As previously mentioned, the mother's alpha function refers to her capacity (meaning unconscious ability) to unconsciously acknowledge and accept the 'sense data' of the infant (their feelings, emotions, their love and their hate) and respond to it by dreaming it, that is being able to unconsciously process the projected feelings from the infant into her own emotional experience. Bion claimed that the infant, in order to think thoughts, needed to change their emotional experiences into aesthetic experience that could be used later in life for dreaming (thinking through tolerating frustrating emotional experience). Bion's theory of dreaming differed distinctly from Freud's to concentrate on unconscious waking thought, rather than the deciphering of infantile and disguised wishes.

Symington and Symington (2008: 168) write that reverie is "which best disposes the mind to make that transition from sensual to mental". Here 'sensual' refers to emotional and unthought (unconscious) experience, and 'mental' to the conscious thinking of what was sensed. Put another way, the sensual is affective and raw, and it requires translation in order to be communicated to another person. It may or may not lead to an embodied response, depending on the success of its transition into becoming thought. The translation of the sensual into a visual, recognizable emotion that can be interpreted (not always consciously) is the indication that transition into the mental has occurred. Indeed such transition is a consequence of reverie, however Ogden offers a more comprehensive interpretation, "I view reverie as simultaneously a personal/private event and an intersubjective one. . . . Reverie is an exquisitely private dimension of experience involving the most embarrassingly quotidian (and yet all important) aspects of our lives" (Ogden 1999: 158–159). The purpose of reverie is to create space for alpha function – specifically, to let the received emotional experiences that we are not conscious of, but which affect us nonetheless, to wander and be aimless in their path so that they may be used for unconscious waking thought (dreaming) later in our lived experiences. Reverie, in this way, can be said to function as aesthetic psychic spacing – to conjoin as well as separate the sensual from the mental in our everyday lives.

What I wish to wander away from is the normative practice of finding examples within cinema where this can be shown, that is to fix (and force) where films can be said to visually represent this process. Instead, I want to consider how moving images offer the intersubjective space for reverie to suggest itself through aesthetic experience. Wandering, then is argued here as an unconscious construction of space through the pretense of physical distance and without any concerted effort or desire to get from one emotional thought to another. As psychic spacing, the aimless passing of wandering in our going to and watching of moving images, our physical receptivity and response to them, returns us to the childlike path where we use such images to turn the sensual to into the mental, affording ourselves the different actuality of creativity that makes possible our emotional experience to be thought, or dreamed. If, as Bion claims, dreaming is what allows us to think the sensual into the mental, then cinema (again whatever it was, is and comes to be) carries the potential of a shared, almost collective, wandering 'dreamed' space. Dreaming, as discussed below within the context of Bionian psychoanalysis has very little to do with decoding a film's latent or implicit meaning and much more about the capacity of moving image experience to elicit new thoughts and the potential to think differently about the inner world of the spectator.

Devious journeying: reverie and spectatorship in *Walkabout*

Bion's concept of reverie offers its own wandering in terms of thinking about spectatorship, aesthetic experience and an audiences' use of cinema. Whereas traditional models of psychoanalysis have focused on the gaze, either as an apparatus that facilitates visual pleasure (Mulvey 1975) or as the dominant structure of spectator identification (Baudry, 1970, 1975; Metz 1974, 1982), Bion's concept of reverie presents a more mystical perspective for the analysis of moving image experience, which looks to account for the range of sensory experience (of which vision is one part) in how we process, think and respond to emotional experience. Given that cinema is a conglomerate of formal aesthetics (sound, light, movement, cinematography, ideology, etc.), such contemporary psychoanalytic theories on experience and thought not only enables us to think about the function of cinema within society as an object, but even specifically how cinema and its parts are used by the filmgoer to unconsciously negotiate their own instinctual lives.

Ogden (1999) observes that the importance of reverie is easy to underestimate given its everyday aspect and idiosyncratic quality, but equally that this is what makes it both extremely significant and necessarily unremarkable in our daily interactions. In his examination of reverie, as a happening as well as an intersubjective structural presence within psychoanalysis, Ogden uses words that mirror a sensibility of wandering. "[Reverie] does not have a clearly delineated point of departure or point of termination separating it" (1999: 160); "The analyst's use of his reveries requires tolerance of the experience of being adrift" (1999: 160); and most interestingly "[r]everie is an emotional compass that I heavily rely on (but cannot clearly read) to gain my bearing in the analytic situation" (1999: 160). Ogden's choice of words illuminates the presence and working of reverie and its wandering potential within the analytic situation, as much as it shows the process of reverie as a wandering process in our unconscious waking thought. Even further, and more specifically for the question of 'being embedded' as a consequence of wandering, reverie is argued to be an essential component in the formation of the relationship between the analyst and the analysand, serving to create what Ogden has termed the 'intersubjective analytic third' (Ogden 1994a, 1994b, 1999), which Ferro and Civitarese view as an elemental aspect of the analytic field. Ogden writes that intersubjective experience is:

> simultaneously within and outside of the intersubjectivity of the analyst – analysand, which I will refer to as 'the analytic third'. This third subjectivity, the intersubjective analytic third (Green's [1975] 'analytic object'), is a product of a unique dialectic generated by (between) the separate subjectivities of analyst and analysand within the analytic setting.
>
> *(Ogden 1994b: 4)*

The duality involved in the actualization and recognition of the analytic third is paralleled within moving image experience, where the screen is no longer simply projected upon (as mirror, or as a sardine can that looks back)[4] but rather that the experience is mutually constructed between spectator, film and the overall engagement of what makes cinema, cinema – forming a cinematic *gestalt* as well as a 'cinematic third' or better, 'cinematic field'.

It is clear that watching moving images is not the same experience as being in an analytic session, however this does not discount the intersubjective role and activity of reverie in the formation of cinematic meaning. Indeed, it echoes the long held notion within film studies that meaning is developed through the hermeneutics of cinema, not simply residing in the film text itself. The reverie in spectatorship then, mirrors Bion's reverie that Ogden explicates via the analytic situation, where we can say that the term reverie refers

> not only to those psychological states that clearly reflect the analyst's active receptivity to the analysand, but also to a motley collection of psychological states that seem to reflect the analyst's narcissistic self-absorption, obsessional rumination, day-dreaming, sexual fantasising, and so on.
>
> *(Ogden 1994b: 9)*

This is similar to the spectator's receptivity of the film and their own 'motley collection' of psychic states. The power of reverie, where it is exercised within cinematic experience, is in the spectator's engagement with the moving image – silent or otherwise. The film is watched, understood and put together within the minds of audience members, or more specifically within the internal world of the spectator, without interruption to "the free play of ideas: images, words, feelings, somatic states, body affinities, jumbl[ing] together in a moving chorus of psychic apprehension" (Bollas 2010: 107). Let us look to two specific films by Nicolas Roeg, *Walkabout* and *Don't Look Now*, as examples that illuminate how the Bionian idea of reverie might echo the qualities of wandering (and being embedded) between the spectator and the moving image.

Walkabout

In Roeg's *Walkabout*, we see wandering as reverie working in a number of ways: 1) as a spectatorship experience within the spacing (visual and aural) of cinema; 2) as a representation of movement; and 3) as a recurring theme within the film where different typologies of wandering (active wandering versus imposed wandering) work to valorize the interconnected spacings of subjectivity and setting. The film opens with the following statement:

> In Australia, when an Aborigine man-child reaches sixteen, he is sent out into the land. For months he must live from it. Sleep on it. Eat of its fruit and flesh. Stay alive. Even if it means killing his fellow creatures. The Aborigines call it the WALKABOUT. This is the story of a 'WALKABOUT'.
>
> *(Roeg 1971)*

In the first instance, we are given the referential code of what a walkabout is but not whose walkabout the story concerns. It is assumed that it is the Boy's (David Gulpilil)[5] that we will witness because it is the most literal and it falls within the given frame of reference, but there are *at least* three others. The walkabout of the Girl (Jenny Agutter), who as a 16-year-old girl, must also learn to survive in her own environment using the resources it offers (verbal and gestural languages that exist as social performativities – a type of symbolic flora and fauna – rendered completely useless in the Australian Outback); of the father (John Meillon), whose walkabout is both a metaphor for the displacement of national identity, as well as the loss of the self as it descends into madness; and third, there is the walkabout of the spectator – who, more than their screen counterparts, is required to tolerate 'being adrift' (as per Ogden) as they must piece together and order all walkabouts in order to interpret and dream the film. It is left ambiguous, the number of walkabouts and their relevant (and relating) potential within the film, and this ambiguity is in itself a way of recognizing reverie at work within the interstices of moving image aesthetic, sensory experience.

Ogden writes, "thoughts and feelings constituting reverie are rarely discussed with our colleagues" (Ogden 1999: 159), and we can speak of other filmgoers here instead of colleagues inasmuch as though we may be willing to discuss what we 'thought of the film', it is rare that we can easily "hold such thoughts, feelings, and sensations in consciousness" (Ogden 1999: 159) at the same time as each other. Indeed, Bion claims that the "term reverie may be applied to almost any content" (Bion 1962a: 36), leaving us to link reverie with actions of interpretation as a wandering that unconsciously distinguishes between what is sensed versus what is thought. Instead of spectatorship identification operating here within an ocular-centric paradigm, Bion's theory of reverie and Ogden's explication of its function within an analytic setting, demonstrate its potential in offering an alternative emphasis, "[i]n our efforts to make analytic use of our reveries, 'I' as unselfconscious subject is transformed into 'me' as object of analytic scrutiny" (Ogden 1999: 159). This transformation assisted through spectator reverie is an intersubjective process – we view *and use* the walkabouts of both the Boy and the Girl to structure our own, and in doing so concurrently structure our reading of theirs.

The wandering sequence of acousmatic (or non-diegetic) sounds (acousmatic sound refers to the sound that is heard by the spectator but is not visually represented (see Chion 1994)) and images in the first fifteen minutes of the film, dreamlike and dream-worked in their relation, begin with an extreme close up of a rock face formation as though it were scarred, red rock cutting through lighter, browner stone. This image is overlaid with acousmatic sound, synthesized tones and technology that sound eerily like the outer-space, 'other world' type sounds from films like *Forbidden Planet* (Wilcox 1956), before becoming radio static. The first acousmatic sounds we hear signal a migration from a different place and space, foreshadowing the narrative themes of the film and the relationship between Girl and Boy, but more immediately the movement of disconnected images that follow. The rock face formation gives way to another extreme close-up, this time of a brick wall, representing shifts in time and materiality of space, a juxtaposition that is quickly supported through the clashing of images and sound: the radio voice speaking French, "*Faites vos jeux, messieurs et madames, s'il vous plait*" ("place your bets, ladies and gentleman, please") against the sound of a didgeridoo over a modern urban setting with no Indigenous person in sight. The invisibility of hearing here (as opposed to the invisibility of seeing what is heard) is an example of the wandering ear, not necessarily an active wandering, but an imposed wandering – where the non-diegetic acousmatic sounds are representative of the two worlds that are about to collide on screen but require the imposed participation of the spectator. Who is placed to hear such sounds if not the audience? Where are the other ears (are there other ears?) located that are supposed to hear these sounds against these images?

As Michel Chion (1994: 296) writes, "[t]he question of point of audition, like that of point of view, involves not just locating the source but also poses the question of who is listening". He argues that the connection and arbitrary relationship between what is seen and heard, and who is hearing, is an adoption that is dependent on a visual "sound barrier, which could be either a material obstacle that impedes the sound (wall, door, windowpane) or another louder noise that masks it (crowd, storm, wind, train)" (Chion 1994: 296) – something that allows us to visually connect sound to referent. In *Walkabout*, it is not until we see Girl's breathing in unison with her classmates that this subjective adoption is formed within the spectator.

Such sounds that are not visually identified or easily relatable require the reverie of the spectator, their free play with what Chion refers to as the "narrative indeterminacy of acousmatic sounds" (1994: 290). The music of the didgeridoo competes with the direct sound of people walking, cars driving in the streets; the girls' breath heard alongside the office sounds of telephones and typewriters, all while we are looking at a man who is slightly visible in his high-rise office building. We cannot see anyone playing the didgeridoo and so we imagine that its narrative function is to assist the mood and setting of the film – effecting Indigenous Australiana to situate 'Australia'. We think the characters cannot hear it, the music being acousmatic, but there are indications that perhaps the man (father of Girl) can. He is shown looking aimlessly upwards (possibly seeking the source of the sound) when he enters a concrete, urban space by himself in central Sydney. This scene is instrumental in challenging not only the point of audition – what is heard and who hears it – within the sequence, but it also questions the normative narrative structure at the beginning of a film. The editing techniques, traditionally invisible and used to establish the style and hermeneutic of the film are left noticeable, confronting and transitory in *Walkabout*, as the wipes switch us three times between urban and outback spaces.

This aural and visual wandering within *Walkabout's* opening sequence uses the narrative indeterminacy of sound and sound effects to affect a dream-like quality to the film, as well as the space to dream the film for the spectator. It is the wandering of movement in images and sounds that permits the aesthetic experience of the 'walkabout' story to develop, a journey to begin, an action to occur. Wandering is movement here, as the wandering ear and invisibility of its hearing linking both the experience of cinema and the happening of the story together. As spectators, we both think and feel the walkabout from the opening of Roeg's film because of the aesthetic, sensory experience formally offered.

Reverie as spacings: the irregular turning of aesthetic experience

Ferro and Civitarese use the word 'spacings' in their analysis of the (psycho)analytic field:

> to put into immediate context space and time as two terms that imply each other and must necessarily live side by side. Replacing the combination of space and time with the concept of spacing (less abstract than *différance*) allows us to simultaneously allude to the temporality of space and the spatiality of time. Spacing is neither the one nor the other, and is both together.
>
> *(Ferro and Civitarese 2015: 69)*

Their use of the term 'spacings' is intended to continue to rethink the analytic situation and relationship between analyst and patient in a post-Bionian context, where the concept of spacing notes not only the things (tactile, visual, spoken, gestural) that keep parts of the situation separate but also acknowledge and evaluate those elements that form what an analytic situation can be and is aesthetically experienced as. As such, everything that is identified is seen as both connected and separate, and as mutually constructive of the space and time (the spacings) that become the 'analytic situation'.

This further connects the interrelationships and experiences of analyst and patient subjectivities, the analytic setting, and the reveries and experiences of these linkings. Subjectivity, the context and the setting are viewed as reciprocated constituents within the exchange, so rather than examining the distinct elements of space and time, Ferro and Civitarese look more to *how* the spacings of these various elements distance, fuse, respond and recreate each other. The notion of wandering is used similarly in this chapter to denote the *function* of Bion's reverie and to show a possible way in which it works as its own spacing within cinema, mimicking the structure and affect of aesthetic experience (and any potential transformation) within the analytic situation. If instead of analyst and patient, we identify film, spectator, audience/community, auditorium or visual space, as occupying physical and psychical distances necessary to "achieve and expand emotional unison" (2015: 69), then just like the analytic field, the cinematic field "may also relate to the past, the present, the future, material or mental reality, conscious or unconscious experience". (Ferro and Civitarese 2015: 73). The idea of spacings, initially appears to ask that we pay attention to the gaps, the in-between spaces that separate each individual element, as well as consider a sensibility of time that is not linear but circular (Ferro and Civitarese 2015). This is a means of acknowledging plurality in a post-Bionian analytic field, as it highlights the networked relativity between any element in a situation that has site (sight?) specificity to its identity (the duration of analysis and the duration of a film both utilize and obey the idea of the limit in time and in space).

The psychoanalytic field is recognized as the analytic field and not as something else because there is a script attached to the relationship of analyst and patient, one that is dependent not only on the physical distance between two people, but also on the close emotional connections that occur within the situation – the high levels of intimacy, the privacy afforded this particular relationship (it is not overheard and it is not recorded for the public). Ferro and Civitarese write:

> The setting of the analysis itself organises the spacing that is meant to help restore a less anxious sense of space and time, to turn back the hands of the clock if they have been moved forward and vice versa. . . . Its concreteness is regulated by the analytic contract, but it is both a dream space and a theatrical space, where the struggle for meaning with ghosts can go on stage in a state of adequate safety.
>
> *(2015: 71)*

The spacings within cinema are similarly constructed and adhered to. The cinematic setting is organized to embody a fantasy of spacings that exist if not outside, at least parallel to that of regular spacings. Our attention is organized – we might say spatially and temporally arranged – toward virtual external worlds that have an immense impact on our internal world. It is an irregular turning of time, this moving image experience – a wandering that permits an insertion of alternative time (not just of the film duration itself but equally of the time within the film text itself) in any given day, as well as a narrative structure that determines such cinematic aesthetic experience. Let us look at how the affect of spacing works as wandering aesthetic experience within *Don't Look Now*.

The affect of spacing in *Don't Look Now*

Don't Look Now responds to and recreates the aesthetics of grief, following the story of an English couple, John (Donald Sutherland) and Laura Baxter (Julie Christie) who are recovering from the trauma of the accidental drowning of their daughter, Christine (Sharon Williams). After Christine's death in England, John and Laura are living in Venice, Italy, where John has taken on the job of artistic restoration of a dilapidated church. Laura meets two sisters, Heather (Hilary Mason) who is blind and psychic, and Wendy (Clelia Matania); John is seduced into believing that they are able to communicate with Christine in the afterlife.

The limited amount of information given about the Baxters is maintained throughout the film – we know they have suffered, we can see that they are making the effort of recovering from the death of their daughter and that they have been scarred by the experience. We are not sure, nor are we ever told, of the time that has passed between Christine's death and the Baxters being in Venice. The vagueness of time is intentional as Roeg uses the lack of clearly stated time to punctuate (or we should say 'to space') the portrayal of grief and mimic its disruption of time throughout the film. Time appears as fog-like, where everything (every space) rests on the verge of closing down or emptying out. It is the off-season in Venice and the hotels are closing, the streets are empty and the footsteps of John and Laura walking through the maze-like streets echo loudly as if they were in a hollow chamber. As in the opening sequence of *Walkabout*, Roeg's treatment and spacing of time throughout *Don't Look Now* has a wandering effect, where the past relates to the present and the future in the cinematic field as both material and mental reality, conscious or unconscious experience.

The opening sequence of *Don't Look Now* is structured very similarly to that of the opening in *Walkabout* in its treatment of cinematic (diegetic) space and time. Roeg's technique of using narrative indeterminacy of sound (the synchronization of acousmatic and diegetic sounds) to create the effect of a wandering ear, produces the same dreamlike and dream-worked aesthetic that was present in *Walkabout's* opening montage of the Eastern suburbs of Sydney and the Australian Outback. *Don't Look Now* opens with Christine and her brother Johnny (Nicholas Salter) playing in a wintry, English country garden. The acousmatic sound of a piano playing is heard at the same volume as the diegetic sounds of a white horse running through the field, birds chirping, Christine wheeling a wheelbarrow and Johnny riding his bicycle through the grass. Once more these sounds, delivered in equal volumes and therefore of seemingly equal narrative importance, are for the spectator's wandering ear to play with and order through their individual reveries. The lack of clear difference between volume levels prevents the audience from using sound to organize sonics into a hierarchy and thereby create a narrative through sound; uncertainty and tension build.

Sound is classically used to offer a way to interpret images, to create the necessary affect that enhances the images shown, but Roeg's technique is to use sound as a wandering technique to create conflictual information in order to create meaning. We are limited to hearing competing sounds, but are given the repeated visual signifier of the color red which allows the spectator to take this limited repetition in visual information (as a spacing within the film's opening sequence) and bring it to a single point of information and interpretation. The spacing of the sounds in the opening sequence are non-linear, they are the visualized sounds of children's play, circular in their repetition, as all that we are left to respond and recreate with the experience of such sounds is the innocence of children absorbed in their own fantasy of play. These sounds are juxtaposed against the linearity of the repeated signifier of the color red (in Christine's red mac, in the stripes on the ball, in the fire, in the stained glass window, in the red hooded jacket in the photograph, in the red wine, in the blood from Johnny's cut finger), whose repetition is not for the characters but for the audience to link them. The repetition is to be interpreted as a spacing, and as relational, where the connections between the signifier of the color accumulates meaning and intensity the more it is repeatedly shown. Through the juxtaposition and repetition in sound and image, Roeg purposefully creates spacings in the diegesis, the multiplicity of sounds running counter to the multiplicity of images which creates an aesthetic conflict within the spectator (tension, anxiety – but of what? At the start, there is no mystery to be solved despite the aesthetic conflict that is established). The repetition of the color red – in all its different iterations – ends up saying the same thing: red equals the trauma over Christine's death, a trauma that pervades the aesthetics of the film (its present, its past and its future). The spacing of the red color unifies the trauma of Christine's death for both John and Laura, as well as the anxiety of what will happen to John and Laura for the audience.[6]

The present and the future are concurrent in many other scenes throughout the film. For example in Venice, John, without realizing what he is seeing, views his own funeral procession passing by on a boat in a canal. John, who we learn has the gift of second sight like Heather, the blind woman, believes that what he is seeing is in the present rather than it being a premonition. John believes he has seen Laura in Venice, when she should be in England visiting her son at school. This use of time, which is not formally indicated in the film as a flash-forward or psychic vision, renders the effect of cinematic time to appear as eerie and anxious rather than dreamlike or hallucinatory. John finds out that Laura is indeed in England and that he could not have seen her on the boat.

Perhaps the most memorable wandering of time working as an aesthetic spacing in *Don't Look Now* is evident in the montage of John and Laura's sex and dressing sequence. The sequence uses post-classical time as a spacing to create focus on the emotional intimacy between John and Laura, but also between the characters and the audience. The sex scenes show John and Laura returning to each other corporeally and psychically, recovering from the death of the daughter and finding happiness and connection with each other again. The scenes of sexuality are interspersed with scenes of getting dressed; again, Roeg is using time (or rather mixing up a sensibility of time) to create an aesthetic of intimacy that transcends nakedness and copulation. There appears to be an opposition between John and Laura being naked and getting dressed, but the sequence uses the different, conflicting iterations of intimacy with their bodies to show their private, and now re-connected and recreated, inner worlds. There are further and more literal examples of spacings within the text of the film itself. Venice is labyrinthine and confusing – Laura and John get lost on their way to a restaurant in the evening, and John has trouble finding the pensione where Laura met with the sisters. In these literal spacings, characters and audiences attempt to make sense of space and time through each other, which exacerbates the aesthetic spacing of grief in Roeg's film. Venice is not only the literal setting for the working through of the Baxters' trauma, it is also the figurative projection of the labyrinth of emotional experience (here anguish and loss).

In reviewing an analytic encounter with one of his patients, Bion (1965) highlights the importance of relying on aesthetic experience in order to find meaning, a strategy that also works in the cinematic field. Bion writes of his patient's violent emotions as being too extreme to be able to expressed adequately or comprehensively in words, "the communication from material from an experience [where the violence, or better – the intensity – of emotions] that is ineffable; the scientific approach, as ordinarily understood, is not available and an aesthetic approach requires an artist." (Bion 1965: 51), and asserts that it was only through aesthetic rather than a scientific experience that he was able to determine the meaning of his patient's emotional intensity. Aesthetic experience, especially within a Bionian psychoanalytic context, turns to focus on emotions and how they are experienced between two or more people, more specifically how emotions are seen to be apperceived within experience of reality (that is, how they connect with thought in order to interpret the reality we see and live). In the analytic field, aesthetic experience refers to the spacing specific to the analysis, what wanders as reverie and what determines the spacings between the analyst and the patient (and their subjectivities, the setting, the intersubjective and networked exchanges of communication that transpire therein). In the cinematic field, aesthetic experience refers to the spacing of spectator, film, audience and the intersubjective reality exchanged within the space-time of the film.

I see the function of 'aesthetic experience' within cinema – as narrative idealization or experiential, embodied reality – as highlighting the potential connections that cinematic spacings organize. These cinematic spacings include: 1) the film (the creative object), 2) the internal and private world of the spectator. For Bion, this *is* dreaming the film, individual unconscious waking thought that processes the experience. For Winnicott (1999), it is individual fantasy – that is, the frame or structure for the interpretation of the creative object; and 3) the intersubjective exchanges between spectator, audience, and film which form the 'aesthetic encounter' that works within cinema to create meaning (specifically emotional experiential meaning). This recognizes that the creativity within the aesthetic experience of cinema comes from the unconscious interactive participation of the spectator and the audience, who through respective reveries recreate, that is dream the film as they live it. The perception is both visual and corporeal ("the body is absolutely the protagonist of the subject's unconscious fantasies" (Ferro and Civitarese 2015: 27)) mirroring and paralleling the creative process that made the films. Outlining the aesthetic experience within cinema is another way of speaking to the wandering that occurs in our interaction with the external objects of our realities and our negotiations of their impact on our internal worlds, instead of leaving cinema to simply exist as a collection of films that are solely external objects to be viewed.

Aimless passing: 'being embedded' through dreaming

For a long time in film studies, the classical psychoanalytic model of dream theory (via Freud and Lacan) evolved through the influential work of Metz, Baudry and Mulvey as a method of interpreting the symbolism, reception and assembly of visual material. It has influenced the analysis of cinema as a social phenomenon as well as the textual analysis of individual films. What Bion's revolutionary theory of dreaming changes is the focus of moving image experience as becoming much more about how we use films to give meaning to our individual (as well as collective) experience, how moving images can reveal a cartography of a cultural (potentially national) unconscious, and even illuminate a spectator's own history of emotional experience. In this manner, moving images can be called dreamings in themselves, which invite and validate wandering as a most vital exercise of thinking.

The films of Nicolas Roeg discussed in this chapter are examples of what Civitarese (2014) calls 'dream films' (2014), although not exactly in the same manner with which he explores Akira Kurosawa's *Rashomon* (1950) (and Donald Meltzer's (1984) treatment of it). He writes that "[i]t is illusory to think of a direct, non-mediated rendering of the dream experience, or of a dream that is not continuously re-dreamt" (Civitarese 2014: 101) to argue that the stories we experience with moving images are "complex object[s] and ambiguous, not unlike a second dream" (2014: 101). 'Dream films' are difficult to identify as the term runs the risk of being prescriptive and of being reduced to any film that represents a 'dream', such as *Inception* (Nolan 2010). Instead, Civitarese's term 'dream films' is better understood as pointing to films that function intersubjectively as dreaming experience, like Roeg's *Walkabout* and *Don't Look Now*, but equally to recognize such potential within possible use of the moving image. Perhaps the term 'dreaming films' offers a more specific, poetic focus, one that attends to the recreation involved with the use of cinema, a spectatorship that plays with formal aesthetics (such as the narrative indeterminate spacings of time and sound) and experiential aesthetics (the bringing forth of emotions, thought within the action of spectating) in order to make meaning out of everyday life.[7]

The main difference between Freud's classical theory of dreams and Bion's contemporary theory of dreams revolves around the encounter and structure of aesthetic experience, which is the centrality of physical and psychical emotional response to our interactions with everyday objects and reality. In Chapter 2,

I discussed the influence of Klein's early work (1923, 1930, 1932) on the theorizing of dreams in order to show how the process of dreaming took on more physical and less (but not discounted) symbolic relevance, that is, the emotional elements of dreams were viewed as more representative of the process of dreaming (how and why we do it) rather than examining dreams as puzzles to be deciphered. It was through Klein's observation and analysis of children at play, specifically the material their play created, that enabled her to concentrate on the development of the inner world, and in turn helped to shift attention and attitudes on the institution of psychoanalysis overall. In this quotation from Klein's "The Psychological Principles of Early Analysis" (1926), we can note the influence of her work on Bion's development of his theory of dreaming, as well as see the impetus for his devious journeying from Freud's theory of dream work.

> My analyses again and again reveal how many different things, dolls, for example, can mean in play. Sometimes they stand for the penis, sometimes for the child stolen from the mother, sometimes for the little patient itself, etc. It is only by examining the minutest details of the game and their interpretation that the connections are made clear to use and the interpretation becomes effective. The *material* that children produce during an analytic hour, as they *pass* from play with toys to dramatization in their own person and, again, to playing with water, cutting out paper, or drawing; the *manner* in which they do this; the reason why they change from one to another; the *means* they choose for their representations – all this medley of factors, which so often seems confused and meaningless, is seen to be consistent and full of meaning and the underlying sources and thoughts are revealed to us if we interpret them just like dreams. Moreover, in their play children often represent the same thing as has appeared in some dream which they have narrated before and they often produced associations to a dream by means of play which follows it and which is their most important mode of expressing themselves.
> *(Klein 1926: 134 fn 1, italics original, except for 'pass', italics added)*

In this we see beginnings of what resulted in the wandering of Bion's theory of waking dream thought – that is, the structure of dreaming (via play – its own type of childlike wandering) as a process that is thinking through experience, the negotiation of inner worlds in the external environment of creative play. I see moving image experience as a modality of creative play, as something that resists fixed meaning, indeed it becomes the aimless passing between self, image and dream, and which uses cinema to "again and again reveal how many different things . . . can mean in play".

This is clearly not dreaming as forming the fulfillment of a wish, but much more dreaming as a way to process reality (Bion's concept of O discussed in Chapter 7) through its aimless passing between emotions and thought. It follows that Klein's contribution to the theory of dreams, her focus on their structure and subsequent affect in the child's activity, is what influenced Bion to link the process of dreaming with the structuring of thought as a way to process and negotiate sense data into embodied thought and experience. Instead of using "conscious material to interpret unconsciousness, Bion uses the unconscious to interpret a conscious state of mind" (Bléandonu 1994: 177). Rather than interpret the content of dreams, or in the case of cinema, concentrating only on what the film symbolizes, Bion's reformation of dream theory and the concept of reverie explores what the entire activity of creative experience (the 'material' produced) means for the individual (or film spectator). Put another way, "the dream becomes the very model for thought" (Civitarese 2014: xiv), it is how we watch cinema, how we use its 'material', the 'manner' in which we use cinema, the cinematic 'means' we choose, which become a revelation for how we think.

Notes

1 See Marks (2000) for a more specific discussion on sensory experience and memory.
2 Still in their infancy, VR and AR are examples of technology that make this application of 'wandering' that is being worked through here a projection of what may occur in the future with moving images. However, such VR technology as immersive art installation already has its own history concerning affective aesthetic experience (see Char Davies immersive VR work *Osmose* 1995, which integrates user movement with their breathing.
3 See Ferro and Civitarese (2015: 22) who list clear differences between free association and reverie, stating that reverie "is characterised by direct contact with the pictogram that constitutes the waking dream thought". Whilst reverie can be free association, not every free association can be reverie as it is subject to the conditioning of "narrative derivatives of waking dream thought".
4 See Lacan (1986: 95) "I was in my early twenties . . . and at the time, of course, being a young intellectual, I wanted desperately to get away, see something different, throw myself into something practical. . . . One day, I was on a small boat with a few people from a family of fishermen . . . as we were waiting for the moment to pull in the nets, an individual known as Petit-Jean . . . pointed out to me something floating on the surface of the waves. It was a small can, a sardine can. . . . It glittered in the sun. And Petit-Jean said to me – You see that can? Do you see it? Well it doesn't see you".
5 The billing of David Gulpilil's character is listed as 'Black Boy' but I have chosen to use Boy, given that Girl (Jenny Agutter's character) is not listed as 'White Girl'. As Sara Ahmed notes, "Not only do you have to become insistent in order to receive what was automatically given to the others; but your insistence confirms the improper nature of your residence. We do not tend to notice the assistance given to those whose residence is assumed". (Ahmed 2014: 149).
6 In terms of narrative structure, *Walkabout* and *Don't Look Now* use death in much the same way. Each film narrative begins with a death and uses death as a denouement. *Performance* (1970) employs a similar structure.
7 Civitarese's treatment of Michel Gondry's *The Science of Sleep* (2006) is a good example of this definition of 'dreaming film'.

References

Ahmed, S. (2014). *Willful Subjects*. Durham: Duke University Press.
Baudry, J-L. (1970). Ideological Effects of the Basic Cinematographic Apparatus. In Rosen, P. (ed.) *Narrative, Apparatus, Ideology: A Film Reader*. New York: Columbia University Press, 1986.

Baudry, J-L. (1975). The Apparatus: Metapsychological Approaches to the Impression of Reality in the Cinema. In Rosen, P. (ed.) *Narrative, Apparatus, Ideology: A Film Reader.* New York: Columbia University Press, 1986.
Bergstein, A. (2013). Transcending the Caesura: Reverie, Dreaming and Counter-Dreaming. *The International Journal of Psychoanalysis,* 94 (4), pp. 621–644.
Bion, W.R. (1962a). *Learning From Experience.* London: Tavistock.
Bion, W.R. (1965). *Transformations: Change From Learning to Growth.* London: William Heinemann Medical Books.
Bion, W.R. (1997). *Taming Wild Thoughts* (ed.) Francesca Bion. London: Karnac Books.
Bléandonu, G. (1994). *Wilfred Bion: His Life and Works, 1897–1979.* Translated by C. Pajaczkowska. New York: Other Press.
Bollas, C. (1989). *Forces of Destiny: Psychoanalysis and Human Idiom.* London: Free Association Books.
Bollas, C. (2010). *Being a Character: Psychoanalysis and Self-Experience.* Hove, East Sussex: Routledge.
Cartwright, L. (2008). *Moral Spectatorship: Technologies of Voice and Affect in Postwar Representations of the Child.* Durham: Duke University Press.
Chion, M. (1994). *Audio-Vision: Sound on Screen.* Translated by Claudia Gorbman. New York: Columbia University Press.
Civitarese, G. (2014). *The Necessary Dream: New Theories and Techniques of Interpretation in Psychoanalysis.* Translated by I. Harvey. London: Karnac Books.
Ferro, A. and Civitarese, G. (2015). *The Analytic Field and Its Transformations.* London: Karnac Books.
Klein, M. (1923). Early Analysis. In *Love, Guilt and Reparation and Other Works 1921–1945.* London: Virago Press, 1988.
Klein, M. (1926). The Psychological Principles of Early Analysis. In *Love, Guilt and Reparation and Other Works 1921–1945.* London: Virago Press, 1988.
Klein, M. (1930). The Importance of Symbol-Formation in the Development of the Ego. In *Love, Guilt and Reparation and Other Works 1921–1945.* London: Virago Press, 1988.
Klein, M. (1932). *The Psycho-Analysis of Children.* London: Hogarth Press.
Lacan, J. (1986). *The Four Fundamental Concepts of Psychoanalysis* (ed.) Jacques-Alain Miller. Translated by A. Sheridan. Harmondsworth: Penguin.
Marks, L. (2000). *The Skin of the Film: Intercultural Cinema, Embodiment, and the Senses.* Durham: Duke University Press.
Meltzer, D. (1984). *Dream-Life: A Re-Examination of the Psycho-Analytical Theory and Technique.* London: Karnac Books.
Merleau-Ponty, M. (1964). *The Primacy of Perception: And Other Essays on Phenomenological Psychology, the Philosophy of Art, History and Politics* (ed.) J.E. Edie. Translated by W. Cobb. Evanston: Northwestern University Press.
Metz, C. (1974). *Film Language: A Semiotics of the Cinema.* Translated by M. Taylor. Oxford: Oxford University Press.
Metz, C. (1982). *The Imaginary Signifier: Psychoanalysis and the Cinema.* Translated by C. Britton, A. Williams, B. Brewster, A. Guzzetti. Bloomington and Indianapolis: Indiana University Press.
Mulvey, L. (1975). Visual Pleasure and Narrative Cinema. *Screen,* 16 (3), pp. 6–18.
Ogden, T. (1994a). *Subjects of Analysis.* London: Karnac Books.
Ogden, T. (1994b). The Analytic Third: Working With Intersubjective Clinical Facts. *International Journal of Psycho-Analysis,* 75, pp. 3–19.
Ogden, T. (1999). *Reverie and Interpretation: Sensing Something Human.* London: Karnac Books.

OED Online. "reverie, n." and "wandering, n." Oxford University Press. http://www.oed.com.libproxy.chapman.edu/view/Entry/164772?rskey=tKbyt8&result=2 Accessed June 2017.
Symington, N. and Symington, J. (2008). *The Clinical Work of Wilfred Bion*. London and New York: Routledge.
Winnicott, D.W. (1999). Creativity and Its Origins. In *Playing and Reality*. London: Routledge.

Filmography

Don't Look Now (1973). Directed by Nicolas Roeg.
Forbidden Planet (1956). Directed by Fred M. Wilcox.
Inception (2010). Directed by Christopher Nolan.
Rashomon (1950). Directed by Akira Kurosawa.
The Science of Sleep (2006). Directed by Michel Gondry.
Walkabout (1971). Directed by Nicolas Roeg.

4
METAPHOR, THE ANALYTIC FIELD AND THE EMBEDDED SPECTATOR

This chapter continues to explore the notion of intersubjectivity as a dynamic element of our emotional experience with the moving image. 'Intersubjective aesthetic experience' is a structuring characteristic of the 'analytic field' – a term contemporary psychoanalysis has developed to identify and address the spatiotemporal, unconscious interaction of two minds and bodies within an analytic situation. George Hagman (2005: 1) writes that aesthetic experience is not a value of sensations or of objects, rather it is what emerges as the 'creative engagement' in our shared lived experience with the world. Without aesthetic experience, the analytic field is ineffective and disintegrated; it does not offer a meaningful or fruitful encounter. The analytic field differs from Freudian and Lacanian conceptions of the analytic situation, being more representative of Kleinian and Bionian models, which regarded the analytic experience as more interactive, corporeal and emotionally dynamic than the traditional analyst/analysand enclave.

Bion's theory of thinking places lived emotional experience at its core and was influential (if not directly cited) in developing initial conceptions of 'field theory' (Baranger and Baranger 2008, originally published 1961–62). Most recently, the Barangers' field theory has been extended and given its stronger Bionian inflection through Ferro and Civitarese's theorization of the analytic field (2015) (see also Ferro and Basile 2009; Ferro 2009, 2011; and Civitarese 2010). The potential of analytic field theory for the study of the moving image is that it foregrounds the experience of dreaming as sensory dynamic interaction within lived emotional experience. It emphasizes the phenomenological aspects within psychoanalytic theory as it specifically places aesthetic experience as its central concern, paying attention to the role and workings of unconscious fantasy, more importantly the sharing of such fantasy as it is shaped between two (or more) minds and their bodies, over time and through their lived experience with each other. In this respect, the 'analytic field' is its own metaphor for the dreaming that is intersubjective aesthetic experience – a metaphor which I extend to the notion of 'being embedded' that transpires with moving images. Cinema is already within the throes of its own field of becoming, its identity shifting rapidly within the 21st century as it responds to digital developments and uses, exploring within its practices and theories what it means to say 'cinema' as it involves technologies of virtual and augmented reality. Bionian psychoanalytic theory offers conceptual devices for thinking about the future of moving images in the 21st century post-cinematic mediascape and our lived experience with them.

I introduced the basic core principles of Bion's theory of thinking in Chapter 2 and explored the role of reverie as it works to sustain dreaming as aesthetic experience in Chapter 3. Here I wish to briefly reiterate that for Bion, dreaming is the founding principle of mental functioning that enables lived experience to be processed as emotional experience. It was through a range of metaphors that Bion outlined and established his theory of thinking. Ferro and Civitarese note that metaphor has driven almost all psychoanalytic theories, from Freud's metaphors of archaeology, to the surgical and 'analyst-as-screen' (2015: xvi) – arriving at their own interpretation of a Bionian field. In this chapter, I also touch on Lacanian discussions regarding the function of metaphor to show how Bion's ideas both connect to and depart from classical psychoanalytic approaches, advancing the function of the field metaphor as an experience of dreaming. In order to make this link between Bion and Lacan relevant for film and media studies, I begin by discussing the emergence of the linguistically inflected classical psychoanalytic application of metaphor within Metz's film theory to note the emphasis that was placed on the positioning of the subject in 1970s film spectatorship theory. In part, this is to highlight how the traditional use of metaphor influenced the development of a particularly classical psychoanalytic model via Metzian thought, but also to lay the groundwork for why Bionian-derived analytic field theories offer a different use of metaphor for aesthetic experience. Ferro and Civitarese's Bionian revisionist concept of 'analytic field',[1] briefly introduced in the previous chapter, is explored further here, looking to its historical development in order to conceive of moving image experience on similar terms, foregrounding such experience as dreaming with moving images as it occurs between minds and bodies.

Ferro and Civitarese's work on notions of intersubjectivity and the analytic field reappraises the long-established concept of metaphor as it has been used within clinical practice. I use their theory of the field and apply it to moving image experience, rather than psychoanalytic, to show how a rethinking of the film theory from 1970s onwards helps to introduce different ways of conceiving aesthetic experience with moving images overall. By no means is this a finalized or exhaustive model, for the main aim is to link Bion more directly to the field of film and media studies and begin to ask how might his psychoanalytic models offer new avenues and conversations for traditional and current questions.

To further relate Ferro and Civitarese's work on the analytic field to the issues and developments within film and media studies, I refer to Francesco Casetti's *Theories of Cinema 1945–1995* (1999), given that what I am proposing – a divergent psychoanalytic theory of moving image experience – links with his survey of theories about cinema and its characteristics. Casetti is one of the very few film theorists that has used the specific term 'field theories' (1999: 179), although other works that explore the models and histories of film theory acknowledge and use this expression (see Temenuga Trifonova 2009). Casetti recognizes that the diversity present within the many schools of film studies established a landscape of "autonomous and interconnected, delimited and yet open" (1999: 179) fields of study – all revolving around the same focus of moving image experience, to which this work contributes. Casetti does not associate 'field theories' with Bionian field theory, yet there are some shared characteristics that I discuss with respect to thinking through the metaphor of the field and moving image experience. Finally, I consider the construct of the 'embedded spectator' as a way to illuminate the intersubjective aesthetic experience of cinema as a dreaming – a version of metaphor that takes up Ferro and Civitarese's revision of the field metaphor, viewed as "an instrument of technique . . . as a conceptual device in theoretical activity" (Ferro and Civitarese 2015: 1) in order to offer a divergent psychoanalytic method for thinking about our experience with moving images.

Metaphor, 1970s film theory and beyond

Philip Rosen notes in his article "*Screen* and 1970s Film Theory" (2008) that by 1975–6, the majority of articles in *Screen* "contested established modes of film analysis and proposed the development of new modes involving a theory of subjectivity in relation to conceptions of film textuality" (2008: 269). The basis for such contestation was the ('non-cinematic') linguistic theories of Ferdinand de Saussure and Roland Barthes, which were appropriated for the subsequent theorization of the spectator in the early semiotic-focused works of Metz (1974), and the later psychoanalytic article "The Imaginary Signifier" (1975) which became its own monograph (1982). Metz's subsequent influence (after Jean-Louis Baudry 1975) on the development of film theory is undeniable, and as Rosen comments, his 1975 article was instrumental in establishing the theoretical trajectory of *Screen* (and by extension the field of film studies) by laying the foundations for the conceptualization and contestation of the "theory of the spectator as a relation between text and subject" (2008: 274). It is worth foregrounding that for 1970s film theory, and for a long time afterwards, the emphasis of such theorizing rested on subjectivity and its construction through the apparatus of cinema, rather than the specificities of lived relational experience, that is, the reception of moving images rather than lived experience *with* moving images. The materiality of film became the textual system upon which codes and sub-codes were organized and analyzed as a "configuration of relationships among a plurality of codes of all types . . . shaped in the flow of images and sounds" (Rosen 2008: 275). Metz's argument moved film theory away from structuralist pursuits and more toward the dynamics of cinema through his debate on metaphor and metonymy, but continued to locate his ideas within the cinematic apparatus and filmic textuality.

There is such a significant body of work on Metz, either as criticism (Bordwell and Carroll 1996; Ambrósio Garcia 2017) or as revision (Rushton 2002), that it is not necessary to repeat such arguments here. Instead I wish to address the underlying assumption, which is the classical psychoanalytic model upon which Metz's argument was formed, in order to offer the alternative metaphor model of analytic field theory. Some contextual comments on Metz's use of metaphor are needed so that the 'systematic deconstruction' (Ferro and Civitarese 2015: xiv) offered by Bionian psychoanalysis is made clear and purposeful regarding cinematic encounter and experience. I lean heavily on Ferro and Civitarese's Bionian treatment of the metaphor and its function within the analytic field, not only because their work remains pivotal in terms of the 'Bionian turn' (yes, another turn) in psychoanalytic theory, but because, as Wendy Katz (2013: 458) has noted, their Italian interpretation of 'field' is a 'radical revision'.

Metz's theories have greatly influenced the subsequent study of film (and film worlds) within terms of transference in spectatorship involving conscious and unconscious processes. His methodology is reflected in Stephen Heath's work – "[f]ilm is not a static and isolate object but a series of relations *with the spectator it imagines*, plays and sets as subject in its movement" (Heath in Rosen 2008: 279, italics added) – indicating how film theorists maintained analyses of cinema as a textual system; a system that positioned the viewer and saw the direction of the transference process as moving unconscious desires into conscious thought. The particular psychoanalytic paradigm underwriting this approach was Freudian and Lacanian, so it is no surprise that the argument ended up concentrating on experience within ocular-centric positioning comparisons – "you don't watch the film, the film watches you" – and even via a metaphor of secrets where the film text was seen to hold hidden, latent meanings that textual analysis could reveal (the transference of unconscious into conscious). A Bionian paradigm offers a reversal of the transference process, suggesting that "we watch/dream *with* moving images", using the aesthetics that cinema affords (audio, visual, haptic – particularly if we extend 'cinema' to include emergent digital media such as VR and AR environments) to make conscious lived experience unconscious (in order to dream). The evolution of analytic field theory serves as a means to show how the conception and application of metaphor has evolved from a Lacanian/Metzian to Bionian use, suggesting that such a critical distinction challenges previous theories of spectatorship within cinematic experience.

The aim here is not to reject or refute the previous work of Metz and related film scholars such as Heath, who utilized classical Lacanian psychoanalysis; rather I ask how might the rhetorical device of metaphor be said to communicate different meanings if it follows a different, that is, Bionian, model of psychoanalysis? To this end, I capitalize on Rosen and Heath's observation and study of "*relation*, which is the experience of being a subject" (Rosen 2008: 278, italics original) and discuss Ferro and Civitarese's Bionian field theory to examine relations with moving images within the context of intersubjective aesthetic experience. In doing so, metaphor continues to signify movement and relation of meaning (Silverman

1983) but is released from the fixing of 'positionality' (Rosen 2008: 278) so that it can be viewed within a more Bionian context without memory or desire (Bion 1967). This shares the intentionality of Ferro and Civitarese's claim that analytic field theory is not interested in fixed positions within an (analytic or cinematic) situation – or even in the transpositionality that results through metaphoric likeness or resemblance. Instead, analytic field theory looks to highlight how relations are "formed instant by instant from a subtle interplay of identity and differentiation, proximity and distance" (Ferro and Civitarese 2015: xiv). As such, analytic field theory offers an alternative psychoanalytic model that attends to the *experience with* a system that includes, rather than specifies or isolates, its materiality as a textual system.

Ferro and Civitarese acknowledge that the term 'intersubjectivity' is misleading (2015: xv) if the emphasis remains on theorizing 'subjectivity'. This is a very clear deviation between the use of metaphor in Metzian film theory and Bionian field theory, as it revises the direction and emphasis of analytic attention. Rosen writes that *Screen* articles began to privilege the idea that films 'address[ed]' the audience in order to argue the existence of a 'filmic enunciation' (2008: 279); metaphor in this capacity belonging to the film text, said to position and "imagine the spectator". Within the model of analytic field theory,

> [m]etaphor and the field are linked in a chiasm: the field metaphor transforms Kleinian relational theory into a radically intersubjective theory, which in turn, places metaphor at a point along the spectrum of dreaming – to paraphrase Bion, it is the stuff of analysis."
>
> *(Ferro and Civitarese 2015: xvi)*

Rather than emphasizing 'subjectivity' then, Ferro and Civitarese look more closely on 'inter' within 'intersubjectivity', shifting the function of metaphor toward relational interests – what happens between, across and through the field – over the metaphor of the 'talking cure'.

Not only does this echo the work of theorists on embodiment, such as Sobchack (2004, 2006), Marks (2000), Maartin Coënarts and Peter Kravana (2016) and Kathrin Fahlenbrach (2016), but it also underwrites the aspect of 'intersubjective aesthetic experience', which seeks to identify the consequence or function of the analytic field and reorient psychoanalytic theories of moving image experience. Marks, for example uses the metaphor of the skin as haptic sense to bring the unknown perceived into the represented known, claiming that "vision itself is tactile, as though one were touching a film with one's eyes" (2000: xi). Marks's metaphor of 'haptic visuality' is used to point to the permeability of the moving image, indeed as a transmission of affect, across cultures.[2] Like Marks's approach, instead of only concentrating on the meanings within a specific film (and how they are arranged or received), analytic field theory foregrounds intersubjectivity which involves exploring the shared unconscious field that emerges in-between the lived experience with moving images. This is in direct opposition to Metz's claim that "the spectator is absent from the screen" (Metz 1982: 48). In many ways analytic field theory aims to note more clearly the role of displacement within the function of metaphor – not dissimilar to the hope of catching something 'in the net' of being idle as discussed in the previous chapter. Sobchack writes that "metaphor is, by tropological nature a *displacement*" (2006: 21, italics original), her view reiterating that metaphor, when used, is about the transposition of attributes from one object or context to another so that the transposition *itself* becomes the meaningful transformation via relation or relating.

Returning to Metz and *The Imaginary Signifier*, we can begin to see where his ideas on the metaphor do not address experience *with* moving images as effectively as they might, in part because they heel too closely to a Lacanian perspective. To begin with, Metz likens the dream to the materiality of film – what it expresses or represents (or misrepresents) – instead of perceiving cinematic experience as dreaming in and of itself. In this capacity, Metz's theories of the cinematic apparatus and the film itself are guided by the Freudian view that dreams are wish-fulfillment and aimed at drive gratification rather than object relations. Cinema remains a signifying process for the spectator, not an experience of dreaming their undreamt dreams (as Bionian type of thinking – see Chapter 2). As such, Metz is arguing that it is the film text itself that predominantly resembles the dream, and not that the entire visual, embodied cinematic experience is, in fact, the dreaming. Ambrósio Garcia has commented that Metz's position stems from his interpretation that "both film and dream promote a narcissistic withdrawal and gratifying experience of phantasy" (Ambrósio Garcia 2017: 25), highlighting its derivation from Freudian/Lacanian psychoanalytic approach as it sees dreaming as limited to being asleep – similar to being immobile and silent in a cinema theatre, driven by wish-fulfillment.[3]

Metz, of course, was not alone in this – much earlier, Serge Lebovici wrote that film images worked like dream thoughts, where a lack of direct reference required the similarity and contiguity of metaphor to create meaning, "a dream as a whole is almost exclusively visual . . . films offer the spectator very oneiric material" (Lebovici 1949: 50). Once again, it is the textuality of the film that is likened to the dream rather than the overall embodied experience itself becoming the spectator's dreaming. The dream metaphor, as conceived via classical psychoanalysis, limited the dream work to systems of materiality, textuality or ocular-centric perception, where the transference process was seen to work through the notion of revelation (unconscious to conscious). Bion's theory of thinking and his revision of dreaming offers a re-scripting of the dream metaphor for moving image experience, reversing the process of transference (conscious experience to unconscious thinking) involved.

Ferro (2009, 2011) combined the Bionian concepts of waking dream thought and reverie with theories of narratology to propose a different perspective of dreaming as aesthetic experience. He argues that within the analytic situation, both patient and analyst are constantly engaging with "an ongoing *baseline activity of reverie*" (2009: 1, italics original) referring to the incessant reception of sensory data that occurs both within (as well as outside) the analytic situation.[4] For Ferro, the purpose of analysis is to use the reveries of both analyst and patient to "weave a fabric of images (which remain not directly knowable) . . . [but which can be] accessed indirectly through the 'narrative derivatives' of waking dream thought" (2009: 1). Dreaming for Ferro therefore is not limited to the analysis of a dream-text recalled in analysis, rather the process of dreaming itself is viewed through a metaphor of digestion – where the mind 'digests' everyday lived experience, and all its sensory data, in order to produce conscious 'narremes' (Ferro 2009) that permit thinkable experience (Katz 2013).[5] Dreaming is therefore extended to include (and emphasize) the corporeal and psychical experience of storytelling, moving beyond the specificity of Freud's dream work while asleep.

For Ferro, the use of narratology furthers the metaphor of the analytic field in a Bionian direction as it emphasizes the patient's capacity to think emotional experience in the immediacy of the field that is *in situ* analysis. Katz views Ferro's model as an "emergent formulation of experience rather than the uncovering of existing repressed material" (2013: 462), and this is the basis for her claim that Ferro and Civitarese's analytic field theory is a radical revision because it reimagines what the purpose of analysis is. As the Italian psychoanalysts see it, the analytic field is no longer about 'textual analysis' of a patient's dreams, but much more an embedding space that enables a patient to develop their capacity to cope with the pressure of aesthetic experience – that is to think through lived experience in order "for more effective dreaming and making narratives" (2013: 463). Dreaming, viewed in this Bionian way, is entirely concerned with our capacity to *tell* stories instead of analyzing their content. The presence and the spacings of stories constitute the field and are supported and furthered through reverie.

The centrality of dreaming (as aesthetic experience) cannot be overstated regarding the function of metaphor; however, the current point of contestation is not how moving images might work like a dream, but rather how aesthetic moving image experience is itself a dreaming. If we acknowledge that Metz developed his ideas via Roman Jakobson's "Two Aspects of Language and Two Types of Aphasic Disturbance" (1956) in order to theorize filmic interaction as a signifying exchange, so must we also remind ourselves that the metaphor/metonymy model he draws on begins with Freud's *The Interpretation of Dreams* (1900). Condensation and displacement are the two agencies that Freud employs to illuminate considerations of representability within the dream work, which were constructive in Metz's theory of metaphor. Ruggero Eugeni writes that Metz's treatment of condensation and displacement differed from Lacan's, "condensation and displacement are kinds of movements of meaning – that is, ways of building relationships between referential elements – while rhetorical figures [such as metaphor and metonymy] are the results of such movements and processes" (2014: 410). Yet, Metz, who claims he was thinking of the entire 'cinema-machine', still regarded filmic interaction within semiotic and discursive means "our point of entry is now more clearly indicated as being that of filmic textuality" (1982: 44). Other writers such as Linda Williams (1981) have taken up Metz's metaphor/metonymy textual perspective in order to think through the implications of his psychoanalytic approach for the question of hermeneutics of cinema, yet they too adhere to a classical psychoanalytic platform, even through their criticism of it. Williams, for example continues to view films themselves as oneiric rather than one's overall embedded experience with moving images. It is the generic classification of films that Williams contests as dream-like.

Given 1970s classical psychoanalytic-informed theories of spectatorship were born from a Freudian/Lacanian conceit of metaphor and metonymy, it makes sense that the cinematic encounter would examine questions of identity "representation, codes and textuality" (Rosen 2008: 280), and not focus on questions of aesthetic experience, affect or emotion. After all, 1970s film theory and beyond treated film (and filmic experience) as a discourse, adhering to the Lacanian idea that the unconscious is structured like a language. Eugeni further reminds us that Lacan rethought the Freudian unconscious in terms of desire and lack, "that is, a discourse uttered by a subject other than ourselves who nevertheless is 'the core of our being'" (Eugeni 2014: 409), where truth can only be known through metaphor (or as Eugeni writes, through "the analysis of dreams" (2014: 409)). But what happens if Freud's theory of dreams is no longer the primary model psychoanalysis itself practices, as indicated through Ferro's and Civitarese's theory of the field? What happens to the debate of metaphor relative to cinema and our experience with it (within the context of psychoanalytic theory)? Civitarese tells us that despite the importance and recognition of Freudian principles in contemporary psychoanalytic practice, "there have been radical innovations in this field – we no longer work *on* dreams but *with* dreams" (Civitarese 2014: xi, italics added). This would mean that the function of metaphor within the cinematic encounter, originally determined and contextualized through Freudian agencies of condensation and displacement, would also need revision, and that such revising may lead to new, different perspectives about cinema and our experience with it – cinema no longer existing as *only* a textual or material system, but more comprehensively, an aesthetic embedding and embodied experience, more indicative of a field. This time, psychoanalysis could be said to work with cinema, and not simply illuminate "the theory of psychoanalysis itself" (Rushton 2002: 107).

Indeed, things have moved on – not just from Metz's influential film theory, or within the scholarship and clinical practice of psychoanalysis; overall classical models of metaphor no longer dominate in the ways they once did. In addition to Ferro and Civitarese's questioning of metaphor in the analytic field, cognitive film studies scholars such as Fahlenbrach (2016) have shown that the 'intermediary structure' of metaphors serve to shift unknown and invisible "ideas, concepts, or emotions in terms of embodied schemata and gestalts", into the representable known, "like exploding containers ('emotion is a container')" (Fahlenbrach 2016: 1).[6] Fahlenbrach states that as intermediary structures, metaphors are a combination of our external worlds and our inner perceptions, and as such are no longer seen as "analogies between two words or pictures" (2016: 1); however, their transformative potential remains. Following George Lakoff and Mark Johnson (1980), she argues that metaphors are better considered as transpositional tracings that work through a series of emotional projections; a combination of how we feel, think and psychically respond to the world, resonating with Sobchack's claim of metaphor's inherent tropological characteristic being a displacement. Fahlenbrach doesn't go so far as to use the terms 'analytic field' or 'dreaming' but there are many echoes within *Embodied Metaphors in Film, Television, and Video Games* that illuminate the revisionist concept of the 'analytic field' that Bionian theory offers, particularly on the question of embodiment and sensoria transference.

An example of such potential 'connection-as-displacement' is evident in Joe Kickasola's "Metaphor Without an Answer" (2016: 162–179) who, through a cognitive approach, discusses the experience of cross-modal perception as sensorial experience. He writes, "metaphor, sensory experience, and the most important experiences of meaning are deeply intertwined" (2016: 163). Again, Kickasola does not refer to any psychoanalytic model, much less 'field theory', and yet many of his concepts are relevant to a Bionian intersubjective field model. Kickasola emphasizes the linking, that is the *dynamic* process, which occurs though embodied metaphors: "They [multisensory processes] affirm the connectedness of the sensory, effectual, and semantic realms of our experience, enabling corporal, felt "meanings" (2016: 173). This is reminiscent of the case study experience Bion recalls in *Transformations* (1965), where he writes on the frustration he felt in trying to interpret a patient's emotional violence.

For context, Bion discusses the potential for transformation as it might occur through experiences of frustration and emotional turbulence within the analytic situation and explores the expectation that analytic interpretation incurs. He speaks of the difficulty in the "communication of material from an experience that is ineffable" (Bion 1965: 51), foreshadowing Ferro and Civitarese's 'analytic field' as going beyond the specific geography of the analytic room by reflecting on his own responses (which are clearly not 'in' the analytic situation at his time of writing, but nevertheless are *with* analytic time and sustain analytic space). Here Bion uses the metaphor of the analytic situation to focus specifically on intersubjective aesthetic experience rather than the analysis of a specific enunciated 'dream-text'. Bion says that despite having a lengthy analytic relationship with this patient, and being very aware of the patient's fear of his own emotional violence, and violence in general, much of the patient's comments were "incomprehensible . . . [and that only by] virtue of aesthetic rather than scientific experience" (1965: 52) was he able to grasp what the patient was communicating. Bion's brief clinical vignette privileges the idea that aesthetic experience *forms and extends* the analytic field, predominantly through reverie – and not that aesthetic experience simply exists *within* the material content of a patient's dreams or memories that are recounted. When Kickasola writes of embodied metaphors as having an "open set of targets [his 'metaphor without an answer']" and that through "the very structure of metaphor, these experiences join two separate "ideas" (or, rather, sensory experiences)" (2016: 173), I associate Bion's aesthetic experience of the analytic field – particularly through their similar application of metaphor as a proto-mental intermediary structure.

In further critique of metaphor, film-philosopher William Brown writes, "[Lakoff and Johnson] outline the way in which the very structure of our thought is the product of our embodiment in the world" (Brown 2013: 127). Here, as with

Fahlenbrach and Kickasola, this 'reorientation' of the function of metaphor for lived experience offers to resolve previous difficulties present in traditional, more rhetorical theories of metaphor. Brown examines the Bergsonian metaphor 'space is a container', extended by Lakoff and Johnson, and in doing so highlights the specific attention cognitive studies assigns to the re-appropriation of metaphor – the notion of 'space-as-a-*physical*-container'. Brown notes that metaphors for emotional or abstract experiences are often assigned 'spatial models' (2013: 127) that do not necessarily possess qualities of space in themselves but reflect our corporeality in how we feel ourselves relating with our environments. Ferro and Civitarese also use this prevalence for the metaphoricity of space in their metaphor of the field; however, their thinking on 'space as a container' differs.

The idea of containment, as per Lakoff and Johnson, is developed through the notion of the *physical* rather than a temporal, dynamic *process*. Coënarts and Kravana (2016) employ Lakoff and Johnson's theory of containment within similar parameters in their analysis of the "visual field as container" (2016: 130), where 'container' is also understood as a vessel and not as a process. They write, "[t]his metaphor [of perception within the visual field as container] originates in the bodily experience of our bodies as containers and as *things in containers*, and states that when we look at some object or entity, we conceptualize what we see as *being something inside it*" (Coënarts and Kravana 2016: 130, italics added), implying that containment is an act of 'holding', even when the visual field is considered via Robert Dewell's theory of the "filmic frame as a *dynamic* container" (2016: 130, italics added).[7] Such cognitive approaches that continue to view 'container' and 'space' through physical metaphors, like a vessel or boundary, run the risk of sustaining the theoretical assumptions discussed in 1970s film theory – which privilege cinema as a material and textual system – because they limit the idea of the 'filmic field' to the screen, its enunciations, and its 'positionalities' (despite there being a strong attention on embodiment). From this perspective, metaphor remains within the cinematic image rather than across, and constitutive of, the cinematic field. Analytic field theory offers a model that views the filmic field as extending beyond such spatial-vessel constructs, treating space more as a container-process. I am not suggesting that these are necessarily oppositional perspectives – indeed, there are a good number of points that seem to be moving toward the same goal, which is to view the function of metaphor as a more sensory, corporeal and fluid experience. For example, Brown's discussion of cliché, as theorized by Deleuze, offers many points of convergence with Bionian theories of thinking[8] (see for example the similarity between Deleuze's idea of automatic viewing and Ogden's (2010) idea of 'magical thinking').

Brown further illustrates that space, despite its varying conceptualizations, has become a primarily corporeal metaphor. He uses the prepositions of being 'in time' and 'in love' (2013: 128) as examples of spatial models, which read as reliant on the abstract understanding of space as a physical container. If instead, these emotional experiences are viewed as spatial processes (argued within Bionian terms) 'in time' and 'in love' appear as relational if they are reasoned as 'spacings' (Ferro and Civitarese 2015: 69) – particularly as we are always '*with* time' and '*with* love'. In the previous chapter, I introduced Ferro's and Civitarese's metaphor of spacings with regard to reverie. This metaphor of 'spacings' refers to the spatiotemporal quality of the analytic field, in order to identify both the mind and body difference and distance between analyst and patient as well as the capacity and ability to achieve and develop harmony within emotional experience. To recall, spacing simultaneously speaks to "the temporality of space and spatiality of time" (2015: 69); it is a processual metaphor that avoids fixing 'space-as-a-*physical*-container' (like a vessel) and looks more to the idea that space itself is an expanding, processural and relational metaphor for our lived emotional experience. With respect to the analytic setting, the geography and temporality of the analysis is said to provide a state of calm and possibility, which Ferro and Civitarese liken to Winnicott's (1956) 'space-womb', and Julia Kristeva's (1974) 'semiotic chora' (not dissimilar to Ambrósio Garcia's theory of 'the retreat in film' 2017). The significant difference of the meaning of the metaphor in the Bionian field, is that the "possibility this space-field-as-*process* has of forming (or not) and of functioning" (Ferro and Civitarese 2015: 71, italics added) lies in the inclusion of the corporeal – as its own lived space and lived time – not just of the patient, or the analyst, or even of the analysis, but equally of the analytic couple together *in situ* and beyond. Therefore a Bionian perspective would regard such emotional experiences of being 'in time' and 'in love' as negotiations of reality (per Brown) and, if viewed further as 'spacings' (per Ferro and Civitarese), they become considerations of bearability and tension as they are thought and therefore felt.

Ferro and Civitarese remind us that 'thinking', in the Bionian sense, is to feel and to dream – it is how we take our everyday day sensory experience and turn it into "psychological work in order to create new emotional bonds and construct mental meaning or space" (2015: 70). Thus, Bion's thinking as emotional experience becomes 'links', which operate as tensions and "generate . . . the force of the field" (Ferro and Civitarese 2015: 73; Bion 1962). Being 'in time' or 'in love', viewed via the metaphor of spacings, transcends the physical aspect of Brown's 'spatial model' as container, and become much more about the emotional dynamics involved in one's tolerance of frustration (rather one's capacity *to* tolerate as a spatial process) over and during time, and must also include what it is to be 'not with time' and 'not with love' – both frustrations that Ferro and Civitarese account for as 'empty spacings'. Brown cites Lakoff and Johnson's theories of embodiment to further their claim that we 'live by' metaphors. In contradistinction, Ferro and Civitarese, via Bion, use the theory of spacing, dreaming and the analytic field to argue we live *with* metaphors (better we dream with metaphors). I speak more on Bion's theory of the container-contained in Chapters 6 and 8, and wish to put this question of containment to one side for the moment in order to return to the issue of metaphor within the analytic field.

Antonino Ferro and Giuseppe Civitarese's metaphor within the analytic field

Let us look more closely at Ferro and Civitarese's very bold claim that Bionian psychoanalysis deconstructs the fundamental concepts of classical psychoanalysis.

They clarify that Bion's theories offer a less rigid, less positional, psychoanalytic model found in classical approaches, and write that analytic field theory is more a model that views analysis as a 'shared journey' with a patient rather than a sequence of dialectical reversals and developments of truth between analyst and analysand (as per Lacan's 1951 "Presentation on Transference"). Before I discuss the specific characteristics of Ferro's and Civitarese's analytic field theory and metaphor, it is necessary to contextualize field theory as it emerged as a technique of psychoanalysis.

The origins of analytic field theory reflect the idea of a 'shared journey' as Madeline Baranger and Willy Baranger (2008) utilized a number of concepts such as Klein's projective identification (1952), Bion's theory of group experience (1961) and Merleau-Ponty's phenomenology of perception (1945) to form their theory of the analytic situation working as a dynamic field. From its conception, the Barangers' field theory sought to transcend the spatio-temporal limits of the analytic situation and think more broadly about "the error of one-sidedness in early descriptions of the analytic situation as a situation of objective observation of a patient" (Baranger and Baranger 2008: 795). The Barangers' field model moved away from the idea that the analytic situation was formed as a sum of its parts and instead saw a "a new gestalt, a bipersonal or basic unconscious fantasy of the couple that is different from the fantasies of the patient or those of the analyst considered individually" (Eizirik in Baranger and Baranger 2009: xii). The field, then, was to reconsider the exchange of transference as something that is "created *between* the two, within the unit they form in the moment of the session" (Baranger and Baranger 2009: xiii, italics original), instead of a to-and-fro relationship. It is interesting to think about how Metzian film theory might have developed had he utilized this psychoanalytic notion of the field to inform his use of transference in the theorization of cinema. The implications for a stronger, more comprehensive psychoanalytic method on the questions of affect and emotional experiences are significant, particularly when we include theories of the gaze that generated a large body of scholarship on the interrelationship between identity politics and the moving image, Mulvey's (1975) and bell hooks (1992) being the most famous examples.

Lacanian film theory models, such as Mulvey's, privileged the gaze as a technique and tool for identification on the basis of pleasure and unpleasure; however using the Barangers' field theory we find the notion of the 'second look' (1961–62), a reflective gaze which they argue is necessary to note (and respond to) the obstacles and resistances that form within the analytic encounter. "This has led us to propose the introduction of several terms: 'field', 'bastion', 'second look'. When the process stumbles or halts, the analyst can only question himself [*sic*] about the obstacle, by encircling himself and his analysand, Oedipus and the Sphinx, in a second look, in a total view: this is the field" (Baranger, Baranger and Mom 1983: 1). In this respect, the 'gaze' becomes part of the field, as it is constituted. The 'second look' engenders the recognition of an analyst's participation in the structuring of the gaze. Here the emphasis rests not on visual pleasure as it informs questions of spectator agency, but more on experience that affects both mind and body behavior as it compels us to think of our own participation in the construction and function of such gazes and looks.

This leads us to an aspect of field theory that I see as most significant. Initially proposed by the Barangers', which Ferro and Civitarese later integrate into their Bionian-inflected field theory, is Merleau-Ponty's attention on corporeality and sensory experience within the field. Ferro and Civitarese note that Bion's work on group experience (discussed in Chapter 5) had already led him to conceive of shared unconscious fantasy as an intersubjective experience (Bion 1961), and through his observations of group experience, had come to view emotional and corporeal experience as linked, inseparable from one other. The Barangers' field theory opened up the possibility of conceiving the situation as a 'new gestalt', and when viewed alongside Bion's claim that "the group can be regarded as an interplay between individual needs, group mentality, and culture" (Bion 1961: 55), it is clear that analytic field theory offers a challenge to traditional thinking of the psychoanalytic situation by prioritizing the proto-mental aspects of the field. By extension, it is clear that field theory offers a similar challenge to the ways in which Metz's 'cinema-machine' has been conceived. Cinematic experience, after Sobchack, Marks and Brown, markedly belongs to a spectrum that involves the simultaneous, shared, lived experience of mind and body – and whilst cognitive film scholars have examined this extensively, similar attention via contemporary psychoanalysis is yet to take hold.

Had Metz followed the Barangers' more field-oriented theory in his theorizing of the cinema-machine, it is conceivable that his critique of the subject's unconscious fantasies – and indeed the overall cinematic apparatus – would have been compelled to move beyond linguistic and scopic paradigms and recognize Merleau-Ponty's attention on "the *carnal* – feeling and felt – aspect of the body" (Ferro and Civitarese 2015: 27 *fn* 3, italics original). It is almost as if Metz was searching for the metaphor of the field as conceived by the Barangers to help him formulate his ideas of the cinematic apparatus and its effects on the spectator, especially as Ambrósio Garcia (2017: 29) notes, he concentrates on the idea of absence in varied ways that flirt with aspects of relation (identification, voyeuristic desire and fetishism) throughout *The Imaginary Signifier*. Metz's attention on absence – informed primarily through the Lacanian frame of lack and desire – bears similarities to the absence that is present in (and which helps to structure) the intersubjective character of the field. Ferro and Civitarese state that the Barangers' essay emerged at the same time Winnicott and Bion were developing their own models of intersubjective experience. These parallels are important as they offer a relative historical context for how thinking about the analytic situation emerged as 'field theory', but equally, this correlation between object-relations theories highlights a different perspective of the function of absence (as desire versus the absence as relation) within models of transference and countertransference – something that Metz might have used to rethink his pleasure/unpleasure emphasis.

Ferro's and Civitarese's metaphor of the field further foregrounds the key principle of Bion's theory of thinking, which is a mind needs another mind in order to think (and as we have also established, this simultaneously means to feel – the proto-mental system); a mind cannot exist or develop in isolation. Following the

Barangers' example, they draw on thinkers from a range of disciplines outside psychoanalysis (Umberto Eco, Jacques Derrida, Luciana Nissim Momigliano) in order to demonstrate that the field is not simply an interdisciplinary or intersubjective idea within clinical psychoanalytic practice. It can only thrive and grow if it links to other minds in other disciplines. A strength of Bionian field theory is that it combines the premise of its intersubjective psychoanalytic models with its design and practice. Much of the metaphor of the field is informed by interdisciplinary thinking (from semiotics, philosophy, narratology; visual culture); indeed Ferro and Civitarese also make associations with the definition of the field from scientific schemas in order to convey its pluralistic qualities and equate them with intersubjective meaning. The field is outlined as 'unstable', '*inclusive, invisible*', '*delimited*' – terms that are used to specify their processural "constant, mutual cross-reference" (2015: 7, italics original). More than anything else, it is this sense of dynamism, system and process that the metaphor of the field is intended to convey – challenging the linguistic and textual emphasis of metaphor present in previous models. This returns us briefly to the previous discussion of containment used in Brown and Fahlenbrach's work.

Ferro and Civitarese claim the field is a container inasmuch as it exists in "dialectical relationship with what is outside it – that is, with other, broader containers (social groups, institutions, ideologies, etc.)" (2015: 7). Therefore, instead of rejecting Lakoff's and Johnson's classical position outright, they argue that revision of the function of metaphor – moving from a linguistic, rhetorical device to an "elementary psychological mechanism" (2015: 16) was necessary in order to show that metaphor has evolved as a technical device that enables us to think of intersubjective aesthetic experience *and* the psychoanalytic situation differently – as a relational, proto-mental field. Elsewhere, Civitarese (2010) has argued that field theory is a response to the "interactive and immersive concept of play" (2010: 74), as it offers a new technique for psychoanalysis at the same time it permits a rethinking of psychoanalysis itself. He explores the emergent media of VR as it highlights the elements of immersion and interactivity inherent in play, but also because its own innovative quality as an emergent digital medium invites 'new hermeneutics' (2010: 74). In the Bionian spirit of linking with other minds in order to grow, we can see similar potential of growth in linking 'cinematic experience' with other media (such as television, gaming and VR) in order to consider creative engagement with such new platforms as well as reappraise what constitutes 'cinema' itself.

The concept of play is vital to the mechanics of field theory as it foregrounds the oneiric quality and potential of the exchange that occurs with the field, whilst holding onto the equal importance of both mind and body. Ferro and Civitarese describe the analytic field as inclusive of all elements that might constitute communication, that is "an event, a memory, a dream, an enactment, a reverie, as association, an emotion, a sensation, or whatever" (2015: 7) to emphasize the particularity of reverie as it transpires in the interplay of the analytic situation. The dream is essential to the metaphor of the field, shifting its hermeneutic away from being a text to analyze, toward a joint proto-mental aesthetic experience. As such, the metaphor of the field as proposed by Bionian field theory allows a reconsideration of spectatorship outside previous theories of identification and reception, instead prioritizing emotional engagement and the sensorial and corporeal embeddedness that occurs through aesthetic experience with moving images. Civitarese states it as "how to let oneself be captured [by moving images] and why" (2010: 74), situating the analytic field as a highly effective metaphor that foregrounds the existence and experience of play which enables and sustains the embeddedness of dreaming.

Analytic field theory and field theories of cinema

'Analytic field theory' as employed here is not to be aligned with Casetti's use of the term 'field theories', although there are some points of similarity between them, and certainly potential for analytic field theory to be included as a method of film theory within such a paradigm. Casetti uses 'field theories' to refer to a range of methodological approaches to the analysis and theorization of cinema, and whilst his term lacks the psychoanalytic specificity present in Ferro and Civitarese's intersubjective 'analytic field theory', his identification of characteristics specific to the field theories of cinema help to relate the Bionian field metaphor within a more cinema-friendly context.

Casetti suggests that there are three main traits to cinematic 'field theories'; the first referencing attention on the "relationship between the observer and the object observed" (Casetti 1999: 179), where the academic author directly acknowledges and considers their own role in the work, making the personal political (as it were). There is a trace of intersubjectivity and reverie within Casetti's first characteristic, evident in his argument that the object of analysis is no longer a distant, 'passive' object under inquiry, rather:

> [cinema] interferes with the gazes that traverses it, often openly resisting it, and always contributing to its orientation. As a result, the boundaries between the roles of observer and the observed, of the theorists and cinema start to blur, and an open dialogue is instituted, in which the two partners exchange positions.
>
> *(Casetti 1999: 179)*

There is some resonance here with Ferro's and Civitarese's metaphor of the field, in that it recognizes the *lattice* of looks involved within analysis (as within cinema) (see the Barangers' 'second look'). Indeed the field metaphor views the gaze as a structuring presence within analysis, but does not center it – as previous metaphors have tended to do (such as Metz's and Mulvey's theories of identification). The field metaphor gives greater attention to the working of unconscious fantasy between people, where we can locate Casetti's 'open dialogue' as mind and body experience, to which we can further include 'enworlded' (Brown 2013) aspects such as space and time within the analytic situation, over specific patterns of exchange, ocular or otherwise.

Casetti's second characteristic of field theories rests on asking 'good questions' (1999: 179), a practice requiring self-awareness of one's own implicit biases in their work. We might say that for film scholars this involves awareness of limits within their area of research and its specific methods and approaches, for psychoanalysts – their school of training. In many ways this second characteristic of field theory better defines Metz's 'cinema-machine' in that it recognizes aesthetic experience as extending beyond textual systems, guiding us to ask things of cinema in order to fully "grasp its meaning . . . [that is] what cinema wants us to ask it, for it to show us its depth" (Casetti 1999: 180). The third characteristic, as Casetti puts it, was the increasing attention on specific films themselves over the practice of using films generally to illuminate theoretical positions about cinema. It is on this final characteristic where analytic field theory and Casetti's 'field theories' requires closer attention, as on first glance there appears to be little to link them.

Casetti's intention is to offer a historical pathway showing how theories of cinema had evolved up until 1995 and he views critique of research methodologies as a significant development within film theory. The capacity to analyze and evaluate previous theories and methods of film theory was "to go beyond each isolated discipline to bring into play something common to all" (1999: 180). In this manner, the understanding of 'field as a process' involves similar interpretive positions – for Casetti it is to see theories of cinema working within the metaphor of the field so that the various methodologies, texts, and experiences that go into constituting cinema are able to remain 'autonomous and interconnected'. For Ferro and Civitarese, the metaphor of the field "is tantamount to the use of a kind of violence, to causing a slight shock . . . as a development of narrations or opening up of possible worlds" (Ferro and Civitarese 2015: 11). I read this as being similar to Deleuze's claim that "with the movement-image, you can't escape the shock which arouses the thinker in you" (Deleuze 2013: 156). In order for new worlds to emerge from the field, which is for the patient to be able to dream effectively (in the Bionian sense) and tell stories, they must face emotional turbulence (what I interpret as Deleuze's violence) in the analytic field, otherwise emotional growth is unlikely to occur. Here, the emotional turbulence is not necessarily derivative of traumatic experience (from sexual or physical abuse – although of course, it might be); rather emotional turbulence – the violence that Deleuze's alludes to – evolves from thinking the unconscious tensions and pressures of emotional frustrations.

This sentiment – where shock is linked to the sensation and production of thought caused by specific films – has caught other scholarly attention within film and media studies (see Perkins and Verevis 2014; Hansen 2004; Cooper 2013; Rizzo 2012). Mark Hansen notes that from a Deleuzian standpoint, shock is something that "forces us to think", placing the experience of thinking seemingly in line with Bion's model, where thinking is seen as the apparatus required to cope with the pressure of thoughts (that is the pressure of raw sensory data which constitutes lived experience). However, Hansen writes that this Deleuzian shock exists "*within the image itself*" (Hansen 2004: 301, italics original), running counter to the more comprehensive principle of Bion's theory of thinking, which is that in order for thinking to be productive it must link to another mind, so outside the limits of a filmic frame – we can only think our most disturbing (shocking) thoughts in connection with other mind in order to grow. Sarah Cooper emphasizes Deleuze's idea of shock more in line with Bion's proto-mental model, "thought is embodied as the cerebral cortex is inextricably linked to the fleshiness of the body. For Deleuze the body takes us through thought to reach the unthought that is life itself" (Cooper 2013: 132). In all respects, it is the use of the field metaphor that facilitates a link between the action of thought (however encountered – via Deleuzian shock or otherwise), a specific moving image experience, and its relation to corporeality in order for growth to occur. It avoids placing a rigid significance on the interpretation of meaning through textual analysis, instead 'field' recognizes the plurality inherent in each discipline as an embodied, embedding dreaming – for Casetti, cinema; for Ferro and Civitarese psychoanalysis – that awakens the thinker in us all.

The embedded spectator

How might the metaphor of the field illuminate the notion of an embedded spectator, particularly as 'embedded' connotes senses of fixity and positioning? I mentioned that Civitarese drew on the example of VR as a metaphor for the field, where he argues, "VR experience is the closest experience to dream" in a waking state and which is possible to be shared (Civitarese 2010: 79). Here Civitarese is using VR to highlight key characteristics of the analytic field as he sees them, immersion and interactivity, and I wish to invert this and use the metaphor of the field to speak to the changing landscape of cinematic experience. The two key notions of immersion and interactivity, which found Civitarese's consideration of VR, are used quite literally, where immersion refers to the body virtually entering into digital space and responding in real time to immediate feedback. Interaction is taken to refer to the capacity to alter or play with the 'system', that is 'digital texts' (2010: 75). Civitarese views the purpose of VR as reconciling these two elements. Inasmuch as VR (and AR) offer new opportunities to rethink our aesthetic experience with moving images, and are indeed immersive and interactive, I am more cautious of linking dreaming (as unconscious waking thought) to specific technologies such as VR. There is a danger of being seduced into the utopia of imminent possibility in such virtual or augmented worlds that the lived experience fails to live up to.

Ferro (2009), Ferro and Foresti (2013), and Civitarese (2014) have all argued that dreaming is not limited to nighttime sleep, but works as unconscious waking thought. This is the revolution of Bion's revision of dream theory for psychoanalysis. Unconscious waking thought is also not able to be shared in the literal manner of direct exchange, but rather through reverie, that establishes intersubjective aesthetic experience across the analytic (or cinematic) field. Further, experiences of dreams and dreaming must exist on a spectrum (or indeed, a field) that includes the 'more real' to the 'surreal' – all of which are the intersubjective aesthetic experiences of dreaming. No dream experience is more or less real than the other, variable certainly, but no less a dreaming.

The concept of the embedded spectator, then, becomes ineffective if it aligns too closely with specific technology, circumstance, or experience. Instead, it serves as a construct to enable Bionian psychoanalytic theory to investigate cinema and its morphologies; and at the same time, allow a second look at cinema as a field that enables us to include Bionian ideas and their challenge to traditional models of film theory and spectatorship. The close relationship between film studies and psychoanalysis has offered a heavy overlaying and cross-referencing of practices and approaches throughout the years (via Baudry; Metz; Mulvey 1975; Doane 1987), often in response to the development of production technologies or socio-political movements. Ferro's and Civitarese's metaphor of the field, as a radical Bionian revision of dreaming as intersubjective aesthetic experience, offers a way to approach the contemporary relevance of psychoanalysis for new hermeneutics of cinema. The impact of Bion's ideas for film and media theory shows very little sign of diminishing, especially as his reappraisals of classical psychoanalytic models link well with the theoretical frameworks of other approaches, such as cognitive studies. Bion's theory of thinking, which includes concepts of reverie and the intersubjective field, are significant because they address affect and emotional experience in a phenomenologico-psychoanalytic context.

Notes

1 Throughout this chapter, I use 'analytic field theory' interchangeably with 'Bionian field theory'. This is to acknowledge the specific direction of Ferro's and Civitarese's revision of the Barangers' initial 'field theory' and, where necessary, to either emphasize the metaphor of the field and its function or the difference Bionian psychoanalysis incurs to the conception of the analytic situation.
2 This resonates with Tomkins's theory of 'inverse archaeology' and his theory of affect being transmitted and motivated through the face and the skin that I discussed in Chapter 2 (see Tomkins 1962 and Frank 2015).
3 See Ambrósio Garcia (2017) who examines Metz's discussion of filmic unpleasure within the context of cinema as bad object and a misinterpretation of Kleinian object relations.
4 I explore this at greater length in Chapter 8 within the context of containment and Deleuze's and Guattari's notion of rhizome.
5 With respect to cinema theory, Deleuze makes a similar statement in *Cinema 2: The Time-Image* (2013: 157) when he writes, "According to Eisenstein, the first moment [of cinematic movement] does from the image to thought, from the percept to the concept".
6 Fahlenbrach's use of the word 'container' in this context – whilst relative to the experience and intersubjectivity of emotion – is applied in a significantly different manner to the way in which Bion develops and uses his term 'container-contained'. I discuss later in the chapter with respect to characteristics of the field (for Bion containment works as a process), but for a more in-depth discussion see Chapter 6 and Chapter 8.
7 See Ogden (2004) for a detailed discussion of the difference between Winnicott's concept of holding and Bion's theory of container-contained.
8 Deleuze's notion of shock as "the very form of communication of movement in images" (2013: 157) links with Ferro's pictograms (2009), particularly as the concept of shock arising "the thinker in you" resonates with Bion's "thoughts in search of a thinker".

References

Ambrósio Garcia, C. (2017). *Bion in Film Theory: The Retreat in Film*. Abingdon, UK: Routledge.
Baranger, M. and Baranger, W. (2008). The Analytic Situation as a Dynamic Field. *International Journal of Psychoanalysis*, 89 (4), pp. 795–826, 1961–1962.
Baranger, M. and Baranger, W. (2009). *The Work of Confluence: Listening and Working and Interpreting in the Psychoanalytic Field*. London: Karnac Books.
Baranger, M., Baranger, W. and Mom, J. (1983). Process and Non-Process in Analytic Work. *International Journal of Psychoanalysis*, 64, pp. 1–15.
Baudry, J-L. (1975). The Apparatus: Metapsychological Approaches to the Impression of Reality in the Cinema. In Rosen, P. (ed.) *Narrative, Apparatus, Ideology: A Film Reader*. New York: Columbia University Press, 1986.
Bion, W.R. (1961). *Experiences in Groups and Other Papers*. New York: Basic Books.
Bion, W.R. (1962). *Learning From Experience*. London: Tavistock.
Bion, W.R. (1965). *Transformations: Change From Learning to Growth*. London: William Heinemann Medical Books.
Bion, W.R. (1967). Notes on Memory and Desire. In Spills, E.B. (ed.) *Melanie Klein Today: Developments in Theory and Practice, Vol. 1*. London: Routledge, 1988.
Bordwell, D. and Carroll, N. (eds.) (1996). *Post-Theory: Reconstructing Film Studies*. Wisconsin: The University of Wisconsin Press.
Brown, W. (2013). *Supercinema: Film-Philosophy for the Digital Age*. New York and Oxford: Berghahn Press.
Casetti, F. (1999). *Theories of Cinema: 1945–1995*. Translated by F. Chiostri, E.G. Bartolini-Salimbeni and T. Kelso. Austin: University of Texas Press.
Civitarese, G. (2010). *The Intimate Room: Theory and Technique of the Analytic Field*. London and New York: Routledge.
Civitarese, G. (2014). *The Necessary Dream: New Theories and Techniques of Interpretation in Psychoanalysis*. Translated by I. Harvey. London: Karnac Books.
Coënarts, M. and Kravana, P. (2016). The Eyes for Mind in Cinema: A Metaphorical Study of the Viewer's Experience. In Fahlenbrach, K. (ed.) *Embodied Metaphors in Film, Television and Video Games: Cognitive Approaches*. London and New York: Routledge.
Cooper, S. (2013). *The Soul of Film Theory*. Basingstoke: Palgrave Macmillan.
Deleuze, D. (2013). *Cinema 2: The Time Image*. Translated by H. Tomlinson and R. Galeta. Minneapolis: The University of Minnesota Press, 1989.
Doane, M. (1987). *To Desire to Desire: The Woman's Film of the 1940s*. Bloomington: Indiana University Press.
Eugeni, R. (2014). Rhetoric and Film. In Branigan, E. and Buckland, W. (eds.) *The Routledge Encyclopedia of Film Theory*. London and New York: Routledge.
Fahlenbrach, K. (2016). *Embodied Metaphors in Film, Television and Video Games: Cognitive Approaches*. London and New York: Routledge.
Ferro, A. (2009). *Mind Works: Technique and Creativity in Psychoanalysis*. Translated by P. Slotkin. London and New York: Routledge.
Ferro, A. (2011). *Avoiding Emotions, Living Emotions*. Translated by I. Harvey. Hove, East Sussex: Routledge.
Ferro, A. and Basile, R. (2009). *The Analytic Field: A Clinical Concept*. London: Karnac Books.
Ferro, A. and Civitarese, G. (2015). *The Analytic Field and its Transformations*. London: Karnac Books. Freud, S. (1900). *The Interpretation of Dreams*. Standard Edition. Translated by J. Strachey. London: Hogarth Press, 1953.

Ferro, A. and Foresti, G. (2013). Bion and Thinking. *The Psychoanalytic Quarterly*, 82 (2), pp. 361–391.
Frank, A. (2015). *Transferential Poetics, From Poe to Warhol*. New York: Fordham University Press.
Hagman, G. (2005). *Aesthetic Experience: Beauty, Creativity, and the Search for the Ideal*. Amsterdam, New York: Rodopi Editions.
Hansen, M.B.N. (2004). *New Philosophy for New Media*. Cambridge: MIT Press.
hooks, b. (1992). The Oppositional Gaze. In *Black Looks: Race and Representation*. Boston: South End Press.
Jakobson, R. (1956). Two Aspects of Language and Two Types of Aphasic Disturbance. In Rudy, S. (ed.) *Selected Works, vol. 2*. The Hague: Mouton.
Katz, W. (2013). Field of Dreams: Four Books by Three Italians. *Contemporary Psychoanalysis*, 49 (3), pp. 458–483.
Kickasola, J. (2016). Metaphor Without an Answer. In Fahlenbrach, K. (ed.) *Embodied Metaphors in Film, Television and Video Games: Cognitive Approaches*. London and New York: Routledge.
Klein, M. (1952). The Origins of Transference. In *Envy and Gratitude and Other Works: 1946–1963*. London: Hogarth Press and the Institute of Psychoanalysis.
Kristeva, J. (1974). *Revolution in Poetic Language*. Translated by L.S. Roudiez. New York: Columbia University Press.
Lakoff, G. and Johnson, M. (1980). *Metaphors We Live By*. Chicago: The University of Chicago Press.
Lebovici, S. (1949). Psychanalyse et cinema. *Revue Internationale de Filmologie*, 2 (5), pp. 49–55.
Marks, L. (2000). *The Skin of the Film: Intercultural Cinema, Embodiment, and the Senses*. Durham: Duke University Press.
Merleau-Ponty, M. (1945). *The Primacy of Perception: And Other Essays on Phenomenological Psychology, the Philosophy of Art, History and Politics* (ed.) Edie, J.E. Translated by W. Cobb. Evanston: Northwestern University Press, 1964.
Metz, C. (1974). *Film Language: A Semiotics of the Cinema*. Translated by M. Taylor. Oxford: Oxford University Press.
Metz, C. (1975). The Imaginary Signifier. Translated by B. Brewster. *Screen*, 16 (2), pp. 14–76.
Metz, C. (1982). *The Imaginary Signifier: Psychoanalysis and the Cinema*. Translated by C. Britton, A. Williams, B. Brewster and A. Guzzetti. Bloomington and Indianapolis: Indiana University Press.
Mulvey, L. (1975). Visual Pleasure and Narrative Cinema. *Screen*, 16 (3), pp. 6–18.
Ogden, T. (2004). On Holding and Containing, Being and Dreaming. *International Journal of Psychoanalysis*, 85 (6), pp. 1349–1364.
Ogden, T. (2010). On Three Forms of Thinking: Magical Thinking, Dream Thinking, and Transformative Thinking. *The Psychoanalytic Quarterly*, 79 (2), pp. 317–347.
Perkins, C. and Verevis, C. (2014). *B Is for Bad Cinema: Aesthetics, Politics and Cultural Value*. Albany, NY: State University of New York Press.
Rizzo, T. (2012). *Deleuze and Film: A Feminist Introduction*. London and New York: Continuum.
Rosen, P. (2008). Screen and 1970s Film Theory. In Grieveson, L. and Wasson, H. (eds.) *Inventing Film Studies*. Durham: Duke University Press.
Rushton, R. (2002). Cinema's Double: Some Reflections on Metz. *Screen*, 43 (2), pp. 107–118.
Silverman, K. (1983). *The Subject of Semiotics*. Oxford: Oxford University Press.
Sobchack, V. (2004). *Carnal Thoughts: Embodiment and Moving Image Culture*. Berkeley: University of California Press.
Sobchack, V. (2006). A Leg to Stand On: Prosthetics, Metaphor and Materiality. In M. Smith and J. Morra (eds.) *The Prosthetic Impulse: From a Posthuman Present to a Biocultural Future*. Cambridge: MIT Press.

Symington, N. and Symington, J. (2008). *The Clinical Work of Wilfred Bion*. London and New York: Routledge.
Tomkins, S. (1962). *Affect, Imagery, Consciousness, Volume 1, The Positive Affects*. New York: Springer.
Trifonova, T. (2009). *European Film Theory*. London and New York: Routledge.
Williams, L. (1981). *Figures of Desire: A Theory and Analysis of Surrealist Film*. Berkeley: University of California Press.
Winnicott, D.W. (1956). The Theory of the Parent-Infant Relationship. *International Journal of Psychoanalysis*, 41, pp. 585–595.

5
GROUP EXPERIENCE, COLLECTIVE MEMORY AND DREAMING

Moving image experience with cinema and media involves the assembly of groups – such as the coming together at a specific screening, participatory fandom, cultural events such as festivals, and even academic exchanges through scholarship and conferences – effecting a wider collective memory of what it is to have seen/experienced screen media across time, cultures and contexts. Cinema, in particular, due to its political and ideological histories, possesses the potential to act as a reflexive social framework for groups, reflecting the tensions that are present within political culture of a nation, or more specifically those that involve individual cultural politics of identity that are "ferried between two worlds" (our inner and outer worlds) (Civitarese 2014). The experience of 'being embedded' when considered within such a context is not defined through any remediation of geographical location or context, or even the literal quality of physical movement, but rather through the more internal and perceptual, yet equally affective, social frameworks of memory and group experience.

In this chapter, moving image experience is explored as an example of a shared social framework of collective memory and is argued to work as a potential type of group dreaming that seeks to unify the psychic life of the group with its lived, bodily experience. Dreaming, when considered through the revisionist paradigm of Bionian psychoanalysis, far exceeds its definition of being "stories when we sleep", and potentially the more abstract 'unconscious waking thought'. For Bion, dreaming was knowledge; a proto-mental process through which we become embedded in everyday lived experience that restores our sensuous lived body experience with our own conscious perceptions and expressions with others.

Ogden writes that "[d]reaming is our profoundest form of thinking and constitutes the principal medium through which we achieve human consciousness, psychological growth, and the capacity to create personal, symbolic meaning from our lived experience" (2008: 25). A knowledge, then, better be described as sensorial knowing which digests the unthought emotions of our lived experience. In Chapter 3 I discussed Bion's notion of reverie as a typology of intersubjective mind-body wandering that occurs with moving images, which Chapter 4 developed with respect to Ferro's and Civitarese's metaphor of the analytic field. In this chapter, I extend the Bionian model of dreaming to the much broader context of group experience and collective memory. There are two main reasons for this; the first is that moving images, like dreaming, however much they are regarded as immersive and individual experiences, are also group experiences and part of wider socio-cultural and socio-political structures. The second is the claim that dreaming as group experience manifests via social frameworks of memory, which includes moving images.

Maurice Halbwachs's (1992) theory on collective memory is positioned here as a philosophy of *group* emotional experience – which I argue functions as a dreaming, that is as an embedding, emotional experience. Admittedly, Halbwachs never intended or indicated that memory (individual or collective) works as a dreaming – quite the opposite. His argument was that memory was only possible through collective relationships, which were sustained through a variety of social frameworks that included groups of people, and (perhaps more importantly) oral reminiscences, national holidays and objects of art that either memorialized or centered on historical events, or significant affective resonance (such as any resulting trauma). I argue that collective memory, when placed within a Bionian psychoanalytic context, can be read as a typology of group dreaming, which seeks to process socio-cultural emotional experience, such as the emotional work done with moving images.

Halbwachs claimed that memories adapt to and are influenced by the visual images we use to construct them (1992: 38). Memory can only ever be in service of the present, not simply because this is where it exists and is at its most relevant, but because memory requires sensuous material in order to thrive. In other words, memory needs sensory data, which Halbwachs says comes from such social frameworks that structure our external environments. Even though there are no direct disciplinary links between Halbwachs and Bion, their respective positions on memory and dreaming nevertheless suggest significant degrees of alignment. Here we can see key principles[1] explicating Bion's theory of thinking as echoing Halbwachs's concept of collective memory, as memory needs interaction with other minds more than it needs the "combination of individual recollections of many members of the same society" (Halbwachs 1992: 39). Further, Halbwachs's claim that memory is used to solve problems in the present is reminiscent of Bion's psychoanalytic function of the personality (1962) which is one's ability and capacity to tolerate frustrations within lived emotional experience – to think and feel them in order for mental growth to occur. As Halbwachs puts it:

> we appeal to our memory only in order to answer questions which others have asked us, or that we suppose they could have asked us. We note, moreover, that in order to answer them, we place ourselves in their perspective and we consider ourselves as being part of the same group or groups as they.
> *(1992: 38)*

Ogden notes that the 'psychoanalytic' part of our personality refers to the ability to view lived experience from both conscious and unconscious viewpoints, and "dreaming (which is synonymous with unconscious thinking) is the principal psychological form in which this work is performed" (Ogden 2008: 24). A Bionian theory of dreaming supports Halbwachs's claim that collective memory (and the social frameworks that facilitate it) is dependent on the individual's participation and membership of the group. Indeed Halbwachs (1992: 40) states that collective memory when formed through such frameworks is a reconstruction of the imagination of the past, which in its own turn reflects the dominant social perspective of its time. It is therefore a distortion because it is adaptable and able to be changed, furthering his claim that collective memory forms along selective and variable lines. My aim here is to consider group experience and collective memory through the framework of dreaming as a common link that exists between Bion and Halbwachs, as both position dreaming as a central structure for collective aesthetic experience, albeit in with different disciplinary and theoretical intentions.

Cinema often plays out versions of collective memory through its film worlds; as a cinematic field that functions as a social framework of memory, which enables group dreaming – particularly as a revisionist, distorting recollection that responds to present-day social issues and concerns. As Daniel Yacavone writes, film worlds possess 'global affective character' (2015: 161) where specific aesthetics are argued to transmit affect, which facilitate individual and audience 'feeling'. Yacavone notes the ambiguity that exists on the subject of expression of emotion and affect in cinema, referring to either the transmission of affect through identity representation, or via formal aesthetics, or authorial intentionality. Even though Yacavone comes to view "*expression* . . . [as] synonymous with any affect, feeling or emotion prompted by a film that is actually felt to varying degrees by an engaged viewer" (2015: 162), his argument often includes reference to an implicit collective audience body (local to global). As a theory that seeks to map affect and emotion as forms of feeling within cinema *worlds*, Yacavone's is also indirectly a theory of groups "what is produced by the 'group', as well as the individuals within it" (Brennan 2004: 51). Engagement with moving images and their worlds then, is participation in 'global affective character', which I see as reflective of Halbwachs's theory of collective memory and Bion's conceptualization of dreaming.

Yacavone's 'cineaesthetic world-feeling' is discussed to contextualize the non-cinematic theories of Bion and Halbwachs in relevant film and media studies scholarship; and Kuhn's (2010) foundational work on memory texts and memory work is used to consider the collective cultural aspect involved with the use and relational value of moving images. The notion of collective experience as group 'memory work' and as a typology of dreaming is examined through two examples, illustrating how moving images guide and direct what it is to remember as much as what is to be remembered. The film *Force Majeure* (Östlund 2014) and the web-based documentary work, *Prisons Memory Archive* (McLaughlin 2006-present) are two very different examples that equally use the group and the moving image as social frameworks of collective memory to exercise comment on group experience, and in doing so they exemplify Bion's claim that the individual is incessantly shaped through the perception of the group to themselves. The narrative in each example involves the co-presence of the group, and the physical and psychical framework of collective memory, which becomes essential in determining the group's value and significance. *Force Majeure* represents the social framework of the family and the tensions that result from neglecting "the rules and customs independent of us that existed before us" (Halbwachs 1992: 55); and *Prisons Memory Archive (PMA)*, through the lattice of reflective testimonies, illuminates elements of Bion's theory of the 'work group'. Both exemplify the interrelationship of Kuhn's memory texts and memory work as they aim to direct memory and group experience within the context of moving image experience. These examples, to varying degrees, foreground the necessity of collective shared knowledge (such as memory) and illustrate the significance of Bion's theory of thinking, that two minds are required in order to think (and therefore feel) each other.

Despite Bion's and Halbwachs's different positions, each thinker views the dream, or the process of dreaming, as a key element between the individual and the group, critical to shared aesthetic experience – emotional or mnemonic. Their respective works are therefore valuable in outlining the specific collective aspect of 'being embedded' that is being postulated here. Dreaming is argued to act as the connective tissue that links theories of moving image experience with those relevant to collective memory and group experience, not just because these 'works' – dreaming and remembering – involve affective aesthetic experience common to both, but because, as Halbwachs writes, "[i]t is not sufficient, in effect, to show that *individuals* always use social frameworks when they remember. It is necessary to place oneself in the perspective of the *group or groups*" (1992: 40, italics added). For him, dreams are sensations that "demand a certain degree of reflexive attention that is in tune with the order of natural relations that we and others experience" (1992: 41), and it is possible to view the collective enterprise of the moving image in a similar context. As Civitarese writes, "the dream ferries us between worlds" (2014: 5), and I use this 'carrier' characteristic of dreaming as a means to link the concept of 'being embedded' to the frameworks of collective memory, group experience and aesthetic experience. Before we look more specifically at the interrelationships between memory, group experience and dreaming within the context of 'being embedded', it is important to establish what the word 'group' refers to and how it is being used here within the context of collective memory and experience. In this next section, I discuss Bion's theory of groups and outline how it links with Halbwachs's notion of collective memory before applying it to the analysis of *Force Majeure* and *PMA*.

Bion's *Experiences in Groups*

Bion's theory of thinking eventually emerged from the group therapy work he conducted alongside John Rickman (the 'Northfield experiments') at Northfields Military Hospital in 1942. From this field work, Bion saw that the emotional life of the individual within a group "illumines both his own personality and his view of the group" (1961: 50), and that such participation with group life will require constant compromise between one's own agenda and that of the group. Bion's theory on groups and the different mentalities, introduced in Chapter 2, outlined psychotic parts of the personality as constitutive of group life – more correctly, it was the clash and negotiation between the individual's emotions and those of the group that constructed group mentality. The study of moving image experience as a 'total affective field' (Yacavone 2015: 169) – involves the critical interplay of individual and group behavior, making Bion's theory of group experience highly relevant as we examine the connection between thinking and feeling, dreaming and remembering with moving images. Bion saw the group as being vitally important to everyday life, which in turn enables us to locate key critical questions of immersion, embedding and collective memory: "[w]e are constantly affected by what we feel to be the attitude of a group to ourselves, and are consciously or unconsciously swayed by our idea of it" (Bion 1961: 32). We must consider the difference between an individual dreaming and the dreaming that occurs within a group – as discussed in terms of the metaphor of the field in the previous chapter – particularly as so much of moving image experience involves (or implies) audiences, both *in situ* and virtual.

Before Bion came to form his theory on group mentality and experience, Freud had previously acknowledged that the individual's relationship to themselves was also reflected in their relationship with others. In *Group Psychology and the Analysis of the Ego* (1959), Freud begins to outline and incorporate a stronger place for the object and its affect within psychoanalysis, "only rarely and under certain exceptional conditions is individual psychology in a position to disregard the relations of the individual to others. In the individual's mental life someone else is invariably involved" (Freud 1959: 3).[2] Through the Northfield experiments, Bion devised two main types of group function, namely, the basic assumption mentality and the work group mentality. These two mentalities, often concurrent but not compatible, were used to identify the ways in which group behavior (and therefore groups themselves) became easily distracted and dysfunctional, or maintained their cohesion and efficacy. One of the issues in Bion's writing is that despite his efforts to define group behavior via psychoanalytic observation, his interchangeable use of the word 'groups' to refer to a collection of people, and also to a group's psychic functioning makes for tricky interpretation. The typologies of group function can be said to refer to the ways in which group mentality reflects its emotional experience about its own existence and relationship to other groups and environments it connects with.

Bion identifies a group as including three or more people. Two people "have personal relationships; with three or more there is a change of quality (interpersonal relationship)" (1961: 26), and while this recognizes what a group is, the focus of this chapter looks more toward Bion's theory of what a group does, or what the purpose of groups are. For Bion, group experience is "an interplay between individual needs, group mentality, and culture" (Bion 1961: 55) – his definition privileging the 'working' of a group, what we might refer to as 'group-work' (like "the working of memory as memory work" or "the working of a dream as dream work"). He begins and concludes *Experiences in Groups* (1961) by acknowledging Klein's enormous influence on the development of his theory of groups. He notes that without her theories of projective identification and the interaction between paranoid-schizoid and depressive positions[3] – key mechanisms that foregrounded the psychotic defenses present within early mental life – his work on groups would not have evolved as it did (1961: 8). Bion took the Kleinian emphasis on individual psychotic (primitive) anxieties and extended it to group thinking and behavior. This was to supplement Freud's claim that the family group is "the prototype of all groups" (1961: 188) and Bion shifted attention to the emotional life of the group, that is its aesthetic, affective life. These anxieties, as Bion saw them, were the basis for his 'basic assumptions' group behavior.

I have previously introduced Bion's three basic assumptions in my overview of his theory of thinking in Chapter 2, but it is worth repeating here that these basic assumptions are the anxieties and emotions that differ in aim from any work group activity "designed to further the task at hand" (1961: 189). Basic assumptions, then, will always be at odds with work group mentality as they are Oedipal in their determination.[4] As assumptions, they express emotion and affect within the group, and because the basic assumptions are reflective of primitive, anxious emotion, the affective experience manifested as an assumption is negative. Basic assumptions, as conflicting aspects of group experience, are the echoes of Klein's envy, hate and aggression sensations and unthought emotions originally directed toward the mother's breast. Klein's theory of splitting, where the hated object is also the loved object, was a means of survival – to distance and separate (split) conflictual emotions to avoid dissociation and disintegration.

It is the interrelationship between these basic assumptions that Bion sees as stitching a group together rather than any specific people, empirical quality or attribute. Bion's definition highlights the fluidity of groups and their transient existence. Just as we can note that memory is an intangible 'glue' that attempts to 'hold' society (as per Halbwachs) and its identity and histories together (despite conflicting and varying accounts and diversities), Bion's consideration of groups is equally collective and interstitial. He writes that the normal state of a group "is mostly perplexing and confused" (1961: 57) which, in its own perplexing and confused manner, is his way of saying that groups can never be any one thing; rather that they are always a combination of mentalities and intersections of attentions. In this way, the basic assumptions within group behavior maintain a group's life even when the group does not meet in real time. Their connection is dependent on the transmission of affective experience rather than the literal physical meeting and gathering.

Equally, Bion views the part that an individual plays within a group as representative of the group overall. That is, if an individual's actions or voice are not challenged by other group members, it is assumed that their actions or voice speak for all those within the group. On this point, we can see how Halbwachs's social frameworks operate via Bion's theory of group experience in support of collective memory, acting as a mirror for the relationship between the individual and the group. Social frameworks are formed externally via repeated exchanges of everyday interaction, stories between people, conscious emotional experiences being made unconscious, and the control of a group is necessary to alleviate its confusion or distraction. Groups and memory operate co-dependently, both requiring shared social space through which they are able to come into existence and be sustained, arguably by each other. Halbwachs writes, "it is in society that people normally acquire their memories. It is also in society that they recall, recognize, and localize their memories" (Halbwachs 1992: 38), thereby foregrounding the significance of interaction between people for not just the invocation and transmission of memory but equally for the action and behavior of remembering as a way to concretize and nourish groups and our individual relativism to them.

Halbwachs notes that social frameworks and collective memory are not the same thing rather they are integrated with one another, or at the very least, work in tandem with one other. Social frameworks then, are not "simply the people around us" (Erll 2011: 15), but they are also the spaces and times that we place ourselves within, abstractly, in order to respond and recreate the perspectives of those around us. Thought and emotional experience go 'into' these perspectives, these frameworks, that are then used in order to participate in acts of remembrance that hold viability and meaning for the groups to which they are presented to. Group memory work is as much about past events as it is about events that ask us to remember how to act – something that Kuhn stipulates in her work on memory texts and memory work that I discuss later.

As Bion's basic assumption group mentality refers to a group's beliefs and subsequent behavior to sustain its existence, the assumptions are said to maintain the group via collective emotional experiences that are projected into/onto the group by its individual members. Group mentalities will utilize social frameworks differently in order to fulfill the assumptions that the group possesses in order to keep it alive. This links with Halbwachs's assertion that collective memories are in themselves selective and variable. Halbwachs states that memories are recalled more easily and to a greater degree when they are shared between friends and family. He writes:

> [w]hat makes recent memories hang together is not that they are contiguous in time: it is rather that they are part of a totality of thoughts common to a group, the group of people with whom we have a relation at this moment, or with whom we have had a relation on the preceding day or days.
>
> *(1992: 52)*

Halbwachs is adamant that memories are located externally to us and that it is only through the adoption of the perspective of the group and its interests that we are able to recall and make sense of such recollections.

Bion's original three basic assumptions – pairing, flight/fight and dependency – have been added to by Pierre Turquet (1974), who offered a fourth basic assumption of 'oneness', and Lawrence, Bain and Gould (1996) who presented a fifth basic assumption, 'me-ness', argued to exist as cultural phenomena rather than individual narcissism. This fifth basic assumption holds particular relevance for the present discussion of dreaming as an embedding emotional experience,

> living in contemporary, turbulent societies becomes more risky so the individual is pressed more and more into his or her own inner reality in order to exclude and deny the perceived disturbing realities that are of the outer environment. The inner world becomes thus a comforting one offering succour [comfort].
> *(Lawrence, Bain and Gould 1996: 24)*

Our participation within group experience, whether conscious or not, is recursive and regulated. Even in the circumstances where one is not part of a specific group, one is placed within the grouping of "not being part of a group". However, time is rarely taken to attend to a group's literal materiality – how via the combination of its members and their own goals and fantasies, is its purpose, value or function determined? Instead, what a group has come together to do, its manifest identity, is the usual focus.

The group as a socio-cultural framework that includes the notion and experience of audience, operates as a vehicle, which we can examine the plural means we embed/dream ourselves within social settings and environments. If 'being embedded' can be said to function as dreaming, then group experience is a very real phenomenon to demonstrate our thinking through emotional experience. One of the contentions of this book is that 'being embedded' is a processing, a dreaming of sensory experience as a response to lived experience in our external worlds, via all our different relationships with such people, places and things. This is why specifying a singular definition of what 'being embedded' is becomes not just difficult, but ultimately meaningless. Rather, placing emphasis on what 'being embedded' does aesthetically as sensorial experience, and considering how such social frameworks like moving images influence us, offers more options and possibilities in how we acknowledge and negotiate our lived emotional experience.

The other mentality of group experience that Bion identifies is the work group, which concerns the focus and application of a group's 'sophisticated' mentality (Bion 1961). Bion writes that the work group "meets for a specific task ... the capacity for co-operation on this level is great ... the psychological structure of the work group is very powerful" (Bion, 1961: 98) but also the work group is "constantly perturbed by the influences that come from other group mental phenomena" (1961: 129). These perturbing influences are the 'basic assumption' mentalities. In her study on the transmission of affect, Brennan asks "[w]hy do psychotic bits of us emerge in groups but not in individual behavior" (2004: 65), in order to propose that groups are agencies for the transmission of affect, particularly – our anxious and paranoid emotions. Psychotic parts of personality also present in individual behavior, but Brennan is looking more to question the emphasis that Bion places on the overt psychotic behavior observed in groups. Perhaps collective memory offers some solution.

Memories are often about the working through of emotional experience – intersubjective and collective – even if the recollection appears to be about something else. As Bion warns, whatever the group is talking about, it is always talking about itself (1961). Brennan's conclusion is that Bion's attention on the psychotic elements of group experience proves "affects are preeminently social . . . [t]hey preexist us; they are outside as well as within us" (2004: 65). This leads Brennan to make the case that groups either exacerbate or restrain psychotic affects, her examples being Nazism for the former and political acts of resistance for the latter. Outside the specifics of psychotic group behavior (heightened or dampened), Bion foregrounded this mechanism in order to develop his meta-theory of thinking, which presented the radical revision of dreaming as centering on emotional and affective experience over wish-fulfillment and drive gratification.

The task of the group

What is the task of a group and how might this be read in terms of moving image experience for an audience? Bion writes that the task of a group is to manage its tensions – the undulations of its behaviors, to contain and direct its own specific idiosyncrasies. The interrelationships involved with this task of the group are critical for overall group experience, which is what determines good, or not-so-good, group health and relies on the relational structure of its members. The group, and specifically its collective subjectivity and mentality, is central to the ways in which we become knowingly and unknowingly embedded in culture and society, here extended to the relationship and establishment of spectator and audience.

Both Bion and Halbwachs, for their own purposes, establish the relationship between the individual and the group (or collective) as one that is fraught and controlled through a series of continual unconscious tensions involving negotiation, conflict and acquiescence. Halbwachs argues that there "exists a collective memory and social frameworks for memory" (1992: 38) and that only by placing our individual thoughts within these social frameworks (to which I include cinema and media), and by adopting the perspective of the group, is memory (or recollection) possible. Placing individual thoughts in group social frameworks then, is to participate in the world and its memories, "when I remember, it is others who spur me on; their memory comes to the aid of mine and mine relies on theirs" (Halbwachs 1992: 38). For Halbwachs, the mechanics of memory serve to insert ourselves into the present social order via selective means, and it is this selectivity, resulting from the various groups that exist (as communities, as nations, and so on), that produces different collective memories, groups cultures and group mentalities. He writes, "the individual remembers by placing himself in the perspective of the group, but [we] may also affirm that the memory of the group realizes and manifests itself in individual memories" (1992: 40). This reflects Kuhn's position on cinema and media objects operating as memory texts and as processes of memory. They, like the

Halbwachian collective, spur the spectator on to remember, to create and recreate memories. In doing so, film and media act as what might be termed Bionian 'combinations'. For Bion, the group is a combination of its culture (the behaviors and practices that define it), its mentality, and the individuals themselves.

Groups are social structures which we join and use to work through our emotional anxieties (whether such efforts are successful or not is another matter), "anyone who has contact with reality is always consciously or unconsciously forming an estimate of the attitude of the group towards himself" (Bion 1961: 43). The difficulty that exists for both the mechanics of memory and the mechanics of the group is that for the individual to *feel* embedded they must negotiate their own freedoms within the limits that define their membership of the collective. Halbwachs writes, "it is only natural that we consider the group itself as having the capacity to remember, and that we can attribute memory to the family, for example, as much as any other collective group" (1992: 54).

The family in *Force Majeure* effectively embodies both Bion's and Halbwachs's positions as it foregrounds the importance of the group in determining perceptive experience and the necessity of memory.

Memory work and memory texts:
Force Majeure and *Prisons Memory Archive*

Force Majeure is the story of a young family in crisis during a winter ski-trip in the Alps. Whilst having lunch on a balcony at the ski-resort, the family experiences a terrifying avalanche from which they emerge unharmed. During the avalanche, Tomas (Johannes Kuhnke) immediately flees inside, looking to save himself. His wife, Ebba (Lisa Loven Kongsli), stays and tries to protect and calm their two children, Vera (Clara Wettergren) and Harry (Vincent Wettegren). The remainder of the film follows the conflict that develops between Tomas and Ebba due to Tomas's reluctance in admitting his actions. 'Force majeure' is, of course, also a legal clause in contracts that releases one from liability and responsibility in fulfilling their duties during an 'act of god' or unexpected event. (Schaffer, Agusti, Dhooge, Earle 2011). This is in effect what becomes Tomas's unspoken defense in not fulfilling the gendered expectations of social masculinity – the 'contract' of father and husband when he runs to save himself from the unexpected event of the avalanche.

Force Majeure is a critical questioning of the family group (as much as it is about the social framework and performativity of masculinity) and how tensions are evoked and possibly resolved through collective memory. It symbolizes how the actions involved with memory are intricately connected to the thinking that occurs within group experience by highlighting how the identity of the group (the family) hinges on the presence and social exchange of visual images. Kuhn's concepts of memory text and memory work demonstrate how an audience's emotional work within moving image experience is enacted through a set of external social frameworks and relationships, as well as a series of visual recognitions that are subsequently introjected, taken into our own consciousness to become part of our individual world view. These introjections, formed here through the social framework of cinema, are then acted upon to result in affirmation of our own agency. This is not without its conflicts of course, but without tensions, there can be no recognition or awareness of another or indeed collective experience of our relationship to other beings.

Force Majeure further correlates Kuhn's assertion that cinema as a memory text is "capable of feeding readily into collective forms of consciousness, and thus of engaging social memory" (2010: 303). Kuhn's 'memory text' is "typically a montage of vignettes, anecdotes, fragments, 'snapshots' and flashes that can generate a feeling of synchrony . . . the memory text embodies a particular approach to, or type of, performances of memory" (2010: 299), fitting within Halbwachs's definition of a social framework. Kuhn extends her definition of cinema as an example of visual media that represents cultural memory, claiming cinema "is peculiarly capable of enacting not only the very activity of remembering, but also ways of remembering that are commonly shared; it is therefore peculiarly capable of bringing together personal experiences and larger systems and processes of cultural memory" (Kuhn 2010: 303). Here Kuhn is arguing that the critical importance of visual media for cultural memory lies outside the general value of historical and archival presentation and much more within the shared capacity of teaching us how, as well as what, to remember.

This emphasis on relational intersubjectivity – of their needing to be other people in order to think and to remember – also informs Kuhn's concept of 'memory work', which she sees as a more active and revisionist engagement with the past. Memory work is an assembly of experience in the service of who is remembering, as it "undercuts assumptions about the transparency or the authenticity of what is remembered, taking it not as 'truth' but as evidence of a particular sort: material for interpretation, to be interrogated, mined, for its meanings and its possibilities" (Kuhn 2010: 303). Through the group tension that results from Ebba's and Tomas's varying recollections, we can see how Kuhn's concept of memory work assists the specific qualities Bion lists as belonging to a group: its common purpose, its boundaries, the freedom of the individual within a group and most significantly, the capacity to acknowledge grievances and resolve them. Kuhn writes that the memory work is found in the collective sharing of the 'visual aesthetic', where images are treated as 'evidence' that help to form the memory work (Kuhn 2010: 303). These visual media aesthetics act as memory texts that are retold and returned to, and help effect the memory work and group-work by incorporating the shared actions involved with visuality, which memory and groups rely on to validate their own respective mechanics and viability.

Throughout the film, Tomas repeatedly fails to fulfill his 'social contract' of protective father and faithful, loving husband. Some examples are: 1) he abandons his family in the event of avalanche and subsequently denies it; 2) he is slow to act in supportive ways for his wife and for his children; 3) he admits to infidelity; and 4) he agrees to the contrived rescue of his wife for the benefit of their family group (we do not see the planning of this rescue, but by this point in the film, Tomas's consistent failure in meeting expected social roles leaves the audience with the dawning realization that the rescue was Ebba's idea). Halbwachs (1992: 58) writes that in the collective memory of the family, there are regulations that the metagroup of society abides by, referring to specific aesthetics of being and thinking within each family that are imposed through form, or what we may consider as Kuhn's 'visual aesthetic'. In the context of *Force Majeure*, the formal aesthetic of how a family behaves is associated with how well it fulfills its social contract. Bion considers this as a group mentality that needs the support or "conformity with, the other anonymous contributions of the group" (Bion 1961: 50). Using the example of Ebba's contrived 'rescue', Tomas becomes reestablished in his social contractual role of protector father and husband, this being a 'landmark' whereby because of such behavior, the family group mentality is once more in unison and conformity of all members. Indeed Halbwachs (1992: 61) states that figures become representative of both form and collective belief "figures . . . coexist as images and notions . . . we feel capable, given this framework, of reconstructing the image of persons and facts". *Force Majeure* demonstrates the family group mentality in crisis, in part because it critiques/parodies the central role of the masculine. However, the family group mentality is a consistent and recurring motif in cinema; this is in part because of the position and ideology of the family in (Western) thought. In this sense, the analysis of the film as a modality of (family) group mentality holds great potential, but it is beyond the direct concerns of this book to examine it in such depth.

Yet *Force Majeure* is more than a story about a family in crisis, or about the conflict that arises in a marriage, however superficially this seems to be the case. It is about the conflict between the individual and the group, shown specifically as conflict within the family group, which acts as a synecdoche of the conflict between individuals and groups within society. It is subtly commented on through the mirroring of banal quotidian events such as the family brushing teeth and napping together. They are filmed in real time and audiences are made to wait and watch without resolve or clear-cut reason. It exposes the ways in which we adopt and play out roles in our lives within social groups (the family again working metonymically here) according to preset memories of social performativities and cultural scripts, subtly highlighting the clash of experience between knowing ourselves through narcissistic self-identification via idealistic visual signifiers (for example, embodied in Tomas and his contrived masculinity) and knowing ourselves through consistent and difficult self-questioning (embodied in Ebba's resisting femininity).

If recollection is, as Halbwachs claims, a collective process exercised through external social frameworks through which we embed ourselves through thought and emotion in group identity, then it has a great deal to offer for the analysis of tensions between groups and their members. In distinct yet comparable ways, Halbwachs and Bion see memories and groups metonymically – as being about other things – specifically our social behaviors and emotions remaining unexamined and unrecognized for what they are. *Force Majeure* positions Tomas in a similar way, by using him as a synecdoche of the individual at odds with group mentality. Many scenes of daily family activity within the film, such as the family coming back from the ski fields, are used to engender the sense of the family as a group unit as well as the quietly growing frustration at the lack of concern for the individual within such a unit. The narrative of friction between Tomas and Elba functions as a memory text that helps to effect the audience's memory work which recognizes and validates such emotional experience of tension within groups (such as the family). Halbwachs (1980) states that we often believe we are the true authors of our feelings, emotions and ideas but in reality, these are created through our membership and agreement with social groups; the memories we have and share are largely under evaluated, dependent on groups that we are a part of. Similarly, Bion writes, "[w]e all live in groups, and have plenty of experience, however unconscious, of what that means" (Bion 1961: 64). Given that so much of our self-knowledge and thinking rests on collective memory and groups, and that Halbwachs and Bion claim these often lack scrutiny, the intersections of memory and groups within visual culture require critical inspection in order to analyze scripts that appear to present knowledge whilst at the same time, offer resistance to such 'knowing'.

Within the experience and sociality of cinema and media, this resistance becomes readily apparent in the retelling of movies that have been watched with friends, either in the same sitting or within the context of relative time. It is a common experience to have points of difference in the interpretation and recollection of a film's narrative, while concurrently sharing agreement on the overall happening of a film. In *Force Majeure*, Ebba is unable to move past the discrepancy that exists between her's and Tomas's version of his reaction to the avalanche. Tomas's selfish escape to safety leaves Ebba and their children to fend for themselves. Ebba's frustration with Tomas is not just that he left her and their children to their own devices, but more that he denies he *did* actually leave. In order to alleviate her frustration (and disappointment) with Tomas, she shares her story with various people in the film in an effort to incorporate other viewpoints. Yet Ebba's retelling of the event, her emphasis on how it has affected her, is not satisfying enough for her. Later in the film, she shares a video recording of the event via Tomas's cell phone with her brother-in-law and his girlfriend, which shows Tomas running away. Ebba is using the social frameworks of other perspectives to concretize the reality of the video with her perceived truth of the event.

The video here serves as Kuhn's memory text and the validation and participation from friends form the 'memory work'. In their watching of the video, Ebba gains supporters for her story. Her friends become her audience and are embedded in the family group mentality. As the audience of the film, we watch them discuss the event, in a manner that we might, and as an audience, we become embedded further in the overall narrative. The video offers confirmation of Ebba's version of the event and in that moment, we witness a shift in the group and its culture. The video has become the memory text that champions the group memory work, and through the practice of sharing images, has transcended its illustrative boundaries. Whether or not Tomas's account of the experience was accurate is not the point – rather the point being made here is that *Force Majeure* exemplifies Halbwachs's theory that collective memory exists within the external perspective and framework of group experience, additionally affirming Bion's theory that there is a continual tension between the individual and the group.

Collective memory or cultural experience is "itself a construct and more of an academic 'invention' than a discovery of cultural givens" (Erll 2011: 13), indicating that acts of recollection become the cohesive links between groups and the people within them, rather than simply the content of each memory recalled. The examination of the concept and actuality of the archive in recent times, particularly within humanities disciplines and its attentiveness toward digital culture, is a testament to the awareness that has been placed on the differences and conflict between memory as an act of recollection and memory as an exercising of power, agency and knowledge (Schwartz and Cook 2002; McLaughlin 2010; Manoff 2004, Taylor 2003; Derrida 1995). Ebba's insistence that Tomas acknowledge his abandonment of the family is not simply to make sure that *she* has remembered the event correctly, but it is so that she can highlight the lack of cohesion that has occurred within their family unit. It is her attempt to resolve the group tensions through the collective framework of memory, and to embed Tomas once more into the family group. To procure Tomas's agreement is also to procure his recognition of the dissolution of his connection and attachment to each family member, as well as the family group overall.

Prisons Memory Archive

PMA, formed of 175 recorded interviews from participants "who passed through Armagh Gaol and the Maze or Long Kesh Prison" (http://prisonsmemoryarchive.com), is an interactive, networked example of collective memory. It exemplifies how the production of visual images (the filmed interviews) and material cultures (the site-specificities of the gaols in Northern Ireland), identifiable as memory texts, operate as practices of grouping that revolve around one's lived emotional experience. As an archive, the various interviews offer accessible and inclusive links between memory and visuality through the interactive viewing made possible through the website and the audiences' own pathway through them. McLaughlin writes,

> [b]y utilising the formats of linear film and interactive documentary on different occasions, we have encouraged audiences to participate in discussions and/or navigate their way through the material online in order to provoke discussions on how a society might manage its conflicted past in a contested present.
>
> *(McLaughlin 2014)*

The well-established documentary practice of recording noteworthy historical events, lives and places, has been the traditional way to archive and collate cultural memory, "media first create memory culture; the trace of the medium is retained in the memory – histories of memory are often written as histories of its changing media" (Erll 2011: 116). The medium of documentary acknowledges itself as a genre that speaks to group experience by engendering a self-reflexivity in audience spectatorship through its visual language, such as the inclusion of archival (real or fabricated) footage, use of testimony or witness statements – at times black and white images – and voiceover narrative.

McLaughlin's filmed interviews function as cultural memory texts that contribute to the wider social group mentality of Northern Ireland's conflict and contested history through the emotional experiences it is discussing. *PMA*'s memory texts are the documentary interviews that contribute to and assist the involved groups' perspective and voices on its topic. The memory work is crafted through audience participation, formed through their linking and viewing of the different voices on the *PMA* website. The stories that are told and heard, the emotions that are experienced are determined by the sequence of the interviews that are watched by the audience, not governed by McLaughlin's direction. In a Bionian psychoanalytic sense, "any contribution to [the work] group mentality must enlist the support of, or be in conformity with, the other anonymous contributions of the group" (Bion 1961: 50). Whether documentary time-based media, such as *PMA*, deviate from or creatively incorporate standard media practice to possess mnemonic relevance for groups within society, they must also rely on conformity within and across shared social frameworks. In part, this is why certain stories and voices are heard loudest and repeated most often; and it is why the *PMA* project is so unique. The success of McLaughlin's memory archive is that it does not aim to manage the tensions of recollected memories from any specific person's experiences with the prisons. Instead, it enables such memories to be located as authentic knowledge by incorporating the social frameworks of memory within creative participation. No specific sequencing of the interviews is mandated. Each memory is weighted equally with others, the spatial technique here offering an intimacy that engages its audience, and it allows them to navigate their own narratives through the interviews.

One of the difficulties in using documentary as an exemplar to consider the interrelationship between groups and the function of memory is that we may become stuck in the position of 'looking at' representations of groups and memories, rather than acknowledging what the cultural production of such media does in terms of reflecting our own idealizations of identity. As memory texts, these images not only proliferate the production of memory narratives via visual aesthetics, but they also sustain the discourses in which we learn to remember. As Kuhn says, photographs materially collate memories as much as they script how to perform acts of remembrance. The memory work that presents itself here as visual and cinematic, are "material forms in which cultural memory is institutionalized [as] objects that in themselves commemorate, or serve as reminders of, a past event or situation." (Kuhn 2010: 7). It is worth noting at this point, Kuhn's term 'materiality' is used to denote a photograph or film's position as a cultural object. Within the digital culture of the 21st century, the virtuality of the digital image has often been conflated with immateriality which is misleading, as despite its not being paper-based, or shot on 35mm film, digital image capture is more easily transmitted as a cultural object, and one that destabilizes the notion of truth. Its status as a meaningful image-object has not changed despite its method of production. Such digitally produced images remain as meaningful cultural objects and are more influential, are more present (despite their screened immateriality) than their touchable counterparts, particularly in terms of their capacity to be exchanged as social and mnemonic goods. The issue of authenticity in this sense is reductive, particularly in terms of memory and group formation as it sidesteps what such objects do in terms of constructing memory work.

Immersion and 'being embedded' with regard to groups and memory

Yacavone's term 'immersion' is relevant to the conceptualization of 'being embedded' under discussion here – not as a synonym for "absorptive cinematic experience" (2015: 186), although there are certainly aspects of absorption involved, but through its recognition of the viewer's "perceptual, imaginative, and affective" experience, which enters "into a film, with the range of (potential) consequences for both mind and body" (2015: 186). My conceptualization of 'being embedded', which is predominantly Bionian in its configuration, relates to Yacavone's individual cognitive-feeling of immersion by attending to the collective group experience that occurs as 'global affective character' in the site-specific watching of a film or other visual media, and the recollection of such experience. The experience of 'being embedded' is further situated within the broader relational consequences of immersion pertaining to dreaming and memory. In this way, the concept of 'being embedded' parallels rather than contests Yacavone's notion of immersion, acknowledging the potential *collective* affective resonances that result from emotional experience with moving images. It is important to emphasize that immersion and 'being embedded' are not used in opposition here. Indeed Yacavone's research on 'cine-aesthetic world-feeling' resonates strongly with the notion of the cinematic field as argued in the previous chapter. The global character of expression he refers to helps to illuminate the 'affective field' of cinema (2015: 204), in that it too addresses the dynamics of cinematic experience that goes beyond site-specificity of screen and theatre.

He notes that the individual and transient quality of immersion competes with the "less immediate and more reflective" (2015: 187) absorptive perceptual engagements with memory, echoing R. K. Elliot's distinction that immersion is "only a part of a picture or a momentary sense of the real presence of the object represented" (Elliot in Yacavone 2015: 282 *fn*. 44). Immersion, therefore, is related but distinct from 'being embedded', looking to the processes involved in the linking of the viewer's cognitive and perceptual experience through identifying specific cinematic practices and techniques (such as cinematography, editing and soundscapes). Yacavone's 'global aesthetic expression' is "strongly *cumulative*, often coming to awareness and increasing in intensity for the viewer as the film progresses" (2015: 196); whereas the notion of 'being embedded' has greater potential in speaking to the stronger connection with group experience as a Bionian dreaming. Yacavone views his quality of immersion occurring in the interstices of film and aesthetic experience, drawing on Mikel Dufrenne's distinction between art work and the hermeneutics of aesthetics; however he does not go beyond the specific feelings of the individual viewer, despite acknowledging "a kind of expressive glue, in the form of a 'common quality of feeling'" (197), what Halbwachs might term 'social framework' and Bion 'experience in groups'.

In the final section of this chapter, I return to the experience of dreaming as the affective field that links Bion's theory of group experience with Halbwachs's theory of collective memory along affective, aesthetic and existential lines. It is the contention here that dreaming works in similar manner to the insertion of thought in Halbwachs's social frameworks – for memory and for groups. Dreaming is positioned here as entanglements of what goes unseen but that are known via sensory perception, through exchanged acts of looking, unconscious acknowledgments of body behaviors and gestural expressions.

Dreams and memories

Halbwachs begins his discussion of the social frameworks of memory by addressing the relationship between dreams and memory images, his interest going beyond a simple distinction (although clearly there is ample attention given to such a delineation – and on this Freud agrees that dreams and memories are not one and the same). When referring to dreams, Halbwachs speaks specifically to the unconscious space (and time) where an individual can be said to live experience that is not dependent on societal exchange, "[i]t is not in memory but in the dream that the mind is most removed from society" (Halbwachs 1992: 42). On the one hand, Halbwachs appears to be presenting the view that when we dream, we draw on "nothing more than raw materials" (1992: 42) that are linked through "random relations . . . based on the disordered play of corporal modifications" (1992: 42), but the most pivotal distinction that exists in Halbwachs's view on the relationship between dreams and memory is that "what we lack in the dream state for the act of remembering is *the support of society*" (171, italics added). After all, we cannot share the same type of experiences or the presentation of the sequence of images within our dreams with other people – although this is the exact purpose of our dream retellings.

Freud's theory of the dream work does not align dreams with memory but acknowledges their seeming attachment and relativity to one another:

> No one who occupies himself [*sic*] with dreams can, I believe, fail to discover that it is a very common event for a dream to give evidence of knowledge and memories *which the waking subject is unaware of possessing*.
> (Freud 2010: 47, italics added)

Being 'unaware' is the key issue here between Halbwachs and Freud. For Halbwachs memory is constructed in order to be recollected – constructed outside our own selves, collectively formed, whereas he views dreams existing within – separated from societal frameworks and participation. Whilst this might appear as superficially correct, Halbwachs's classical Freudian reading (and positioning) of dreams fails to recognize that whilst dreams may be fragmented, indirect and incoherent recollections of emotions, sensations and images worked into jumbled narratives, they nevertheless bridge internal and external acts of recollection through lived emotional experience. Through the two agencies of condensation and displacement, Freud's theory of dreams separates the story of the dream (its manifest content) from the 'dream thoughts' that underwrite it (latent content). Dreams are not able to create new images, and equally are not synonymous with memory due to their disguised, and often inaccurate, coming together. These 'raw materials' that Halbwachs sees as laying the seeds for dreams are impressions that have been drawn from waking life, stored in affective memory – their emotional impact being stored, waiting to be called upon to present itself in a disguised form. This was Freud's theory of displacement (and subsequently revised by Bion as beta elements – 'raw sensory data' for alpha function) which within it, illustrates that what helps to create a dream is *collectively* assembled – ultimately because the disguise that is the dream's manifest content is permitted to enter the collective consciousness, where we are want to speak about it and share it with another. Put in Halbwachs's terms – insert it as thinking into a social framework that can be exchanged.

The main contrast between Halbwachs and Freud lies in the relativity between dreams and memory as frameworks. Freud's classical view of dreams were that they were disguised communications of wish-fulfillment that came from our unconscious and required an analyst to help interpret them. The presence and involvement of the analyst and pertinent psychoanalytic methodologies were required to make sense of the analysand's dreams. Freud was adamant on the importance and role of the analyst, without whom dream interpretation could not take place. The analyst was essential, in Freud's view, to return the analysand's words to them in order facilitate the exposure of repressed wishes. The analysand's dream becomes collective meaning – as it is shared by the social relationship of analyst and analysand.[5] Unlike Halbwachs, Freud argued that for memories and dreams to enter into the conscious part of our minds so that we are able to think them and talk about them, they must undergo repression. In this way, Freud associated memory with the unconscious. Within this classical psychoanalytic account, memories that we are able to recall are recent distortions that have been formed in connection with memories that were stored from childhood. This was Freud's 'screen memory' – where we draw on early childhood memories that have been archived for possible use in later life. When a connection presents itself as a workable disguise, then that will permit memory to enter into the conscious mind. The association between the early memory and the present memory allows a disguise to form, to contain and transmit the unconscious tension. The memory we recall is crafted around it. In this way, the memory itself is part displacement that Freud saw as an agency of the dream work. Simply put, Freud saw memory and dreams as equally requiring psychoanalytic interpretation in order to determine their meaning, whereas

Halbwachs did not see memory as a disguise. Let us look to the specific difference Bion's revision brings to Halbwachs's interpretation of dreams in order to return to the connections between individual and group experience.

The relevance of Bion's revision on dreaming

Halbwachs's position on dreams is in marked contrast to that of Bion. For Halbwachs, dreams occur in a sleep state that isolates the individual from society, but as discussed in Chapter 4, Bion argues that dreaming is intersubjective, not isolated and not bound to sleep. If Halbwachs saw dreams as a separate experience similar to being isolated from society, then this is the first direct challenge and contestation Bionian psychoanalysis presents. Dreams and the experience of dreaming as set out by Bion is highly intersubjective requiring another mind to think and feel emotional experience. Dreaming involves the desire to know as an emotion that frames all experience, and Bion argued that to be able to grow from lived difficult and frustrating experience, we must face it and think it. Halbwachs uses his distinction between the dream and memory as a means to make clear the difference between the individual and the group. In saying that the sleeping dream state mimics social isolation, where the individual is "no longer capable – nor has need – of relying on frames of collective memory" (1992: 39), Halbwachs is aiming to show how the *coherent* recollection of memory can only be determined socially, not internally. His entire position is based on Freud's classical psychoanalytic theory of dreams (which Bion deviates radically from); Halbwachs notes that the "dream is based only upon *itself*, whereas our recollections depend on those of all our fellows, and on the great frameworks of the memory of society" (1992: 42, italics added). This is no longer the only way – indeed even the most authoritative way – that dreams are viewed or interpreted (Civitarese 2014). It is no longer the specific dream-text that is of central importance to psychoanalysis, but rather the desire to share the experience of the dream – *the recollection itself* – that is very similar to Halbwachs's social frameworks of memory.

Therefore in direct contradiction, Bion's theory of thinking states that dream (and dreaming) are entirely about how we connect with others – this is the capacity for our thinking/feeling – and that without dreaming as 'unconscious waking thought' we could not form social frameworks of memory. Civitarese writes:

> we no longer regard the dream as the royal road that helps reveal the disguises dreamwork imposes on latent thoughts; rather, we valorize its function of transformation and symbolic creation. The ambiguity of the manifest text of the dream no longer arouses suspicion. We consider it instead the expression of its poetic function. In clinical practice the recounting of the dream no longer occupies the privileged position it once always held over the other contents of the patient's discourse, even simply the banal retelling of the events of everyday life. But we should not deceive ourselves. If this happens,

it is because, *when we hear them recounted within the framework of analysis, we also interpret the events of material reality and the past as if they were waking dreams.*
(Civitarese 2014: xiii, italics added)

Civitarese states that dreams exist as a co-presence of thinking – requiring the reflexivity of what he refers to as 'framework of analysis'. Dreams, like memories, and like cinema, are revised, being retold and shared between two minds. For this reason, the theorizing of dreams and dreaming as group experience emphasizes the collective social experience and demonstrates the integral relationship between dreaming, thinking and knowing relative to the qualities of 'being embedded'. Halbwachs is clear that collective memory is made possible due to external social frameworks, which construct stories of the past via the group mentality, not the individual's. Therefore, it is possible to see a connection between Halbwachs and Bion, if dreaming is restated as group experience. Bionian dreaming, like Halbwachs's collective memory, works as a conscious to unconscious transference, not unconscious to conscious. In Halbwachs's view, an unconscious to conscious "framework supposes the existence of memory" (1992: 39), and his point is that "the past is not preserved but is reconstructed on the basis of the present" (1992: 40).

Bion's emphasis on affective psychic life offers fresh insight for emotional experience with moving images, which can be aligned with Halbwachs's theory of social frameworks and collective memory, certainly more closely than a Freudian one. Our emotional life strongly depends on social frameworks, particularly the immersive frameworks of cinema and media as affective associations that facilitate dreaming through our interactions and experiences with others. The potential of dreams manifests once we can say we have had them, and secondarily, when we begin to discuss the fragmented and oddly connected images. In this way, the purpose of dreams is that they are to be remembered and recalled in the presence of another (even if this other is our conscious self), for it is in the telling of dreams that the tensions of affect can be 'thought', much like the practice of oral tradition, wherein the telling of memory is what keeps it alive, transmissive and collective. The difference between the two, however, is that oral tradition recounts stories from the past for the future (of a people, of a belief, etc.), conscious that it is a cultural memory that is being spoken and transmitted. The stories are known to be memories, shared for the specific purpose of remembering within a context of preservation.

In the telling of a dream, what is expressed is not clear or logical (or even able to be trusted for what it is said to be). Dreams are not recollections of memories, but for Bion, the transformations of "emotional experiences into alpha-elements" (Bion 1962: 7). According to Bion, "alpha-elements . . . resemble, and may in fact be identical with, the visual images with which we are familiar in dreams" (Bion 1962: 7). What Bion's revision offers for the present study of 'being embedded' in moving image experience – relative to collective memory and dreaming – is that if dreams are thinking, that is the 'working through' of individual emotional experience, then perhaps it is cultural and collective memory, in this case with cinema, that is the working through of the collective and represented emotional experiences of culture and audience groups.

The major departure from the classical psychoanalytic position of dream interpretation is Bion's statement that dreaming occurs all the time in everyday life, not just in sleep, and that it is primarily concerned with the thinking through of our emotional experience and its 'truth'. He writes,

> [t]o learn from experience alpha function must operate on the awareness of the emotional experience; alpha elements are produced from the impressions of the experience; these are thus made storable and available for dream thoughts and for unconscious waking and thinking.
>
> *(Bion 1962: 8)*

Bion's reversal of the relationship of conscious and unconscious thought in the process of the dream work, makes it possible to view memory and dreams as the alpha function of emotional experience, with each psychical activity being a realization of what Bion terms 'learning from experience'. This 'learning from experience' is dreaming and requires 'awareness of emotional experience' for the individual. Memory is the cultural and collective equivalent to a group's learning from experience, working on the awareness of its group emotional experience and the dominance of visual images (as alpha elements) that form part of both cultural and collective memory and dream-thoughts. Films and other moving image experiences are not only avenues for daydreaming or material to facilitate awareness of emotional experience, but they are also an integral structure of social frameworks and a way to develop social group cohesion, becoming ways to transmit collective cultural memories, as well as provide resistance and alternative voices to dominant paradigms.

Notes

1 See Chapter 2 where I refer to Ogden's "four principles of mental functioning" within Bion's theory of thinking.
2 This is also a premise in Freud's *Jokes and Their Relationship to the Unconscious* (1905).
3 See Chapter 2 for a more thorough discussion of these Kleinian positions.
4 The three basic assumptions: dependent, fight/flight and pairing reflect the key emotional uncertainties and anxieties of early mental life. As Bion writes, they are not 'wholly pleasureable' (1961: 93). Children are dependent on their parents for love and a sense of self; they believe that growth (potentially satisfactory) results from pairing off with others (here we can see Kleinian influence via her 'splitting' mechanism). Children are fearful of and aggressive toward anyone who threatens their emotional and ego security, and of the forceful pressure to confront 'magical thinking' (per Ogden), that is to face difficult emotional turbulence – something much preferred to be avoided. Therefore, 'Oedipal', as used here, is shorthand for referring to one's capacity to tolerate the frustrations that are involved in the negotiation between the individual basic assumption emotions and the behavior and life of the group.
5 See Chapter 4 where I examine the analytic field and intersubjective aesthetic experience that is of relevance to the discussion here.

References

Bion, W.R. (1961). *Experiences in Groups and Other Papers*. New York: Basic Books.
Bion, W.R. (1962). *Learning From Experience*. London: Tavistock.
Brennan, T. (2004). *The Transmission of Affect*. Ithaca and London: Cornell University Press.
Civitarese, G. (2014). *The Necessary Dream: New Theories and Techniques of Interpretation in Psychoanalysis*. Translated by I. Harvey. London: Karnac Books.
Derrida, J. (1995). *Archive Fever: A Freudian Impression*. Translated by E. Prenowitz. Paris: Éditions Galilée.
Erll, A. (2011). *Memory in Culture*. Basingstoke: Palgrave Macmillan.
Freud, S. (1900). *The Interpretation of Dreams*. Translated by J. Strachey. New York: Basic Books, 2010.
Freud, S. (1905). *Jokes and Their Relationship to the Unconscious*. Translated by J. Strachey. London: W.W. Norton and Company, 1990.
Freud, S. (1959). *Group Psychology and the Analysis of the Ego*. Translated by J. Strachey. New York, W.W. Norton Publishers, 1922.
Halbwachs, M. (1980). *The Collective Memory*. Translated by F.J. Didder and V.Y. Ditter. New York: Harper & Row.
Halbwachs, M. (1992). *On Collective Memory*. Translated by L.A. Coser. Chicago: The University of Chicago Press.
Kuhn, A. (2010). Memory Texts and Memory Work: Performances of Memory in and With Visual Media. *Memory Studies*, 3 (4), pp. 298–313.
Lawrence, W.G., Bain, A. and Gould, L. (1996). The Fifth Basic Assumption. *Free Associations*, 6 (37), pp. 28–55.
Manoff, M. (2004). Theories of the Archive From Across the Disciplines. *Libraries and the Academy*, 4 (1), pp. 9–25.
McLaughlin, C. (2010). *Recording Memories From Political Violence: A Film-Maker's Journey*. Bristol: Intellect Books.
McLaughlin, C. (2014). Who Tells What to Whom and How: The Prisons Memory Archive. *p-e-r-f-o-r-m-a-n-c-e*, 1 (1). www.p-e-r-f-o-r-m-a-n-c-e.org/?p=139.
Ogden, T. (2008). Bion's Four Principles of Mental Functioning. *Fort Da*, 14, pp. 11–35.
Schaffer, R., Agusti, F., Dhooge, L. and Earle, B. (2011). *International Business Law and Its Environment*. 8th edition. Mason: South-Western Cengage Learning.
Schwartz, J.M. and Cook, T. (2002). Archives, Records, and Power: The Making of Modern Memory. *Archival Science*, 2, pp. 1–19.
Taylor, D. (2003). *The Archive and the Repertoire: Performing Cultural Memory in the Americas*. Durham: Duke University Press.
Turquet, P. (1974). Leadership: The Individual and the Group. In Gibbard, G., Hartmann, J.J. and Mann, R.D. (eds.) *Analysis of Groups*. San Francisco and London: Jossey-Bass.
Yacavone, D. (2015). *Film Worlds: A Philosophical Aesthetics of Cinema*. New York: Columbia University Press.

Filmography

Force Majeure. (2014). Directed by Ruben Östlund.
Prisons Memory Archive (2010). Directed by Cahal McLaughlin.

6
LINKING, INTENTIONALITY AND THE CONTAINER-CONTAINED

In *Learning from Experience*, Bion writes, "[a]n emotional experience cannot be conceived of in isolation from a relationship" (Bion 1962a: 42), indicating that interaction is necessary for emotional experience and that such experience is created through our relations with others. In the heterogeneous processes of 'being embedded', the encounter with the moving image, as argued here, mimics the emotional experience that results via interaction and relation from such relationships. Both the analytic and experiential processes of emotions, and their complex relationship forming, are an inherent part of psychoanalytic theory and practice. However, there is further analytic benefit in turning to certain ideas in phenomenology, locating Bion within the larger project of phenomenological film theory. To remain true to the core intention of this book, the emphasis here will be on linking Bionian concepts to current methods that investigate moving image experience, and to demonstrate how his approach differs from classical psychoanalysis.

Phenomenology has grown into an exciting area of theoretical inquiry within film and media studies regarding lived emotional experience and the relationship between inner and external reality. In the previous chapter I discussed Marks's work on haptic visuality (2000), which followed the seminal film-phenomenology of Sobchack (1992) and Allan Casebier (1991), serving to orient much of film theory's attention toward embodiment, sensuous and cultural experience with the moving image. Since then other scholars (Yacavone 2016; Sorfa 2014; Stadler 2013; Barker 2009; Sobchack 2004) have contributed to this growing field. Each of these works explores moving image experience within the parameters of consciousness, perception and sensation and whilst they offer considerable insight into the transmission of affect and the intersection of corporeality and culture regarding moving image experience, almost all have eschewed psychoanalysis as a useful method and focused primarily on what Yacavone calls 'first generation' film-phenomenology (2016: 161). My aim here is not to dismiss or refute any of these works. Indeed, such scholarship has made the "revaluation of film, affect and the embodied role of spectator" possible (Stadler 2014: 5), and without them Bion's contribution links less effectively to the overall field. Rather I make the claim that psychoanalysis still has more to offer, particularly on the issue of embodied and emotional experience with the moving image. Given that much of Bion's work is precisely about 'learning from experience' rather than drive gratification, this chapter looks at the similarities that exist between the use of phenomenology as a method within film theory, and Bion's theory of thinking as a method to examine experience, specifically the proto-mental experience of emotion and thought.

Therefore, this chapter will consider the following: 1) Bion's theory of thinking and his conceptualization of links as emotion; 2) Bion's activity of 'linking' within the apparatus of thinking, highlighting that such links occur between perception, thought and appearance, contributing to our emotional experience with moving images. This will be discussed within a phenomenological frame that addresses aesthetic experience with moving images; 3) an exploration of Bion's container-contained theory (previously introduced in Chapter 4) as an alternative psychoanalytic model that prioritizes affective, sensory experience to show that not all psychoanalytic theory is focused on "pleasures including masochism, sadism, and voyeurism because of unconscious drives or repressed psychosexual fears and desires" (Stadler 2014: 151). Bionian psychoanalysis relates to phenomenology's notion of intentionality precisely because it shares similar priorities and positions on consciousness and corporeality. By associating these areas of study, my aim is to contextualize the experience of 'being embedded' involved with moving images as a practice of perceptive, sensory dreaming (unconscious thinking).

David Sorfa writes, "[p]henomenology is the philosophy of experience. Film both records experience and presents itself as an object to experience" (2014: 353), addressing the double agenda of phenomenological inquiry, which examines the links between the self and the experience of reality. As Sorfa sees it, film is a "medium that functions at the very border between ourselves and the world" (2014: 353), locating the moving image encounter as an experience that potentially offers something on our relationship to (we should say with) reality, but also offers comment on how we learn to think reality. Bion argues that "a sense of reality matters to the individual in the way that food, drink, air and excretion of waste products matter" (1962a: 42), showing that for him, our need for truth and capacity to think emotional experience is as fundamental to human existence and vitality as air itself. Phenomenology is used as a method to investigate moving image experience – what happens when we watch a film, television or other visual media – and is useful in understanding emotional experiences that exist through cinema, with moving images, as they occur within the cinematic encounter. I discuss Bion's attempt to notate emotions through his theory of 'links' (his word for the activity of containing emotions) later in the chapter, but for now it is enough to acknowledge this is a further example of Bion's theory of thinking that viewed thinking as a means to reduce tension, shifting away from the Freudian position. For Bion, thinking is an unconscious activity that negotiates tension found in experience. As Symington and Symington write, "Bion saw thought as in the service of truth where the individual uses it to understand him- or herself" (2008: 8), clearly marking a break from the classical psychoanalytic emphasis on pleasure. Bringing Bion and theories of phenomenology together then, takes up Sorfa's proposal, which is to use phenomenology to "point to the flaws and joins in the mirror that allow us to see something we are not" (2014: 358). By utilizing key concepts from Bion's theory of thinking such as 'linking' and his 'container-contained' model, contemporary psychoanalysis contributes to the phenomenological perspective that examines emotional experience with moving images, offering a psychoanalytic phenomenological method.

Phenomenology: experience, consciousness, intentionality

Since their inceptions, both cinema and psychoanalysis have been phenomenologically engaged, that is, they have been concerned with what it is to experience reality, more specifically questioning what the associations are between thinking, thoughts, truth and experience. In 1916, on the art of the photoplay, Hugo Münsterberg wrote, "[t]he act of attention which goes on in our mind has remodeled the surrounding itself" (1916: 87), noting that the moving image, and all it contains, has an effect on our experience of it. Münsterberg was a psychologist, not a psychoanalyst or phenomenologist; nevertheless, his pioneering work centered on the issue of what it feels like to watch a film. His study of cinema focused on the description of key cinematic characteristics, which included discussion of the differences that occur within the experience of cinema depending on the different films that were watched: "[a] characteristic content of consciousness must be added to such a series of visual impressions" (1916: 61). Münsterberg outlines the differences between theatre-going and film-going spectatorship, moving to separate the apparatus (from theatre to film) as well as the types of films themselves (between art and entertainment) and what such differences demand of our consciousness and subsequently yield for our experience. The point here is even though Münsterberg does not specifically offer a phenomenological inquiry, the emphasis he places on describing the environment and technicalities of film, as distinct from theatre, speaks to the influence on emotional experience and illustrates the originary association between consciousness, affect and the moving image. Without overt intention, he employed one of phenomenology's key strategies – description – which involves "systematic reflection on, description, and critical analysis of objects that make themselves available to consciousness, and reduces objects to their essence by means of exact attentive observation, suspending (or 'bracketing') all extraneous influences or presumptions" (Kuhn and Westwell 2012: 309). It is possible to read Münsterberg as one of the first film theorists in light of his attention to cinematic representation, that is the specificity of cinematic experience as determined by its technical elements, and also consider him as one of the first film phenomenologists. I mention his formative work briefly in order to illustrate the very early links that existed between the moving image, theories of perception and emotional experience.

More recently, the works of Edmund Husserl and Merleau-Ponty have had the most influence on phenomenological film theory (Yacavone 2016; Sorfa 2014; Sobchack 1992; Casebier 1991). Through their respective works, the core terms and concepts specific to phenomenology have been developed – intentionality, self-reflexive consciousness, horizon of expectation and being-in-the-world – and as we will come to see, used for the purpose of describing cinematic experience via Sobchack and Casebier. However much less attention has been given to the work of Hannah Arendt, who in her (incomplete, posthumously published) *The Life of the Mind* (1978), offers an arguably more relevant phenomenological theory of thinking which she claims emerges out of everyday experience, where such experience is inextricably linked to what she calls a 'world of appearances'. She writes:

> Nothing could appear, the word 'appearance' would make no sense, if recipients of appearances did not exist – living creatures able to acknowledge, recognize, and react to- in flight or desire, approval or disapproval, blame or praise- what is not merely there but appears to them and is meant for their perception. . . . Nothing and nobody exists in this world whose very being does not presuppose a *spectator*. In other words, nothing that is, insofar as it appears, exists in the singular; everything that is is meant to be perceived by somebody.
> *(Arendt 1978: 19)*

For Arendt, thinking is based on human interaction, an activity that constitutes experience itself. Her own thinking about thinking acknowledges its debt to metaphor "which bridges the gulf between the visible and the invisible, the world of appearances and the thinking ego". She sees senses as cognitive and argues that if they are viewed as 'activities' they "have an end outside themselves", which is to learn from experience in order to be in the world (1978: 123). Arendt distinguishes her phenomenology of thinking from 'knowing', which is a similar distinction Bion makes. For each author, 'knowing' *is* thinking – that is a sensory, emotional experience. As we will come to see, whilst there are differences between Bion and Arendt, such points of convergence between each other's theory of thinking revolve around human experience, particularly on their conceptualization of knowing as a sensory, emotional experience that seeks truth.

This is an apposite moment to reference (albeit a passing one) the key phenomenological aspect of *epoché*, or 'bracketing', and its position in Arendt's theories of thinking and experience. This, in turn, will provide a further line of connection to Bion and a contextualization of their respective ideas. If phenomenology can be said to have a recurring motif, a critical issue that it constantly returns to, then a primary contender would be ontological status. The quote by Arendt can be seen precisely as an example of the centrality of ontology, in this case how it determines issues such as appearance and knowing. Phenomenology's core concern is how we can distinguish different ontological orders and understand our relationships to them. For phenomenology, the ontological order that dominates all our senses is the *lebenswelt* (lifeworld). This is the realm of everyday objects as perceived through the senses, or what we might be most tempted to call the real world and our being in it. This is filled with what Roman Ingarden (a phenomenologist who contributed significantly to aesthetic theory) termed 'autonomontically existing objects' (1973: 156). Inside the *lebenswelt*, filled with these objects, is the ontologically distinct, yet highly connected world(s) of the aesthetic text. These texts (the example used here is the moving image) are constituted of what phenomenology calls quasi-judgement based objects. In brief, these are the objects (and actions and events) that have the *appearance* of real objects but are ontologically distinct. Therefore, the created world of a film, with all the objects that 'match' the appearance of the real world, are viewed as quasi-real objects.

We can keep these distinctions and yet still be affected by a film precisely because of the (emotional) links between the ontologically distinct realms, that is, the real world and the created filmic one. When a character dies in a film we may cry even though we know it is not a real death; we are thus linked through the affective processes that allow us to treat fictions as if they are real (and somewhat increasingly vice versa). (It is for this reason that Ingarden can make the following claim: "[t]he ontically heteronomously existing objectivity . . . has no ontic basis in itself but rather refers to a different entity, indeed ultimately to an ontically autonomous entity" (1973: 362)). The argument here is that Bion's – and Arendt's alongside – concept of thinking and linking positions us more astutely to critically engage and understand these processes and their emotive components when we undertake this phenomenological issue of ontological status and our psychical processes.

In these terms we can locate Bion's theory of thinking in his conceptualization of 'links' as emotions, which he divides into six categories Love (L), Hate (H) and Knowing (K), and their negative equivalents $-L$, $-H$, $-K$. For Bion these categories are 'factors' that contain the "link [the emotional activity] between objects considered to be in a relationship with each other" (1962a: 42). Symington and Symington have observed that six categories for the multiplicity of human emotions able to be experienced seems very general but are quick to point out that Bion's intent is not to be prescriptive, rather to foreground the activity that such 'factors' contain and include. They note by way of example "trust goes under L and greed goes under H" (2008: 28), demonstrating the rationale behind Bion's notation L (-L), H (-H), K, (-K) as being concerned with marking the factors of emotional activity. As such, these six notations are meta-categories that contain the plurality of emotional activity and experience.

Husserlian beginnings and Casebier's 'in-between' qualities

A Husserlian phenomenological approach which considers 'cinema' as an apparatus, as an experience, and as an object, looks to describe the essence of cinema and of cinematic experience – it asks what makes 'cinema' cinema? This is what Husserl and followers such as Ingarden termed the eidetic reduction, allowing us to determine the *eidos*, or essence, of the thing in itself. In *Film and Phenomenology*, Casebier states that a phenomenological approach on the study of cinematic experience will highlight that there are "*more qualities than we have names for*" (1991: 57) and that such qualities are what generate and transmit affect to audiences and facilitate their varying intuitive responses. Significantly, Casebier seeks to find names for such 'in-between qualities' because only by finding names for them can description and generalizations about cinematic experience occur. Naming these in-between qualities in our cinematic experience is how Casebier attempts to indicate what the various affects of individual filmic representation are, which Sorfa interprets as a model that allows "others easier access to that perceptual possibility" (2014: 356). The many interpretations that are possible from cinematic experience necessitates that we include terms for 'in-between qualities' that identify transmission of affect and emotion with moving images. For Casebier, it is the film theorist who is able to "activate [the film-goer's] intuitive processes so that they grasp these in-between qualities" (1991: 57), which then enables audience members to react and communicate their own observations.

We can think of these 'in-between qualities' as being those feelings and emotions that we can't quite explain; or as those states of being that require refuge, or a structure through which sensations can begin to take shape, forming our perceptions and expressions. Such 'in-between qualities' that are beyond naming, that are there to acknowledge if not identify affect, are similar to Bion's 'linking' activity, and what he terms as the 'contained' (or the unknown thought and/or feeling – discussed later), and what Arendt views as 'inherent potentiality'. She writes, "appearances always present themselves in the guise of seeming, pretense and willful deception on the part of the performer, error and illusion on the part of the spectator are, inevitability, among the inherent potentialities" (Arendt 1978: 36). What Casebier identifies with his 'in-between qualities' is that there is something that links us with what we perceive and what affects us in our watching of cinema, and that despite not having enough words to name this 'something', we are also aware of the 'something' being there despite the normalcy of error and illusion in our interpretations.[1]

Here, as in previous chapters, we can locate core tenets of Bion's theory of thinking, which is that a mind needs the presence and interaction with another mind in order grow and think experience, and that we seek out such experiences in order to find truth, despite their difficulty.

> It is almost as if human beings were aware of the painful and often fatal consequences of having to act without an adequate grasp of reality, and therefore were aware of the need for truth as a criterion in the evaluation of their findings.
>
> *(Bion 1961: 100)*

Casebier formulates his film-phenomenology by incorporating this notion of difference in spectatorship, where he "illuminates the experience of film representation"

(1991: 4) through the work of Husserl. Casebier sees any *legitimate* inquiry of cinema as requiring a 'viable realist theory' that examines the relationship of cinema to the world, one which outlines the specific process(es) involved in making cinema 'cinema' in order to show what makes cinematic experience different from any other aesthetic experience. These are, as noted above, the relations and distinctions between the ontological orders of the *lebenswelt* and the created world order of a film. They may share many common appearances, yet we are continually required to contemporaneously distinguish them and bind/link them together.

I do not wish to restate Husserl's theory of artistic representation via Casebier here; rather my aim is to indicate how some of the key elements in his phenomenology informs or relates to Bionian psychoanalysis, specifically to the notion of 'linking'. Husserl's approach is noted as 'transcendental' and as the 'transcendental egological state', meaning that in order to comprehensively and accurately speak of experience, we must rise above (transcend) our own subjective consciousness and describe things as they appear, and in their essence 'are', rather than how we personally view them. This allowed Husserl to separate the act of interpretation (as a participation and modification of the world) from the object's actual being in the world. This is what Husserl articulates as the natural attitude – a position in the world that requires phenomenological analysis to transcend. Husserl describes being in the natural attitude thus:

> I find myself continually present and standing over against me the one spatio-temporal fact-world to which I myself belong, as do others found in it and related in the same way to it. This fact-world, as the word already tells us, I find out there, and also take it just as it gives itself to me as something that exists out there.
>
> *(2002: 51)*

Using a cinematic example, in *Rabbit-Proof Fence* (2002) the story of Molly Craig's forced removal from her family and her escape home, as screened and depicted by Philip Noyce, is not the same as the real abduction and escape of the Molly Craig who lived and existed in the world. Her appearance on screen becomes the key focus here, as it is through our capacity to note the difference between the appearance and the real object, that Husserl argued that we are able to experience the representation and recognize its meaning. It is precisely because we can distinguish the representations *as appearances* that enables us to link the cinematic representation with the 'real' object in the outside world. This is a good example of the complexity of quasi-judgements – their ontological status is never simple, which is why they are so affectively powerful. Casebier uses Husserl's approach to argue that the experience phenomenology is concerned with is the link "between experiences of certain sorts that is the source for the representation" (1991: 11). Therefore, what makes *experience* possible is our consciousness that separates the appearance (representation) from the real object.

For Husserl, this capacity to make such distinction involved intentionality, which he views as the property of consciousness, "[t]he essence of consciousness, in which I live as my own self, is so-called intentionality" (Husserl 1964: 12–13); without it we have no awareness of our own existence. Casebier points out that the term 'intentionality' is not to be misread as willfulness but rather it refers to the idea of "extending or stretching out to" (1991: 15) and as such involves a linking activity between the perception of the appearance and the object itself. The intentionality is present in the differentiation between representation and the object itself, but equally acts as the link that makes apprehension possible. The forward direction of our gaze toward the screen demands our conscious attention for the duration of the film – the experience of the film world is, in Husserlian terms, made possible because we know its cinematic representation is based on real objects and places that exist outside it.

Bion uses the term 'linking' as a way to describe the activity of emotional experience we have with each other. "L or H may be relevant to K but that neither is by itself conducive to K. x K y, the analyst K the analysand, I K Smith, these are statements that represent an emotional experience" (Bion 1962a: 47). In this pared down schema, we can note a phenomenological method in Bion's psychoanalysis. He is not interested in typifying the emotions themselves but much more concerned with describing how these emotions, these 'links' occur via intentionality. In themselves, *L*, *H*, *K* are his way of containing Casebier's in-between qualities of affective sensory experience. Husserl's two key elements of intentionality in consciousness are the *noēsis* (the act of consciousness) and the *noēma* (the object toward which the conscious act is directed).[2] The intentionality of consciousness includes the object that one's consciousness is directed toward, such as the moving image. Intentionality enables experience to be seen as something that is shared between everyone as well as something that is subjective for an individual. "It is intentionality that characterizes *consciousness* . . . the unique peculiarity of experiences 'to be conscious *of* something' . . . perceiving is the perceiving of something" (Husserl 1952: 242–243). It is the intentionality behind our conscious perceptions and expressions, that is, the practice of 'becoming embedded', as it is something that we constantly do to ourselves and to others with variability and difference. Equally, we receive perceptions from others and respond to them, by either turning away from or turning toward such intentionalities.[3] Intentionality then, works as a linking activity – Bion's '*K* link' – which seeks to unify experience, perception and sensation as an 'emotional catalyst' (and I add characteristic) of consciousness. Bion places *K* as a sensing activity where emotion is the intentional activity of knowing as "getting to know the other in an emotional [thought and felt] sense" (Symington and Symington 2008: 28). It is not to be confused with obtaining facts about someone or something (which, in Husserlian terms would involve interpretation). If phenomenology, a philosophy about experience as Sorfa states, requires intentionality to determine and describe experience, then Bion's *K* link is the psychoanalytic equivalent, as he views *K* (knowing or knowledge) as the emotional link "that is germane to learning by experience" (Bion 1962a: 47).

Reversible intentionality: phenomenology and cinematic experience in Philip Noyce's *Rabbit-Proof Fence*

Extending Casebier's notion of the 'in-between quality' and Bion's *K* link, we might consider how intentionality works as a reversible in-between quality of experience in order to describe its characteristic of exchange with respect to our aesthetic experience with moving images. Sobchack draws on Merleau-Ponty's term 'reversibility' in order to acknowledge this exchange between perception and expression. She writes, "the reversibility of perception and expression is neither instantiated as a thought nor synthesized from discrete and separate acts of consciousness. It is *given* with existence, in the simultaneity of subjective embodiment and objective enworldness" (Sobchack 1992: 4), drawing attention to phenomenology's emphasis on being-in-the-world as being concurrent with our experiencing it. The 'reversibility' that she highlights is a marker of self-consciousness specific to and necessary for experience (what Casebier would call 'a condition of' 1991: 11). It is a way for Sobchack to foreground corporeality and pay closer attention to the intersectional experience of body, sensation, emotion and perception.

As Sorfa writes "[p]henomenology attempts to identify this structure in our experience as precisely as possible: What do we see? How do we see it? Who is it that sees? These three questions cannot be separated" (2014: 355). As such, perception has often been worked through via these different modes and types of direction in consciousness. On the one hand, perception is a conscious placement of our bodies in space and in time. One example would be the perception involved in recollection, where memory works precisely in this way – as a perceptive intentionality with its main purpose to focus on the present within a conscious temporality (a self-awareness of it being 'now' for you, and equally it being a 'memory' of the collective – as discussed in Chapter 5). Our having memories and sharing them with others through social frameworks such as cinema, is always already about now and who we are with at that historical moment, than it is a specific recounting of the past. Our perceptions consciously anchor ourselves to the immediate present, the now of wherever, and whenever, we are.

One of Sobchack's greatest legacies for film-phenomenology is that she centers the body in her theorizing of cinematic experience; indeed it is her desire to involve the lived, embodied (and later carnal) experience in her film-phenomenology that leads her to prioritize Merleau-Ponty's approach over Husserl's. Such a shift is critical to her claim that perception is intended toward other sensory experience (in the phenomenological sense of 'extending' or 'stretching out to'),

> the body in its finite, situated, and sensate materiality objectively expresses intentionality in the world as a subjective *inscription* of time and *description* of

space. In this sense, the lived-body is both a *speaking* and *writing* of intentionality as being-in-the-world.

(Sobchack 1992: 59)

The presence of the body is linked to its intentionality and becomes a core concern, not only in the classical phenomenology of Merleau-Ponty but also in contemporary film-phenomenology. Intentionality then, is indicative of self-consciousness and the subjective reversibility of perception and expression as it describes the subject's lived experience, and Sobchack tirelessly returns us to attending to the body. "The body allows sensation and intellection to emerge as perception . . . [which is] lived by the body [and] not reducible to either intellection or sensation" (1992: 77). The consequence of this, as Yacavone notes, is that cinematic experience "entails the self's embodied and always reciprocal perceptual engagement with other selves and inanimate objects" (Yacavone 2016: 164). If at the cinema we look directly into the screen, it follows that this is where our awareness (perhaps this can even be called consciousness) is directed – our gaze intentionally looks to the immediate space in front of us, to the screen, its content, and its own space(s). We know that we are watching a film, even if throughout we momentarily relegate such awareness in order to embed ourselves in a film's story world.

As an in-between quality, intentionality is the activity that enables the subject to move from perceiving the world as something that is universally shared (Husserl's natural attitude) to perceiving a specific object that brings forth self-consciousness, or awareness of the object's (the *noēma*) relativity to the subject. Husserl's aim is to demonstrate how a phenomenological consciousness is reached, to separate it from 'regular' consciousness.[4] In Bion's terms, this is the conceptualization of links as emotional experience. As the subject's consciousness develops her or his intentionality, the relativity of what is perceived becomes more and more within the perspective of the self, that is, as a dreaming of emotional experience. This becomes important for moving image experience as it denotes the formation of intentionality within spectatorship, and even further, foregrounds the attention to affect within a Bionian psychoanalytic model. The intentionality, as an 'in-between quality', links the spectator to the film through the self-conscious perception of viewing the film (here as the *noēma*, the object that the *noēsis* is directed toward), not as an external separate object, but as an object that is part of its lived emotional experience.

For phenomenology, consciousness is a person's awareness of their inhabiting of the world, their spatial and temporal physicality in the world. Through this awareness, a lived reality is formed through how one experiences their physical being within the limits and laws of space and time. It is this emphasis on the physicality of lived experience, bodies as perceiving bodies, that signifies the main difference between a Husserlian and Merleau-Pontian phenomenology, and subsequently between the filmic approaches of Casebier and Sobchack respectively. For Merleau-Ponty, it is precisely because we are 'beings' that we can know our place in and our relationship to the world – that we can perceive it – and that we can perceive other bodies, beings and their place and relationship to the world. Here we can note an association between the ideas of Merleau-Ponty and Bion's theory of a mind needing another mind in order to think reality. The existentialism of Merleau-Ponty's intentionality is entirely threaded through 'being' equaling 'knowing', where such knowing is an emotional activity. Stephen Priest refers to the distinction as being "between questions of essence and questions of existence" (Priest 2003: 17), and this means an Husserlian phenomenological consideration of cinema privileges the essence of cinema over its linking, that is the in-between qualities specific to essence and existence. Put another way, a Husserlian approach focuses on what the aesthetics of cinema *are* that make 'cinema' cinema, whereas Merleau-Ponty's approach is more interested on the cumulative lived experience of the cinematic encounter, that is its affective potential. Let us look to a specific example to see how intentionality as a linking emotional experience works within the context of cinema.

Rabbit-Proof Fence

Rabbit-Proof Fence (*RPF*) is the retelling of the forced removal of Molly (Everlyn Sampi), her sister Daisy (Tianna Sansbury) and their cousin Gracie (Laura Monaghan) from their home community Jigalong in Western Australia in 1931. The three girls are abducted from their mother and taken to an internment camp at Moore River, which sought to place mixed-race children with white families to train them for servitude. Lead by Molly, the three girls escape and make their way back to Jigalong, using the rabbit-proof fence as a way to navigate their 1500-mile journey home. Whilst set in 1930's Australia, *RPF* also offers a cinematic interpretation of Molly's journey through the contemporary social response of the early 2000s in Australia, which looks to make social and cultural reparation for the Stolen Generations. The 'Stolen Generations' refers to the mixed race Indigenous children who were forcibly removed from their parents by apparatuses of the Australian State.[5] Although the film is framed as an historical retelling of Molly's, Daisy's and Gracie's escape, it also reflects the national and international debates regarding the Stolen Generations that were taking place 50 years later. The reversible intentionality of *RPF* is evident in its expression of a specific individual history, but through its cinematic representation it also expresses Australia's contemporary 2002 attitude and perception of the events that occurred in 1931. *RPF* transcends the description of Molly's 1500 mile journey back to Jigalong, and the traumatic experience of the Stolen Generations, by also expressing a specific statement about how the girls' experiences (as synecdoches of all Indigenous peoples affected by these abductions) are to be responded to and remembered (perceived) by those who watch the film.

In telling Molly's story via cinema, Noyce uses the appearance of Molly and the narrative of her journey in order to link to the reality and aftermath of the Stolen Generations. Is it possible to watch a film like *RPF*, which describes the happenings of the Stolen Generations in the 1930s, and not at the same time describe what it now means for the world today? Merleau-Ponty's view of intentionality suggests that it is not possible, "a movie has meaning in the same way that a thing does: neither of them speaks to an isolated understanding; rather, both appeal to our power tacitly to decipher the world or men and to coexist with them" (Merleau-Ponty 1964a: 58). In *Film and the New Psychology*, Merleau-Ponty develops this interconnection using Gestalt theory to say our perception of the external world is formed via a 'system of configurations' (1964b: 48) which exist outside and prior to the mind. Indeed, he views the linking between things in the world as,

> [t]he idea we have of the world would be overturned if we could succeed in seeing the intervals between things (for example, the space between the trees on the boulevard) as *objects* and, inversely, if we saw the things themselves-the-trees-as the ground.
>
> *(Merleau-Ponty 1964b: 49)*

Instead of consciousness only being an activity that is directed outwards then, it is an activity that uses intentionality to create and develop links into order to think experience along emotional and affective lines. This is a core aspect of phenomenological theory that informs the various processes of analysis in this approach.

Such linking is evident in the opening sequence of *RPF* where, via voiceover, Molly begins the recollection of her story. In her native language, she says:

> This is a true story of my sister Daisy and my cousin Gracie and me when we were little. Our people, the Jigalong mob, we were desert people then, walking all over our land.

The authenticity of Molly's story is further embodied through the veracity of her Indigenous language and voice. Her voice is heard as voiceover that opens to recount the 'true story'. These signifying practices of authenticity have distinctive attributes in terms of quasi-judgments, for this is where the ontological slippage has its greatest affective values; meaning that when we watch a film such as *RPF*, the phenomenological processes (of eidetic reduction, quasi-judgments and bracketing) are complicated by the merging of ontologies. In the memories and narratives of this true story, continually tracked back (like the sisters' journeys along the fence line) to the actuality of Molly's experience, the status of quasi-judgments are challenged. We, as spectators, cannot contain (in the Bionian sense) the affective investments in the ontologies either of the created world of the film or the *lebenswelt* of real spaces and times. The spoken words we hear are Molly's, laid over the tracking bird's eye shot, that links the red and barren outback of Australia to her memory of the event, and to the spectator's eye and ear. Cinema often associates socio-political statements and explorations of identity through the use and attachment of sound (voiceover or direct sound) to its cinematography (the use of wide-angle shots, deep space and deep focus) to formally integrate and adhere landscape to subjectivity, both as an action of placing and an action of discovery within the film's story. From the start of *RPF*, we are shown that Molly and the Australian outback are physically and psychically linked, each identity embedded in the other. The story is about them both. The voiceover continues, speaking over the visual introduction of Molly, representing her as a little girl who looks over her Jigalong home, her eye grazing over a landscape that is familiar to her as it is unfamiliar to the (white, non-Indigenous) spectator.

When we are presented with moving image experience as offered through *RPF*, with its complexities of ontological orders, and consequentially, a bleeding of one system of judgments into another, we are almost inevitably positioned in a moment of self-consciousness. In such moments of self-reflexivity and self-awareness, we witness the contesting of previously established relations of container-contained experience. The structures of such relations are foregrounded because our own sense of self is foregrounded. A phenomenological questioning of the experience of 'being embedded' considers the conscious and the self-conscious moments of experience, and the individual's self-reflection on such experience. This is precisely the enterprise of Husserl – to understand the *eidos* of being – that became the central issue for subsequent phenomenologists (including Jean-Paul Sartre's existentialist readings and Heidegger's metaphysical ones). The fundamental movement of consciousness to self-consciousness lies in the distinction that everyone can experience self-consciousness but such experience is unknowable outside yourself – only you can experience your own state of self-consciousness, existentially. Put more simply, you can share in the general perception of a film as well as have your own specific thoughts about it, which may or may not contradict the universally shared perception. Self-reflexivity is a turning of attention to either subject or object in order to engender conscious awareness.

For Heidegger (1973), consciousness depends on its 'being-an-issue'. He writes, "Dasein is an entity for which, in its Being, that Being is an issue. The phrase 'is an issue' has been made plain in the state-of-Being of understanding – of understanding as self-projective Being towards its utmost potentiality-for-Being" (Heidegger 1973: 235–236). Heidegger's uses *Dasein* to distinguish between the Being of human existence from that of animal existence or the existence of lifeless inorganic matter. *Dasein* is significant to human existence as it denotes the potentiality for self-reflection, the self-consciousness that permits thinking on experience to occur. Heidegger's emphasis here is that Being is linked with projection as well as existence. It is not just that we exist that is the issue, but that our being is projected – onto others, into space and through time – that is what continues and furthers our Being. Contained within Heidegger's 'Being is an issue', is the in-betweenness of intentionality. The issue is that Being is directed to something, specifically *projected*. Merleau-Ponty shares this conception of projection within conscious, writing:

> consciousness projects into a physical world and has a body, as it projects itself into a cultural world and has its habits: because it cannot be consciousness without paying upon significance given either in the absolute past of nature or in its own personal past, and because any form of lived experience tends towards a certain generality whether that of our habits or that of our 'bodily functions'. These elucidations enable us clearly to understand motility as basic

intentionality. Consciousness is in the first place not a matter of 'I think that' but of 'I can'.

(Merleau-Ponty 1964a: 137)

This sense of 'I can' is not to be misread as a motivational mantra but more as a physical self-awareness of our place in external reality and to others. Merleau-Ponty's 'I can' is a *linking projection* of a bodily existence and self-consciousness, so that a definition of consciousness is developed through ontological and epistemological relativity. Being and consciousness, as they matter to sensory perception, are the links that lead to capacity for self-conscious and self-reflection. On this path, of being self-aware and able to think reflexively about its value, is the awareness of 'motility as basic intentionality'. As Sobchack notes, "intentionality shows itself through the lived body as it perceives and gestures in the world and genetically constitutes the human phenomena of meaning and signification" (Sobchack 1992: 66), which is her way of identifying the difference in approach and application of intentionality as it is conceived by Husserl and Merleau-Ponty.

Perception is an integral part of what the experience of 'being embedded' contains as it helps to create a 'language'[6] through which we can form such links between what we feel, what we see and how that becomes experience. This is the fundamental process of becoming a film spectator, for when we watch a film we are embedded in an audio-visual language, co-creating experience that links us to those on the screen. Arendt (1978: 23) differed from Merleau-Ponty, who argued that being can only flee 'into being'; her position was that Being and Appearance were concurrent as lived experience, requiring a link or a form of intentionality in order to be meaningful and conveyed to someone else. She argued that language was inadequate as a means to accurately express mental activity; "[n]o language has a ready-made vocabulary for the needs of mental activity" (1978: 102). Nevertheless, its capacity for metaphor served as a link between appearance and appearance, making the concurrence of Being and Appearance possible: "[language is] the only medium through which mental activities can be manifest not only to the outside world but also to the mental ego itself" (Arendt 1978: 102). Indeed, what makes linking experience an actuality (mental and not necessarily conscious) is the metaphor, or what Kant referred to as speculative reason (Kant 2007). The metaphor allows the transfer of abstract thought to the experience of being, "the transition from one existential state, that of thinking, to another, that of being an appearance among appearances" (Arendt 1978: 103). As per Bion, it is thought that requires the vehicle of the metaphor, as it impresses on the conscious mind, in order to move from the abstract 'unknown' to the 'linked' known.

Bion and Arendt: linking, emotion and thought

Considerable symmetry exists between Bion and Arendt's questioning of the relationship between thought and appearance. Both thinkers make powerful statements on the correspondence between the influence of emotions, thought and perception of aesthetic experience. For Arendt, we are caught in the syllogism of metaphor – where appearance is brought to bear on the formation of thought and where thought uses, joins with appearance to form consciousness and sensory experience. She writes:

> If the language of thinking is essentially metaphorical, it follows that the world of appearances inserts itself into thought quite apart from the needs of our body and the claims of our fellow-men, which will draw us back into it in any case. No matter how close we are while thinking to what is far away and how absent we are from what is close at hand, the thinking ego obviously never leaves the world of appearances altogether.
>
> *(Arendt 1978: 110)*

Here, she is suggesting that thoughts are not dependent on what we may physically need, but are still attached to both the body and the *world of appearances altogether*. Indeed, she asks if thought and thinking are ever meant to be known, appearing as entities to us and although Arendt is not writing about cinema, her ideas on the linking between thought and appearance are deeply significant for a medium that depends entirely on such association. After all, moving image experience is sustained by the insertion of thought via appearance.

Bion's theory of thinking revolves around the interrelationship between thought and emotional experience, which is why Arendt's phenomenology of thinking fits well with a Bionian approach as she also views thinking as occurring from emotional experience. Arendt also makes a very clear demarcation between thinking and the inability to think, similar to Bion's 'attacks on linking' (1959), or -K that involves the avoidance of thinking in order to defend against emotional turbulence. Bion's K link is not to be read as Arendt's 'knowing', as it is much closer to her use of the word 'thinking'. She notes that the search for knowledge as a '*quest for meaning*' is not the same as emotional thinking, which she describes as a '*quest for truth*' (1978: 15). This aligns with Bion's position that the K link, as an emotional activity, is concerned with knowing someone in a sensory, relational way. Previous chapters have discussed Bion's theory of thinking in terms of how we link with others and through such linking come to feel emotional experience in response to relationships. This then develops into a process of thinking to shape the impressions of thought (thoughts making their appearance through the structure of thinking in our psyche). We link to feel, to think and to dream.[7]

As noted in Chapter 2, Bion views thinking as an activity that is "forced on the psyche by the pressure of thoughts and not the other way round" (1962b: 307). Ogden (2008) terms this Bion's third principle of mental functioning, that is, thoughts are not unconscious libidinal desires seeking to be known in the conscious mind, but are responses to tensions that result from different affective and sensory experiences. Tension here results from new or unexpected experience, not necessarily traumatic. In the circumstances where we are unable to tolerate frustrations or think through tensions, thoughts are either modified or ejected (as the

-*K* activity). This is evident in the tension that demonstrates an inability to reflect another's view (omnipotence): "[r]eality view from a single vantage point represents a failure to think" or through 'excessive projective identification' (Ogden 2008: 17, 22). For Bion, our lived experience accumulates sense data that results in emotional experience requiring the process of thinking. It is important to emphasize that Bionian psychoanalysis sees sensory data (beta-elements) as the primary link to reality. Without sensory activity informing our being-in-the-world, Bionian psychoanalysis states that we have no connection to reality. This is why for Bion, dreaming is the process that makes the links connect together; that is, dreaming enables sensory lived experience "to cope with thoughts" (Bion 1962b: 307).

Bion's idea of linking echoes Arendt's claim,

> I can flee appearance only into appearance. And that does not solve the problem, for the problem concerns the fitness of thought to appear at all, and the question is whether thinking . . . [is] meant to appear or whether in fact [acts of thinking] can never find an adequate home in the world.
> *(Arendt 1978: 23)*

'Being embedded' within moving image experience involves making links between appearance (and our emotional experience of it) and thought through the activity of thinking, with the hope of it finding "an adequate home in the world". 'Thinking as linking' then refers to the emotions we feel in our everyday associations, so it is worth considering how emotions are linked with the space and experience of moving images. It would be inconceivable to watch a film and not be affected by an emotion, even boredom is an emotion.[8] As Symington and Symington have stated, "[i]t is out of this emotional experience that either a thought process or a discharge will take place. . . . Without the links there would be no emotional experience and without that no development of thought" (Symington and Symington 2008: 30). The links, or the activity of linking, can be viewed as the intentionality that directs perception, which results in the self-conscious feeling we experience in our relationships with people and its metaphoric translation into emotion.

Cinema, as embodied experience, what Sobchack addresses as "cinema as life expressing life, as experience expressing experience" (1992: 5), is also the linking of emotional experience to the metaphor of thought within a contained process of thinking. Whilst the term 'thought' is (at times) used for different purposes by Bion and Arendt, their consideration and treatment of its function for perception and lived experience shares the same emphasis concerning emotion. Arendt's view is commonly held, that thought follows thinking, whereas Bion views thinking following thought. Each writer however, views thought as requiring a psychic structure in order to make itself known, so that it can 'appear'. Compare the following quotes from Arendt:

> Thought with its accompanying conceptual language, since it occurs in and is spoken by a being at home in a world of appearances, stands *in need of metaphors*

> *in order to bridge the gap* between a world given to sense experience and a realm where no such immediate apprehension of evidence can ever exist.
>
> *(Arendt 1978: 32, italics added)*

> The language of the soul is in its mere expressive stage, *prior to its transformation and transfiguration through thought*, is not metaphorical; it does not depart from the senses and uses no analogies when it talks in terms of physical sensations.
>
> *(Arendt 1978: 33, italics added)*

With this from Bion:

> The theory of functions and alpha-function [the mental activity that attempts to arrange and express unknown thought impressions – beta elements] are not part of psycho-analytic theory. They are working tools for the practicing psycho-analyst to ease problems of thinking about something that is unknown.
>
> *(Bion 1962a: 89)*

Here we see the concept of exchange from impression to expression, of transformation from unknown to known. Sobchack articulates such exchange within the context of film experience, "the film has the capacity and competence to signify, to not only *have* sense but also to *make* sense through a unique and systemic form of communication" (Sobchack 1992: 6). Clearly, the concept of capacity, as processural rather than simply spatial is a key determinant in the description of 'being embedded' as well as the reversible intentionality between thought and appearance. Arendt's phenomenology of thinking relates to Bion's theory of thinking as it addresses the bringing forth of emotional experience as embodied perception. Both thinkers are heavily influenced by philosophical systems of thought (specifically Kant, Locke and Hume) and in particular phenomenology (Husserl, Heidegger and Merleau-Ponty), with Bion's psychoanalytic theories in particular focusing on the centrality of a person's need to self-reflect on their place in the world in order for mental growth to occur. Bion's particular psychoanalytic approach brings the phenomenology of perception and the world of psychoanalysis in closer alignment.

Sobchack's examination of the relationship between psychoanalysis and phenomenology for film experience concentrates on the contributions of Lacanian psychoanalysis. Her work follows the classical psychoanalytic model rather than the more contemporary version Bion offers. She writes, "psychoanalysis has explored the act of seeing in its relation to the constitution of the Self 'from the outside in' – thus positing, through the influential work of Jacques Lacan, the visibly *seen* as that Other who originates the visual seer" (Sobchack 1992: 99). Viewing psychoanalysis as possessing an homogeneous schemata, as it relates to the positioning of and by the subject to the object – here in the activity of vision as it relates to perception – does not account for diversity and challenge across the schools of psychoanalysis itself. Sobchack's work is undeniably pivotal in its bringing forth psychoanalysis's relationship to phenomenology within the context of film experience. The project here is to continue this association by including Bion's psychoanalytic model for the development of thought, one that moves from sensory impression to conscious expression, emphasizing that it offers a different perspective for the 'outside-in' model. When it comes to negotiating the expression of emotional experience, his exigent but stimulating theory of the container-contained offers a different perspective to previous Lacanian models.

Cinema as container-contained

Bion's container-contained model (1962a, 1962b, 1965, 1970) is viewed as one of the most significant developments within psychoanalytic thought since Freud (Ogden 2004; Grotstein 2007; Symington and Symington 2008). Bion used the container-contained model to identify the processes involved with the mental activity of transforming sensory impression to emotional conscious expression, or as Ogden puts it, "how we process lived experience and what occurs psychically when we are unable to do psychological work" (Ogden 2004: 1354). It is a term that Bion invents to refer to the psychoanalytic function of the personality, which when healthy, is the thinking of lived emotional experience from both conscious and unconscious perspectives simultaneously. This is Bion's process for dreaming which I discussed in Chapter 5. Influenced by Klein's theory of projective identification (1952), the container-contained refers to affective exchange between thoughts and cognitive capability for thinking (dreaming). As such, the intentionality within the intense projection involved within containment (container-contained) is the transformation of sense data into thoughts that can be dreamt and used for mental and emotional growth. The projection here resonates with Heidegger's (1962) and Merleau-Ponty's application of projection of being-in-the-world and its relationship to consciousness, where the concept and action of projection is as much a linking as it is an in-between quality that affects embodied consciousness.

I have discussed the impact of Bion's revision of the psychoanalytic theory of dreaming in the previous chapter, but I wish to put it in context for his model of the container-contained. For Freud the dream work was psychic work that distinguished unconscious dream thoughts through considerations of representability and agencies of condensation and displacement. Only by being disguised can infantile wishes and unconscious desires enter into the mind as dream thoughts, for secondary process thinking. For Bion, dreaming is a work, or rather a psychic process that transforms conscious lived experience into unconscious thoughts. Dreaming in this Bionian frame is not about the release of unconscious phantasies; rather it is the dominant psychological work we do in order to process the raw sensory data from our lived experience so that we might incur psychic growth. It is on this premise that Bion formed his container-contained model.

The container, as Bion conceives it, is a receptive process that enables dreaming (unconscious thinking) to take place. Cinema, inclusive of the entire lived experience of watching, listening, feeling and remembering the moving image can be regarded as a containing process, which processes the emotionality of lived experience. The contained, also a process, is one that foregrounds unconscious thoughts as a dynamic set of feelings and sensations that result from affective sensory lived experience. The containing process can be simply stated as the mental activity of transforming sensory impressions (beta-elements) to emotional conscious expression (via alpha function). The container-contained is an ongoing process and exchange of unbearable experience into bearable experience that Bion uses to formulate his container-contained model. Here we see the implication of 'being embedded' as occurring through transfer and transformation and, somewhat problematically, through words 'container-contained' that suggest spatial holding (discussed previously in Chapter 4). However, this would be to miss the point of Bion's model, "I shall abstract for us as a model the idea of a container into which an object is projected and the object that can be projected into the container: the latter I shall designate by the term contained." (Bion 1962a: 90). It is his way of identifying the potential capacity for the transfer of emotional experience from a source, such as the moving image (as container) to the capacity to process and eventually think them (this is the contained because to think something requires a form or structure for Bion).

Bion recognized that using words like 'container' and 'contained' for the different agenda of psychoanalysis would bring problems, and to avoid this he used symbols ♀ (container) and ♂ (contained). "These signs both denote and represent. They are variables or unknown in that they are replaceable . . . ♂ and ♀ are dependent on each other for mutual benefit and without harm to either." (Bion 1962a: 90–91).[9] These two aspects of our personality 'denote and represent' our capacity for reverie and self-reflective thought. When they are effective, when a ♀ and ♂ work together to allow the transference of emotional experience through projective identification and introjection, self-reflection can occur and growth in thought is possible. Let us look at an example of how Bion's container-contained process works in cinema.

Container-contained in *Unforgiven*

Clint Eastwood's *Unforgiven* (1992) is a critique of the social idealizations of masculinity and the lived experience with such idealization, illuminating Bion's container-contained model. We are introduced to William Munny (Clint Eastwood) via two perspectives, the first belongs to the film's story-world and is predominantly feminine (that of his wife, his mother-in-law and the women of Big Whiskey); the second being of our own perception, which can be read as the contained seeking a container. The film offers a cognitive dissonant experience as it presents a challenge to normative identifications of masculinity within an established cinematic masculine context (the Western genre); and is authored by masculine sources (directed and acted by Clint Eastwood and written by David Webb Peoples) in order to be thought through by the audience. Before we visually meet Munny, we are given the following perspective:

> Of good family, albeit one of modest means, she was a comely young woman and not without prospects. Therefore it was at once heartbreaking and astonishing to her mother that she would enter into marriage with William Munny, a known thief and murderer, a man of notoriously vicious and intemperate disposition.

This description is followed with the cutting of Delilah's (Anna Thomson) face (a woman who works in the town's whorehouse) and the capture of the two offending cowboys. From the start, we are embedded within patriarchal time and space, with feminine perspectives positioned as oppositional and marginalized: through the mother-in-law's unhappiness at her daughter's marriage; through the assault on Delilah's face; and through the lack of justice in response to the cowboys' criminality. It is the proprietor of Greely's Saloon, Skinny (Anthony James), who is offered compensation because his 'property' (Delilah is a prostitute) was damaged. There is no reparation made to Delilah herself. The threat of violent masculinity remains.

> ALICE
> You . . . you ain't even gonna . . . whip 'em?
> LITTLE BILL
> I fined 'em instead.
> ALICE
> For what they done? Skinny gets
> some ponies an' that's . . . ?

These opening scenes establish the exchange between perception of patriarchy and its expression via masculinity within the film. The lore of Munny is at odds with the current reality we find him in and with the dominant masculinity of other characters presented by the film. In the film's legend, Munny is a violent outlaw to be feared and revered. In the present time of the film's story world, he is a failed farmer, all his pigs are sick and he is not able to separate them or control them, falling in pig muck over and over. Munny disappoints as a farmer in every scene. The Schofield Kid (Jaimz Woolvett), who has come looking to partner with Munny says, "you don't look like no meaner than hell cold-blooded damn killer"; and Munny even has trouble mounting a horse. He chooses to leave his two young children to fend for themselves in order to follow the Kid, avenge Delilah, and be paid for murdering the two cowboys responsible for her tragedy. Masculinity is on trial here; or rather, it is the representation of masculinity against its lived experience that is up for reflection.

Whether the masculinity is personified through the different male characters embodying different masculine types, or through the more abstract version of masculine space of the town of Big Whiskey or Greeley's saloon, one of the main container/contained interplays within the film is the being violent and the becoming violent within masculinity. Indeed the crux of masculinity within *Unforgiven* hinges on the thought – it is a "hell of a thing to kill a man". As a container, the film *Unforgiven* functions as the capacity to rethink stereotypes and the consequential experience of representing violent masculinity for men and women. The audience's use of cinema – their experience watching the film – as the contained, becomes the opportunity to think, self-reflect about the stereotypical representation of masculinity and its association with violence and grow from it, reaching new thought about each equally.

The Schofield Kid wishes to be like Munny, who embodies the capacity that makes the Kid's dreaming of becoming a man possible. This dream of becoming (a man) in turn makes Munny a container for the Kid, and thus he can only feel like he has agency and existence by being contained in this way. The Kid uses the myth of Munny's violent past to construct and express his desire for masculinity. Munny does not deny his past, or the Kid's requests for validation of the myth, always responding with ambiguity: "I don't remember". For the audience, his past remains an unknown impression, only expressed through the legends told by the other characters. As spectators, we recognize that Munny will become a killer again, a violent man because he is the unforgiven, he cannot escape what he has done (been a violent man). In addition, Munny is unforgiven of the self – he is not looking for redemption, he breaks the generic Western convention by not actually seeking redemption via forgiveness. The container-contained is interplayed throughout the film demonstrating that in order for cinema to be able to bring forth the possibility of conscious self-reflection about its topic (in this case masculinity and its relationship to violence), there is a consistent exchange between emotions, experience and thought. Characters equally take up the position of container/contained, serving to lead to new thought and new perspective. Remembering that the container is a capacity for emotional transfer that allows dreaming (as unconscious thinking) to be possible, and that the contained offers a structure to 'denote and represent' unknown thoughts that have come from our emotional lived experience so that they can be thought through, moving images have the potential to be the most influential and affective visual experiences. Cinema-as-container makes possible spectator reflection, and in the example of *Unforgiven*, this reflection concerns the mythologizing of masculinity, engendering similar self-reflection within spectatorship. There is the scope to reflect on the misrepresentation of violence as being a desirable and embedded masculine trait.

Applying Bion's container-contained to the reversibility of perception and expression within cinema enables "searching for realization" and as contained-container "thoughts seeking a thinker" (Symington and Symington 2008: 52). Cinema as an apparatus is the one of the closest forms of representing dreaming as it occurs in waking life. If dreaming is the mental activity through which we process and self-reflect on all lived emotional experience, then how we perceive cinema is instrumental in how we introject such presented self-reflection. Bion's theory of thinking is presented as a method for transformation, to follow the process (exchange) of how thought and emotional experience develop and are linked before they are known and able to be perceived. These 'places' and developments however are not in parts of the mind (as it were). It is more effective to view Bion's (many) terms as fulfilling a function. Indeed, many of his key concepts are denoted using a symbol, as exemplified above in the container-contained model.

This progression stands in stark contrast to the classical psychoanalytic perspective on the development of thought, particularly as Bionian psychoanalysis does not work from the "premise that the *structures of language determine the structure of being*" (Sobchack 1992: 100), as Sobchack recognizes in Lacanian psychoanalysis, but rather from the premise that activities of thinking (especially dreaming) express lived emotional experience, and through this thinking can reflect on their being and come to know 'truth' (Bion 1965). Cinema, when considered from a Bionian perspective, is an effective exposition of the container-contained, in that as a 'container' process, its films offer the spectator the structure and form of audio-visual material, space and time to create the capacity to dream. Cinema presents shared lived emotional experience that allows the spectator to use for their own self-reflections of the emotional and embodied experiences they encounter through the films that they watch. In this way, it is possible to view cinema as container-contained in Bion's model. It offers the capacity to experience dreaming in a waking state through embodied perspective. Cinema therefore works as a function of the contained as it is a vehicle for unconscious thoughts of (individual and collective) social emotional experience. What phenomenology, particularly in this context of moving image experience, lends to this approach is a dialogue based on issues of ontology, affect and frames of consciousness. The capacity to explore lived emotional experience at the analytic level is a crucial part of this Bionian approach and phenomenology's recent theoretical turn in film. This issue of the sensory process is taken up in the next chapter.

Notes

1 See Slavoj Zizek (2001), who writes on the threatening 'something' over the dread of 'nothing' in "The Thing from Inner Space: *Titanic* and *Deep Impact*".
2 See Casebier (1991: 25–34), who outlines the concept of Husserl's *noēma* in detail.
3 See Sara Ahmed (2007), where her queering of phenomenology reflexively comments on the lines of conscious orientation (turning) in our relationship to and with others, "what we could call 'the politics of turning' (and turning around), and how in facing this way or that the surfaces of bodies and worlds take their shape" (Ahmed 2007: 201 fn. 5).
4 See Patrick Fuery (2004: 103–5) who writes on the 'as-if' phenomenon. Fuery's 'as-if' example refers to Husserl's phenomenological suspension, the *epoché*, or bracketing, where a suspension of disbelief contributes to the formation of a particular attitude toward everything outside the realm of consciousness. This is the first step Husserl sees as moving away from the natural (that is given and therefore naïve) attitude and the beginnings of an internal (abstract) consciousness that intentionally perceives that world and the subject's inhabiting of it.
5 See A.O. Neville's 1930 eugenic article "Coloured Folk: Some Pitiful Cases".
6 The term 'language' used in this sense brings its own difficulties. I am using the very general sense of language as a system of communication that is exercised in all typologies,

formal, informal, verbal and non-verbal. 'Language' as I am discussing it here is to denote an activity of linking and transfer between abstract affect and thought to the expression of communication.
7 As I discuss in Chapter 2, this is not as straightforward as it appears. It is a best-case scenario. Sometimes we cannot link, or the link between people is unconsciously destroyed, what Bion refers to as 'attack on linking' (1959).
8 In fact, boredom is an exceptionally interesting emotion that is entirely about linking, particularly in terms of creativity and ideas of frustration and satisfaction. See Adam Phillips, where he writes, "moods, of course, are points of view" (1994: 71), and that "[b]oredom is integral to the process of taking one's time" (1994: 73).
9 Bion's concept of containment is explored further in Chapter 8.

References

Ahmed, S. (2007). *Queer Phenomenology: Orientation, Objects and Others.* Durham: Duke University Press.
Arendt, H. (1978). *The Life of the Mind.* New York: Harcourt Brace Jovanovic.
Barker, J. (2009). *The Tactile Eye: Touch and the Cinematic Experience.* Berkeley: University of California Press.
Bion, W.R. (1959). Attacks on Linking. *International Journal of Psycho-Analysis*, 40, pp. 308–315.
Bion, W.R. (1961). *Experiences in Groups and Other Papers.* New York: Basic Books.
Bion, W.R. (1962a). *Learning From Experience.* London: Tavistock.
Bion, W.R. (1962b). The Psycho-Analytic Study of Thinking. *International Journal of Psycho-Analysis*, 43, pp. 306–310.
Bion, W.R. (1965). *Transformations: Change From Learning to Growth.* London: William Heinemann Medical Books.
Bion, W.R. (1970). *Attention and Interpretation: A Scientific Approach to Insight in Psycho-Analysis and Groups.* London: Karnac Books.
Casebier, A. (1991). *Film and Phenomenology: Toward a Realist Theory of Cinematic Representation.* Cambridge: Cambridge University Press.
Fuery, P. (2004). *Madness and Cinema: Psychoanalysis, Spectatorship and Culture.* Basingstoke: Palgrave Macmillan.
Grotstein, J. (2007). *A Beam of Intense Darkness: Wilfred Bion's Legacy to Psychoanalysis.* London: Karnac Books.
Heidegger, M. (1962). *Being in Time.* Translated by J. MacQuarrie and E. Robinson. New York: Harper & Row.
Heidegger, M. (1973). *Being and Time.* Translated by J. Macquarie and E. Robinson. Oxford: Basil Blackwell.
Husserl, E. (1931). *Ideas: General Introduction to Pure Phenomenology.* Translated by W.R. Gibson. London and New York: Routledge, 2002.
Husserl, E. (1950). *The Paris Lectures* (ed.) Strasser, S. Translated by P. Koestenbaum. The Hague: Nijhoff, 1964.
Husserl, E. (1952). *Ideas Pertaining to a Pure Phenomenology and to a Phenomenological Philosophy. Second Book, Studies in the Phenomenology of Constitution.* Translated by R. Rojcewicz and A. Schuwer. Dordrecht: Kluwer Academic Publishers, 1989.
Ingarden, R. (1973). *The Literary Work of Art: An Investigation of the Borderlines of Ontology, Logic, and Theory of Language.* Translated by G. Grabowicz. Evanston, IL: Northwestern University Press.
Kant, I. (1790). *The Critique of Judgement* (ed.) Walker, N. Translated by J.C. Meredith. Oxford: Oxford University Press, 2007.

Klein, M. (1952). The Origins of Transference. In *Envy and Gratitude and Other Works: 1946–1963*. London: Hogarth Press and the Institute of Psychoanalysis.
Kuhn, A. and Westwell, G. (2012). *A Dictionary of Film Studies*. Oxford: Oxford University Press.
Marks, L. (2000). *The Skin of the Film: Intercultural Cinema, Embodiment, and the Senses*. Durham: Duke University Press.
Merleau-Ponty, M. (1964a). *The Primacy of Perception: And Other Essays on Phenomenological Psychology, the Philosophy of Art, History and Politics* (ed.) Edie, J.E. Translated by W. Cobb. Evanston, IL: Northwestern University Press.
Merleau-Ponty, M. (1964b). Film and the New Psychology. In *Sense and Non-Sense*. Translated by H.L. Dreyfus and P.A. Dreyfus. Evanston, IL: Northwestern University Press.
Münsterberg, H. (1916). *The Photoplay: A Psychological Study*. New York and London: D. Appleton and Company.
Neville, A.O. (1930). Coloured Folk: Some Pitiful Cases. *The West Australian Newspaper*. 18 April 1930: Page 9. *National Library of Australia*. Web. June 5th 2015.
Ogden, T. (2004). On Holding and Containing, Being and Dreaming. *International Journal of Psychoanalysis*, 85 (6), pp. 1349–1364.
Ogden, T. (2008). Bion's Four Principles of Mental Functioning. *Fort Da*, 14, pp. 11–35.
Phillips, A. (1994). *On Kissing, Tickling and Being Bored*. London: Faber and Faber.
Priest, S. (2003). *Merleau-Ponty*. London and New York: Routledge.
Sobchack, V. (1992). *The Address of the Eye: A Phenomenology of Film Experience*. Princeton, NJ: Princeton University Press.
Sobchack, V. (2004). *Carnal Thoughts: Embodiment and Moving Image Culture*. Berkeley: University of California Press.
Sorfa, D. (2014). Phenomenology and Film. In Branigan, E. and Buckland, W. (eds.) *The Routledge Encyclopedia of Film Theory*. London and New York: Routledge.
Stadler, J. (2013). Cinema's Compassionate Gaze: Empathy, Affect and Aesthetics in *The Diving Bell and the Butterfly*. In Choi, J. and Frey, M. (eds.) *Cine-Ethics: Ethical Dimensions of Film Theory, Practice, and Spectatorship*. London and New York: Routledge.
Stadler, J. (2014). Affect and Film. In Branigan, E. and Buckland, W. (eds.) *The Routledge Encyclopedia of Film Theory*. London and New York: Routledge.
Symington, N. and Symington, J. (2008). *The Clinical Work of Wilfred Bion*. London and New York: Routledge.
Yacavone, D. (2016). Film and the Phenomenology of Art: Reappraising Merleau-Ponty on Cinema as Form, Medium, and Expression. *New Literary History*, 47 (1), pp. 159–185.
Zizek, S. (2001). The Thing From Inner Space: Titanic and Deep Impact. In Gabbard, G.O. (ed.) *Psychoanalysis and Film*. London: Karnac Books.

Filmography

Rabbit-Proof Fence (2002). Directed by Phillip Noyce.
Unforgiven (1992). Directed by Clint Eastwood.

7

TRANSFORMATION

The idiomatic encounter and use of moving image as object

There are two phases to Bion's oeuvre, what Ogden (2004b) has called 'early' and 'late' Bion, and what Bléandonu (1994) refers to as the epistemological and mystical periods. Despite the somewhat arbitrary division of Bion's works into these two phases, there is a reason for such a distinction, one that is tied to the premise of the theory itself. All of Bion's work up until *Transformations: Change from Learning to Growth* (1965) offer divergence from Freudian approaches, most notably emphasizing his conception of dreaming as a form of thinking that facilitates learning from experience. Ogden states that the early period of Bion's writing was equally interested in crafting what learning from experience feels like, as well as clarifying the process as "a progressive dialectical movement between obscurity and clarification which moves toward, though never achieves, closure" (Ogden 2004b: 288). *Learning from experience* (1962) both outlines and obscures the specific psychoanalytic functions Bion proposes so that the reader is released from cold-categorization of analytic specificity (of a dream, of a text, and as argued in previous chapters, this can be extended to a film and the cultural experience of moving images). Bion effectively defamiliarizes his own ideas and terms so that concepts such as dreaming and container-contained are made strange, enabling and encouraging the reader to use them for their own purpose and process of emotional experience (and learning). The obscurity is important in Bion's theory of thinking as it is fundamental to his overall position, which to recall, is that in order for psychic growth to occur we must put ourselves in the way of frustration. Avoidance of difficult thought or emotional turbulence, otherwise termed as 'not thinking', will not lead to any learning from experience and subsequently no psychic transformation. Therefore using words that carry previous connotations incurs the frustration that Bion wishes us to encounter so that new growth and new knowing of psychoanalysis as an experience can occur.

I have left Bion's most radical theory, the concept of O, to the penultimate chapter because it is simultaneously one that eludes definition and which is the most frustrating and resistant to outline. He begins *Attention and Interpretation* (1970) with this warning: "I doubt if anyone but a practicing psycho-analyst can understand this book although I have done my best to make it simple" (1970: 1). Bion refuses to offer the seduction of magical thinking. He does not specifically state what O means, indeed he entertains for as long as possible the 'not knowing' of O. This is because Bion wants to emphasize knowing, the *K* link discussed in the previous chapter, as an activity that shapes emotional experience rather than knowledge as fact acquisition. He writes, "[r]eason is emotion's slave and exists to rationalize emotional experience" (Bion 1970: 1). Similarly, I have attempted a more subtle frustration throughout this book by alluding to the experience of 'being embedded' with moving image experience rather than specifically prescribing what this might be, or what it might represent as. Yet even though Bion advises his readers to "disregard what [he] say[s] until the O of experience of reading has evolved" (1970: 28), the concept of O and what it presents for psychoanalysis remains the focus of his late, mystical period.

This chapter first explores the Bionian conceit of transformation and its role in contemporary psychoanalysis before taking up Bollas's concepts of idiom (2010) and the "Transformational Object" (2011). To explore such themes, I begin by discussing 'transformation' via the concept of O, contextualizing Bion's own advice on how to conceive it before turning to Michelangelo Antonioni's film *Blow-Up* (1966) as an illustration of Bion's notion of invariance and its significance within his theory of transformations. Toward the end of the chapter, I refer to HBO's television program *Westworld* (2016) to consider how the moving image as an external object influences our self-experience and perception of it. It is here that the 'use' of film and media is discussed, arguing that moving images as 'external objects' are worked with to engender transformative self-experience within the spectator, unconsciously and consciously. The examples are purposefully taken from two different media in order to resist medium-specificity, as well as illustrating the diverse potential of Bion's ideas, and to further the point that audiences work with the moving image, to 'work through' lived experience. This draws on the work of Caroline Bainbridge and Candida Yates (2011, 2012, 2014; Bainbridge 2012; Yates 2010) who have employed a psycho-cultural approach in studying the interrelationship between culture, emotional experience and the moving image, what is often referred as "therapy culture" (Bainbridge, Ward and Yates 2014: 3).

Bainbridge's (2012) analysis of television as a transitional object is highly relevant for this discussion as it emphasizes the transitional qualities specific to object-relation psychoanalytic theory, privileging what it means "to 'live a life in the world of objects'" (Winnicott in Bollas 1989: 26). Following on from Bainbridge, I argue that the moving image extends beyond a conceptualization of Winnicott's transitional object, functioning more in terms of Bollas's transformational process as an evocative and intermediate object. Bollas argues that the mother, as Winnicott's 'environment' mother (Winnicott 1965), is more identifiable as a process than an object, particularly as her adaptations and interactions with her infant effects "cumulative internal and external transformations" (2011: 1). As such, Bollas states that the first transformational object experienced by the infant establishes a sensory knowing (similar to Bion's K link) that is associated with 'altered self experience' (2011: 2). The transformational process that occurs with moving images is argued in a similar fashion, in that the emotional experience is not a representational process but a "recurrent experience of being" (2011: 2). I outline how such 'use' of moving images mimics the psychic movement involved in Bollas's transformational process, where such use is an attempt to "articulate and elaborate [our] personality idiom(s)" (Bollas 1989: 8).

There is a distinction to be made between Winnicott's transitional object (which, like Bainbridge, Kuhn's *Little Madnesses* explores in depth as it informs "aspects of cultural experience" (2013: 1)) and Bollas's transformational object. I posit that this can be seen in the development of one's 'idiom' via the destiny drive, that is, the compulsion to express 'the true self' (Bollas 1989: 3). There will be the desire and expectation for textual analysis of transformation in *Blow-Up* and *Westworld* but, as the reader will come to see, the aim of the chapter is to prioritize the possibility of transformative self-experience with moving images through Bion's intention with the concept of O. O is not able to be universalized, or reduced or expressed; it is ineffable. Ogden also refuses to prescribe O, preferring to let its "meanings to emerge" (2004b: 291) as he follows the trajectory of Bion's theory. This is to both expose the experience of reading Bion's concept of O (which arguably is to frustrate), as much as it is to argue a specifically Bionian consideration of the moving image, as aesthetic experience and as cultural object, that facilitates the potential for O. Further, it promotes the processual quality of transformation as argued by Bollas.

Bion's concept of O

To attempt to present what the experience of O might mean for a cinematic encounter then, is antithetical to Bion's overall project – especially as he spends a significant amount of time describing how O 'becomes' rather than what it means. His emphasis on O as an experience of becoming reads similar to Brian Massumi's questioning of the body. In *Parables for the Virtual: Movement, Affect and Sensation*, he writes:

> When I think of my body and ask what it does to earn that name, two things stand out. It *moves*. It *feels*. In fact, it does both at the same time. It moves as it feels, and it feels itself moving. Can we think a body without this: an intrinsic connection between movement and sensation whereby each immediately summons the other?
>
> *(Massumi 2002: 1)*

For Massumi, the 'qualitative difference' between bodily movement and sensation is "change. Felt and unforeseen" (2002: 1), and whilst this is not able to work as an exact mirror for Bion's O, it does highlight the core affective quality involved with the experience of psychic transformation and the inescapable difficulty of being able to specifically speak to how it makes a body feel. There already exists such a large amount of work on affect and embodiment (Sedgwick and Frank 1995; Hardt 1999; Shouse 2005; Clough and Halley 2007; Gregg and Seigworth 2010; Berlant 2011; Ahmed 2014) that it is beyond the scope of this chapter and the project of the book to trace and discuss the directions and turns that have been taken. As discussed in previous chapters, affect is intersubjective, not easily controlled, and as Lisa Cartwright has observed, is often associated with and contextualized by aesthetics, the classical position being "nature's 'harmonious' lines and colors are the inspiration for architectural form – as if nature 'speaks' directly to our feelings through its forms" (2015: 32). As I discuss later, Bion similarly uses geometrical figures as metaphors that can be interpreted in the same capacity as Massumi's 'qualitative difference', to advance and inform his concept of O, particularly as such forms refer to the affective experience of transformation (although Bion does not express it as such). This scholarship regarding affect theory is mentioned briefly only to associate Bion within wider, non-psychoanalytic contexts and to suggest a broader application of his ideas to the reader, particularly as they relate to the complex affective and ineffable qualities of O.

In *Forces of Destiny: Psychoanalysis and Human Idiom*, Bollas, whilst not directly referring to Bion's O, similarly speaks to the affective and resonant presence within the experiencing of psychoanalysis, saying that it is 'impossible' to state what occurs within psychoanalysis (1989: 7). He focuses specifically on the analytic encounter, noting the failure of words to account for the 'sheer unconsciousness' that structures and transpires in a session, equally the indescribable value of tone and silence, indeed the embedding atmosphere of the intersubjective analyst-analysand field. This is the affect that Brennan has referred to where the "'atmosphere' or the environment literally gets into the individual" (2004: 1),[1] and which can be further extended to Bainbridge's claim that media objects are forces which "shape our lives and our attendant sense of self" (2012: 166). To specify its affective becoming, Bion posits that O is 'the unknown and unknowable' (1970: 27) emphasizing its felt and sensuous properties; the symbol O 'designates reality' (Bléandonu 1994: 200).

In 'Notes on Memory and Desire' Bion writes that the "only point of importance in any session is the unknown. . . . Out of the darkness and formlessness something evolves. . . . It shares with dreams the quality of being wholly present or unaccountably and suddenly absent" (1967: 136–7). In this short statement, Bion is laying down a most significant distinction that becomes specific to his use of the term 'transformation' and concept of O – the difference between knowing and becoming as an intuitive style of thinking. It is this difference particular to 'the experience (thing-in-itself)' that Bion denotes as the 'sign O' (1965: 13), which I later link to Winnicott's (1999) 'capacity to use an object'. Bion's primary concern is to theorize as well as identify the presence of a sensory reality that informs but precedes emotional experience. The complexity and possibility of O lies in *not* being able to know it, as a fact, thing, or even emotion, but rather we can only become it. "O does not fall in the domain of knowledge or learning save incidentally; it can be 'become', but it cannot be 'known'" (1970: 26). As it will hopefully emerge throughout the reading of this chapter, Bion's concept of O informs my conceptualization of 'being embedded' as a transformative process within moving image experience that evolves as a transformative becoming, contributing to the growing body of work that employs psycho-cultural approaches for the analysis of film and media.

The concept of O within moving image experience is, as Ambrósio Garcia states "made in and through the cinema, as well as at a certain distance from it" (2017: 57). Ambrósio Garcia rethinks the cinematic apparatus with Bion's concept of O, stressing its potential as a 'space of retreat' (2017: 56). She writes that Bion's O offers a challenge to the previous traditional film theory perspective on reality, noting that for Baudry (and Metz), much more attention was given to the creation of reality within and through the cinematic apparatus itself, rather than viewing "the impression of reality in the cinema [as] connected with the emotional links established through processes of projective and introjective identification" (2017: 56). The concept of O offers a way of conceiving moving image experience that exists beyond the apparatus and processes of identification, focusing much more on affective, sensory experience. O involves the spectator's multiple and varied experiences with moving images themselves "[the spectator] becomes the O that is common to himself [sic]" and the experience of thinking and feeling cinema beyond the site specificity of viewership that is '[common to] myself' (Bion 1970: 28); locating O as experientially ephemeral and elusive. Ogden writes "[w]e register experience (O) and are altered by it; we hold experience (O) in our being, not in our memory" (2004b: 291). Bion's emphasizes that sensoria and corporeality form emotional experience, again quite a different position from previous psychoanalytic theories that have been used to conceive of spectatorship, which concentrated on pleasure, illusion and fantasy (Kaplan 1990; Mayne 1993; Williams 1995; Elsaesser and Hagener 2015). In offering Bion's concept of O for a new theorization of the spectator, it is necessary to foreground the problems that exist with the 'interpretation' of the emotional experience of spectatorship.

Prior to *Attention and Interpretation*, Bion had established that the concept of O "cannot be known, loved or hated" placing O as beyond the categorization of specific emotions. O therefore was only able to be represented through mystical conceptions such as 'ultimate realty or truth', making 'interpretation' a problematic association with O. He writes that all "qualities attributed to O, the links with O, are all transformations of O and *being* O" (1965: 140) which he later terms as '*evolutions* of O' (1970: 27). O then includes all objects (people, places, things, emotions, spaces, times, etc.) within our lived experience that we are able to know (feel, think and dream). As evolutions of O we may not be able to know (feel, think or dream) their ultimate reality or truth, yet we are still able to know them in emotional experience. Put more simply, Bion saw the transformation of O to K (becoming to knowing) as the psychoanalytic communication of one's personality to another. O to K is Bion's attempt to identify the capacity to relate an unknown part of one's inner self to another person. Ogden impresses that O is not to be interpreted as a philosophical concept and that Bion intended it for use as a specifically psychoanalytic concept

(2004b: 293), but to my mind, this is so readers will not forget the sensoria and corporeality involved with O. As a specifically Bionian psychoanalytic concept, O relies on proto-mental emotional experience (as I have discussed in previous chapters, concurrent thinking and feeling). In the context of moving image experience, we can extend the concept of O to rethink our sensory capacity for dreaming (being, thinking, feeling) with emotions of people in different places, times, spaces, histories and cultures without the need for instruction on how to do so. Bion's O is a helpful concept then in developing Bainbridge's psycho-cultural theorization of 'media as psychological object[s]' (2012: 62) as it emphasizes the crucial role of transformation in the reasoning and desire behind our continued engagement with moving images. Let us look at the specific characteristic of O – its transformative capacity – to consider its potential for self-experience with moving images.

The importance of invariance in transformation

Bion claims that the transformative characteristic of O is 'becoming', that is to be at one in the moment of an encounter, here argued as the encounter with moving images (for Bion this occurs in the analytic session). He asserts it strongly, "[w]e can only have a K link with *transformations* of O" (Bion 1965: 152). Watching a film, a television program, engaging with social media, or playing a video game all varyingly involve encounters that move us psychically and physically. Their respective affections might be shared with friends, others might write about their experience, some may participate via fandom by creating memes, or we may simply re-present it to ourselves in self-reflection. As Symington and Symington (2008) put it, the core of the original experience forms part of the new expression and that this marks a transformation of the emotional experience of the first encounter. This is one of the potentialities of the moving image, its ability to offer sensory aesthetic material for transformative self-experience. Cinema and media use many formal rules of time, space, sound, light and perspective to create an audio-visual language that not only tells a story, but also creates affective aesthetic experience.

Bion begins *Transformations* with the following anecdote:

> Suppose a painter sees a path through a field sown with poppies and paints it: at one end of the chain of events is the field of poppies, at the other a canvas with pigment disposed on its surface. We can recognize that the latter represents the former, so I shall suppose that despite the differences between a field of poppies and a piece of canvas, despite the transformation that the artist has effected in what he saw to make it take the form of a picture, something has remained unaltered and on the *something* recognition depends. The elements that go on to make up the unaltered aspect of the transformation I shall call invariants.
>
> *(Bion 1965: 1, italics original)*

(This is similar to the story of Picasso when a spectator of his work berated him. The man accused Picasso of being a bad artist and that he should paint images that look like what they represent. He took out a photograph of his wife and said "like this . . . this is what my wife looks like". Picasso looked at it and said, after a long pause, "she is very small, and quite flat"). Bion uses the above example as a metaphor for the transformation that occurs within psychoanalytic experience as specific psychoanalytic knowledge. Transformation for Bion is something that has been altered, yet retains part of what it once was. It is not a complete change, but an alteration that includes an unchanged element. Symington and Symington interpret Bion's anecdote as showing the link between self-experience and transformation. They state, "an artificial blinding to what one knows, is necessary to convey the original experience with some accuracy" (2008: 106). This is similar to the 'evolutions of O' that Bion refers to, as one experience has evolved into another – the 'chain of events'. There are difficulties within Bion's analogy between real life and painting as a representation (rather than an interpretation and modification) of the external world. As Bléandonu has also noted, Bion disregards the challenge to the notion of truth in representation presented by photography and conceptual and abstract art, suggesting that even in the earlier stages of *Transformations* there are indications that the 'aesthetic solution' will not be sufficiently argued (1994: 197). However the notion of invariance is helpful in identifying unchanging elements in the before and after of psychoanalytic experience, and this is what I am using to consider a contemporary psychoanalytic approach regarding the before and after of emotional experience with moving images.

A sequence of moving images uses the rules of formal composition that create film language in order to create and convey meaning. Moving images, while clearly belonging to different media than painting, equally hold potential for psychic transformation, as they must depict emotional experience via a screen; emotional experience that must be realized and interpreted by audiences or individuals. Specific interrelationships between formal techniques (cinematography, lighting, sound, editing) are used to create a film grammar that is interpreted as cinematic language. Regardless of the moving image's immateriality, what is represented on screen, via artistic choices of time and space "something like prior knowledge has imposed itself and interfered with the accurate rendering of the original experience" (Symington and Symington 2008: 106). Bion wished to emphasize, via his italicized '*something*' that the transformation of which he speaks is a psychical process and necessarily involves elements that do not change; these are the invariants that he then seeks to explore via the metaphor of geometric form.

Rafael López-Corvo defines invariants as "specific characteristics of an object that, by remaining unaltered regardless of any transformation experienced by that object, will allow the identity of the object" (2005: 153). Whilst Bion's example refers to a painting, such medium specificity is not the relevant part of the anecdote. Instead, the observation of transformation, as a connection and as a process between what is real and belonging to the external world (the field of poppies) and the inner world that is emotional, sensory and interpretive (the recognition of poppies in the painting), is what is important. Bion viewed psychoanalysis as a series of transformations and that the analytic experience was formed through "the transformation of a realization (the analytic experience) into an interpretation or a series of interpretations", which Bléandonu has noted is the "fundamental thesis of [Bion's] second epistemological cycle" (1994: 197). The argument I am making here is that similar emotional experience is creatively known with moving images, which are realizations of the human condition and emotional experience that become the representations via images in film and television. Bion uses the concept of invariance to show how transformation is a progression of a "realization into an interpretation or series of interpretations".

Civitarese points out that Bion takes the term 'transformation' from the field of geometry and appropriates it for his psychoanalysis, "using it to stand principally for psychic transformation (for example, an emotion which gives rise to visual images and thought)" (2016: 1092). Bion's choice to use geometric terms to conceive a theory of psychoanalytic transformation is intentional. It furthers one of his fundamental premises discussed in the previous chapter, that emotional experience is not possible outside a relationship; for Bion, a line is a representation, a metaphor of a relationship "points and straight lines . . . are not things-in-themselves . . . [they] have to be described by the totality of *relationships* which these objects have to other objects" (Bion 1965: 2). It is another example of Bion's recurring strategy to take a familiar term and reposition it in such a way that it becomes defamiliarized. In doing so, it is hoped that the reader comes to Bionian psychoanalysis without memory or desire, meaning that they must free themselves of previous understandings and the fixity of other connotations and associations, allowing an open, intuitive sense of mind to receive how the terms are now being used and what they are being used for. Bion's use of geometric terms, such as point and line (and even the 'painting' in the above anecdote) in themselves do not mean anything specific. Rather, if we heed his warning and 'disregard' what he says, it is possible to view the use of such terms as being about relationships, more specifically as repositioning psychoanalysis as "being concerned with the relationships between objects" (Symington and Symington 2008: 108). Such geometric terms are another tactic Bion uses to show that psychoanalysis itself contains invariants, elements that remain unchanged and unknown.

We can say therefore that Bion's intention with the concept of O, and his work *Transformations*, is to postulate a critical, obscure, yet comprehensive theory for a psychoanalysis that centers emotional and affective experience. In part, the above painting example, whilst containing the specificity of what transformative self-experience aesthetically involves, additionally works as a metaphor for the invariants between Freudian, Klenian, Lacanian, Winnicottian and Bionian – all psychoanalyses – as well as the invariants within his own different stages of work. There are psychoanalytic elements that do not change (dreams, the analyst and analysand, emotions, objects, unconscious) but have been transformed through his own contemporary models. In drawing an analogy between the artist and the analyst, Bion involves a much broader link between theories of perception, expression and reception; the invariance of the self in lived experience permitting association and the linking of transformation to emotional experience.

Invariants are solely formal elements that do not change and yet cannot be known; they are also elements that are shared between people and within social and cultural experience. In part, invariants are purposeful as they refer to the unknown sensory impressions which are exchanged between people that lead to (and are essential for) psychic transformation. Invariants which are not recognized and are not shared do not result in transformative experience. This is because there must be an invariant in the before and the after – a relational, linking element – that effects transformation. Bléandonu states that Bion's metaphor of geometrical figures as invariants includes variations of transformation "including translation, rotation or projection" (1994: 196); and, like Symington argues, invariants can be determined as geometric forms that appear in one image and then again in another. Symington writes the

> invariant lies in the geometric relations that are manifest in the lakeland setting and in the painting. So there is an invariant and then the differing manifestations of it. The invariant exists in one form – the lakeland scene – and can be transformed into another – the painting on the canvas.
> *(Symington 2007: 272)*

This relates to Cartwright's point, which observes that scholarship on affect and aesthetics has related 'lines and colors' to our feelings.[2]

Further, Bion stipulates 'invariance under literacy' (1965: 3), claiming that in order for invariants to have any meaning or currency, there must be a hermeneutic competency that is shared, but not only as an interpretative aspect. There must also be a sharing of aesthetic form, "invariants in photography are not the same as invariants in impressionist painting" (1965: 3). A strength of the moving image is that its formal practices can apply to a range of audio-visual, time-based media. The cinematography (close-up, wide-angle, medium shot, etc.) does not need new configuration (that is a new 'language') for television, for example. A close-up denotes audience attention and narrative importance both in film and television. A variety of generic narratives and structures are shared across visual media using the same geometric and fundamental film forms – of light, the manipulation of space and time, the creating and illusion of depth and movement. Such formal techniques and elements of cinema make it possible for invariants to be shared across genres of cinema and visual media precisely because the same forms and phenomena are used. Yet to regard invariants only as geometric figures that serve to construct a visual, shared language would be to miss the entire enterprise of Bion's argument, and indeed the agenda behind his theory of transformations.

P.C. Sandler extends the metaphor of invariants stating that they are part of our personality and whilst transformations may be widely different, the invariants involved are not. He writes that myths (cultural narratives) "depict human invariants; they are methods of apprehending invariants devised by the group. Invariants are also specific to each individual to the extent that they characterise how each one's personality realises, structures, phantasises, or denies the species-specific invariants."

(Sandler 2009: 167). Roland Barthes's *Mythologies* (1972) informs Sandler's correlation between myth and human invariants. Myths, as Barthes argued, function as semiotic codes of cultural sense-making and what is shared here in this project with Sandler's interpretation of myth is the idea that the moving image exists as a virtual, projected space that contains the thoughts of a society ready to finder thinkers (spectators). For the psychoanalyst James Grotstein, emotion carries an invariant from one form over to its transformation. He writes: "emotions are slaves to (containers of) truth. Thus, truth [as a need to know] is the invariant, and emotion is its vehicle or container" (Grotstein 2007: 218). This recognizes Bion's use of invariance as a quality of transformation, to argue, "relationship and properties remain the same under a projection" (Symington and Symington 2008: 108).

It is significant that Bion wishes to couch the idea of 'transformation' in the context of a process despite using aesthetics and geometric form as his introduction. For Bion, the experience of transformation is much more about the communication of one's personality (what I later connect to Bollas's idiom) than it is about identifying specific formal qualities which solicit transformation. He places an emphasis on the *capacity* to relate an unknown part of one's inner self to another person – this is the process of O, how we use invariants within cultural myths to communicate our personality to another. This is the 'realization' that Bion speaks of when nominating O as something that cannot be known but is able to identified through transformative experience. We are able to 'share in something' (Bléandonu 1994: 199) of another's experience even though we may not have experienced the same thing ourselves. In the following example of Antonioni's *Blow-Up*, I explore how invariance might work within cinema as a stylistic and narrative process that informs the encounter with the moving image. I wish to foreground that transformation, as argued in the particular psychoanalytic sense, is not conscious or even always accessible to consciousness, nor is it always pleasurable or gratifying: "aesthetic moments are not always beautiful or wonderful occasions – many are ugly and terrifying but nonetheless profoundly moving because of the existential memory tapped" (Bollas 2011: 12). As we will see later with regard to Bollas's transformational object, the theory of transformation from an object-relations approach concentrates on the process of communicating one's personality to another, that is, it is a perceptual-based rather than desire-based process.

Antonioni's *Blow-Up*

As a counter to Bion's painting example, *Blow-Up* presents a different way of considering the role invariants play in the process of transformation. Bion's theory of transformations intended to focus on the experience of observation within psychoanalytic experience. He saw what transpired in the analytic situation (patient and analyst statements and even the psychoanalytic methods themselves) as representations of emotional experiences, and by understanding "the process of representation it helps us to understand the representation and what is being represented" (1965: 34). His theory therefore intended to highlight how a series of circumstances might lead to transformation that is mental growth. For growth to occur, the transformative process must incur frustration that can be tolerated by the individual (Bion 1962). The intent here is to use the premise of Bion's theory that views transformation as a process as well as an experience to consider what is invariant within moving image experience, as well as the films themselves (the apparatus and the film forms used) to facilitate spectator thinking and emotional experience.

Amelia Jones has noted that *Blow-Up* explored "structures of a modernist way of seeing and knowing" in cinema and that audiences are offered 'at least' a dual perspective throughout the film (2008: 185). She sees the duality existing in the parallel between Thomas (David Hemmings) and Antonioni as creative 'authors' of their photographic and cinematic work respectively; in the doubtful character of Thomas himself; and I add that the duality extends to the different gazes that the film effects through its cinematography (what we can also relate to Bion's binocular vision, discussed in Chapter 2). Antonioni plays with the audience's conditioned practice of film viewership, the dependence on narrative cinema and the lack of frustration that normally exists within such narrative films. He is specifically reflexive with photographic representation by exploring the act of looking and the dominance and control of the male gaze, which I argue, act as invariants within the film. Through the technique of the wandering camera (Chatman 1985) and realist aesthetic within both photographic and cinematic frames, Antonioni also effects a hermeneutic, receptive gaze that frustrates the audience by denying narrative resolution and therefore facilitates a transformative environment for the spectator through its intentionally challenging film style. The conflict between the types of gaze within the film works as a transformative function which frustrates the audience, facilitating a capacity for 'seeing differently' (Jones 2008).

Thomas, an arrogant fashion photographer with little morality, believes he has inadvertently photographed a dead body in a London park when taking illicit photographs of a couple for a documentary book project he is working on. On returning to his studio and enlarging the photographs, he thinks he can see this dead body in the photograph. Thomas interrogates his black and white photographs, establishing one of the gazes that we are presented with throughout the film, which Jones terms the 'photographic gaze' (2008: 185). Antonioni intermittently uses another gaze, the camera as narrative entity, what Jones calls the 'cinematic gaze' which I view as a disruptive structure. Jones states that the film's narrative is more innovative than its style, however I argue that interwoven points of view that consistently contradict each other throughout the film present a subtle reflexivity for the spectator, inviting them to doubt the dominance and authority of the male, that is Thomas's, gaze. These shifts in perspective represent further duality, or multiplicity within the film; the juxtaposition between Thomas's shallow commercial photography and the more artistic endeavor of documentary photography, which we see mirrored in the difference between the photographic and cinematic gaze.

Jones reads Thomas as both a 'figure of power' and 'disempowered' (2008: 185) through the lattice of gazes, using Lacanian theory to inform her argument. Whilst a Lacanian reading of power and the gaze offers a solid and articulate analysis of

Blow-Up, I am more interested in the pursuit of truth that Jones notes and how the film's form, predominantly its cinematography, enables a transformative environment for the audience. By observing cinematography as a process, we are able to understand the intentionality of the representation and what is being represented. Jones writes: "*Blow Up* is about chasing down the truth with the photographic apparatus, and within the photographic image" (2008: 186), noting that the idea of truth – the process and experience of finding it – is at the core of the film, but instead of interpreting Thomas's doubt and inability to resolve his frustration as potential for mental growth, she reads it as evidence for the 'charade' of the male gaze. This is why we should always be cautious of such declarations. It is a charade, but it is also equally 'about' the ambiguity of perception, the illusion and falsehood of existence, and the problematics of morality in private and public domains.

For Jones the "not knowing, or at least not knowing fully" (2008: 186) is not seen as transformative, at least not in the way that Bion intends it. Her argument is informed by classical psychoanalysis and therefore the gaze is observed and interpreted as sexual rather than relational, leaving the possibility of it being a 'need to know' as emotional experience unexamined, "the failure of the gaze is marked explicitly as a sexual failure; vision is thus enacted as sexualized" (Jones 2008: 187). Jones's analysis of *Blow-Up* is contrasted against Shezad Dawood's revisionist project *Make It Big* (2005), and her argument articulately concentrates on the power dynamic as it manifests between older and emergent structures of vision within media. In contrast, I see the structure of the gaze (cinematic and photographic) within *Blow-Up* as an invariant – the element that exists within the film that remains unchanged in order to effect transformation. This is not contesting Jones's argument, rather as invariants vary "according to style and technique", different theories and techniques will produce "as many different transformations" (Bléandonu 1994: 197). Through this contemporary Bionian model, an alternative interpretation of the function of truth and the gaze in the film becomes available.

The most significant of all Thomas's blow-ups is the very grainy image of what he believes is the dead body lying on the grass behind some bushes. As Thomas's prints become closer and larger images, their form, shape and appearance become more distorted the closer we get. Antonioni's formal use of this realist aesthetic is purposefully playful (again another duality within the film seen in the clash of realist and formalist tendencies (Gunning 1986)); indicative of André Bazin's 'immanent ambiguity of reality' (Aumont et al. 2009: 54) and Rudolf Arnheim's claim that "all perceiving is also thinking, all reasoning is also intuition, all observation is also invention" (Arnheim 1974: 5). The gaze functions as an invariant in photographic representation as it is an absent present structure of looking applied to both Thomas's photographs and our own viewing of the film. The form of the gaze has not changed, both the film and the photograph contain the same elements of looking, rather the blow-ups themselves highlight the difficulty in forcing interpretation, that is the complexity of power (for Jones) and need to know as emotional experience (for Bion) through the gaze. These enlarged pictures are extremely effective in demonstrating how invariants offer the promise of transformation by facilitating thought, the audience questions what it is that Thomas is seeing and therefore are self-reflexive of what they see.

As Jones notes, the doubt that Thomas (and subsequently the audience) begins to feel about the dead body is also a metaphor for the "supposed indexical 'truth' of the photograph"; yet to see it only as a comment on experience of the 'real *as* representation' (2008: 186) is to miss out on the other, more affective potential that the film offers. The difference here is that Bion's concept of O, as ultimate reality or truth, preexists our emotional experience, whereas for Jones, "the 'real' only exists in and through ... acts of representation" (2008: 187). *Blow-Up* does expose limits of the gaze, but instead of arguing that this is failure, I view it as a frustration that Antonioni intentionally creates, enabling us to consider what Thomas himself uses his photographs for. Instead of seeing (interpreting) the blow-ups as Thomas does, Antonioni's cinematic gaze allows us to think about what the blow-ups mean for Thomas. Both truth and the gaze can be read as invariants that facilitate transformative emotional experience, the textuality and ontology of the blow-ups are concurrent with their use as objects to create truth and meaning.

If we permit that only Thomas sees the dead man, then it is possible to ask why Thomas constructs the problem of the 'dead man' as a mystery to solve. Does Thomas uses the construction of the dead man in order to hide a truth about himself, a transformation that he seeks but cannot bring about within himself? His documentary book project is shown very briefly in a restaurant meeting with his editor at the start of the film; the images we are shown are black and white, realist and very different from Thomas's editorial fashion work (formalist, glossy, in color). This private project is an object as well as process of transformation for Thomas, we are never shown it in its entirety or even learn of its name or context; it is enough that we locate it as photography separate from his commercial work. As such, the use of photography in the film acts as an invariant, where the specific mechanism of photography has not changed, but its intention and modality of representation has. This places our relationship to Thomas and his work in a context of value derived from form; his detachment and disinterest from fashion increases our attachment and value (and therefore meaning) to his documentary work. Antonioni's intentionality (phenomenologically speaking) here is emphasized in the use of silence when Thomas studies his blow-up sequence. Through the cinematic gaze, we relate attachment and interest to Thomas's photographic gaze that acts as the invariant apparatus that mirrors our own, as it is the structure of looking that offers continuity between Thomas's photographic gaze and our own cinematic gaze.

In *Blow-Up*'s final scenes, Thomas participates in the mime artists' tennis match, running to pick up what appears to be the imaginary ball and throws it back to the players. The camera (as cinematic gaze) does not follow the ball; the ball remains only seen by Thomas, yet we close in on Thomas's face and hear the off-screen sound of a bouncing tennis ball. Antonioni offers resistance to the notion of truth in photographic representation, reminding us to challenge what we see and this is the frustration that the film's invariance provides allowing the audience to question the relationship between form, shape and appearance. By not allowing the camera to follow Thomas's return throw of the ball, Antonioni frees the spectator from verisimilitude, suggesting that Thomas has also begun to question what he sees in the photographs, confirming the ambiguity of the dead body. We have seen Thomas wrestle with his relationship to reality via his need to determine value and meaning through his use of various external objects in the film – fashion models, the camera, the propeller from the antique shop and the guitar from The Yardbirds concert. Even though Thomas is successful in obtaining all of these objects, his winning of the broken guitar is the most telling, as he ends up discarding it as soon as he sees it is no longer an object that others desire.

Jones interprets *Blow-Up* as being about the "failure of photographic representation to secure truth" (2008: 187) and therefore sees Thomas's doubt as an extension of this uncertainty and the film's inability to offer a stable 'subject of vision' (2008: 187). If viewed through the theoretical paradigm of invariance, I argue that the two gazes are used in the film to engender frustration in the audience, permitting an alternative interpretation of Thomas's struggle with his photographic problem of the dead body. The clash between the photographic and cinematic gaze within the film reveals our desire to know, that is the need for truth as an emotional experience, and this is the experience that offers Thomas a transformative self-experience. The 'object' that is the dead man photograph is the constructed problem that displaces Thomas's desire to leave the vacuousness of fashion, move to the 'more real' world of documentary photography (that is, his need to be taken seriously, for his work to have social rather than commercial value). Just as the fashion models struggle to gain validation through Thomas's commercial photographic gaze, so does Thomas struggle to find validation of his work through the documentary photographic gaze. It is Antonioni's ironic statement that meaning is created through taking up, playing with and discarding of forms, or what we might refer to as relationships between objects. The Yardbirds' guitar loses its significance and transformative capacity for Thomas because there is no invariance for its use outside the concert. Once outside, the guitar no longer offers transformation (or power as it becomes devoid of use and therefore desire) for Thomas, and so he discards it.

The invariance of the gaze in Antonioni's *Blow-Up* draws attention to the influence of external objects for transformative self-experience and in doing so resonates with Bion's theory of transformations and Bollas's transformational object. Both authors examine the use of objects in order to consider what it means to "live a life in the world of objects" (Winnicott in Bollas 1989: 26). In different ways, the prominence that Bion and Bollas give to object relations in their psychoanalytic thinking offers innovative ways of thinking about moving images and what it means to work with and through moving images. In the next section, I consider Bollas's transformational object and concept of the idiom alongside Bainbridge's psycho-cultural approach regarding the 'object use' of cinema that is the emotional work of cinema (2014), and television as a psychological object (2012) to further apply Bion's concept of O to study of the moving image.

The moving image as transitional and transformational object

An area of interest in this book has been the analytic field, that is, the intersubjective space formed in the interstitial relationships between analyst and analysand; here likened to the cinematic field, or more broadly, the shared cultural experience we have with moving images. This metaphor of the field, as argued in Chapter 4, is similar to Winnicott's 'potential space' or 'place where we live' (Winnicott 1999: 107; 104). Here Winnicott examines not only the 'places' where we experience life, but begins by identifying the difficulty in expressing and locating such experience. He refers to being '*in* a muddle', being '*at sea*', where home is 'a castle', and feeling happy is said to be '*in* a seventh heaven' (1999: 104, italics original). Winnicott makes note of such everyday expressions to draw attention to the use of language as a form that negotiates our inner and outer realities, but equally notes the inefficacy of clearly stating what is felt and where we feel it. Bainbridge has linked this articulation in intermediate space to "the creative dimension entailed in both making and consuming films" (2014: 55) and associates the emotional, creative work that transpires in Winnicott's potential space to the same emotional experience that occurs with our use of moving images. In a Bionian frame, this can be said to also highlight the difficulty and frustration that is involved with articulating embodied emotional experience and the transformative capacity of O.

As Lesley Caldwell (2013: xv) notes, Winnicott was interested in the "unconscious links between body, mind and cultural experience established in a mental space that emerges simultaneously with the materialization of the earliest sense of self", and that this intermediate space between us and others was where Winnicott saw our creative work developing via transitional phenomena. Kuhn's *Little Madnesses* (2013) discusses the significant impact Winnicott's theories on creativity and play have had in film and media scholarship, particularly emphasizing the object use of cinema. In Kuhn's edited work, Tania Zittoun argues that

> the use of films, which develops through cultural experience taking place in potential space, engages in a sort of creativity in which an individual may actually change her relationship with the two other spheres of experience: her inner life and her relationship with the external world.
>
> *(Zittoun 2013: 145)*

echoing Bainbridge's point that moving image objects, (her example is television), "can be used to facilitate an important (and perhaps therapeutic) space of working through" (2012: 156). As such scholarship suggests, there are many similarities that exist between the psychoanalytic approaches of Winnicott and Bion, particularly with respect to their view on the primary task of the individual, which each author sees as being about establishing relationships with others. Winnicott writes, it "is creative apperception more than anything else that makes the individual feel that life is worth living" (1999: 65). In this next section, I wish to focus on the specific point regarding the 'use of an object' where I see the ideas of Bion and Winnicott coming together, particularly as they contribute to previous study and use of the moving image.

In "The Use of an Object and Relations through Identification", Winnicott makes a distinction between object use and object-relating, where object-relating refers to a series of projections and identifications that allow "certain alterations in the self to take place" (1999: 88), and where object use however "must necessarily be real in the sense of being part of shared reality and not a bundle of projections" (1999: 88). In this distinction, Winnicott is making the argument that the use of an object must be seen to exist as a 'thing in itself' (1999: 88), to which we can link moving images as 'things in themselves' (see the previous chapter on Bion and phenomenology), and therefore as objects to be used in the service of a creative expression of a sense of self. Winnicott's 'use of an object' was written to refer to the analysand's using of the *analyst as an object* in order to develop a capacity to think through emotionally turbulent experience. The 'use of an object' then more specifically refers to the tools that are required within psychoanalytic experience to help develop a capacity that enables an analysand to dream, or think, by using the analyst as an object.

> In teaching, as in the feeding of the child, *the capacity to use objects* is taken for granted, but in our work it is necessary for us to be concerned with the development and establishment of *the capacity to use objects* and to recognize a patient's *inability to use objects*.
>
> *(Winnicott 1999: 87, italics added)*

Winnicott's 'capacity to use objects' and Bion's theory of thinking (specifically the alpha-function) each address the emotional experience involved in 'object use' and the expression of a "self able to engage with and make use of the world" (Caldwell 2013: xviii). Indeed, Winnicott's thesis on object use specifically refers to the development of a '*capacity* to use objects' (1999: 89), a capacity that is not innate but rather reflective of the 'maturational process' (1999: 89) that occurs within a facilitating environment (Winnicott 1965). This is similar to (but not the same as) Bion's work on the psychoanalytic function of the personality, which as discussed earlier, speaks to not only what is specifically communicated as a part of our inner world, but more importantly how it is communicated and what happens in the instance of our 'inability' to do so. It is beyond the scope of this chapter to discuss further connections between Winnicott and Bion on the 'inability to use objects' and incapacity to tolerate frustration respectively (such as their close attention on the psychotic parts of the personality (1999: 87)). For now, it is enough to note that the purchase of Winnicott's theory on the use of the object was to emphasize the "subject is creating the object in the sense of finding externality itself" and that "this experience depends on the object's capacity to survive" (1999: 91). I return to this within the context of HBO's television program *Westworld* later in the chapter.

Bollas extends Winnicott's 'capacity to use an object' through his notion of the 'transformational object' which he views more in terms of a process than object as it refers to the primary subjective experiential relationship the infant has with the mother. Bollas contends that prior to the formation of the transitional object, the infant-mother relationship establishes the foundational process of interaction and adaptation that leads to an experiential knowing of transformative self-experience within the 'environment-mother', "because for the infant, [the mother] is the total environment" (Bollas 2011: 1). Further, Bollas states that the mother offers an "aesthetic of being that becomes a feature of the infant's self" (2011: 1), referring to the highly sensory, tonal and behavioral exchange of non-verbal and gestural communication that occurs between infant and mother, which Bollas terms as the "idiom of gesture, gaze and intersubjective utterance" (2011: 1). This aesthetic of mothering is shaped in all her 'doing' for the infant (feeding, bathing, nurturing) which becomes the infant's being. In identifying the mother as transformational object, Bollas is recognizing that an ego memory is laid down in our pre-verbal lives that never leaves us; instead, it forms a platform for the sensoria of transformative self-experience that we seek though object use in later life.

The transformation that is discussed both within Bollas's and Bion's psychoanalytic models is not intended as a conscious awareness of how we feel, or even that the transformation(s) are knowingly satisfying (despite that we may come to be aware of it and their satisfactions). Winnicott's transitional object, Bollas's transformational object and Bion's concept of O are more focused on our capacity to use objects to alter our inner worlds in an unknown, mnemonic manner. Just as we cannot consciously recall the ways in which our mothers facilitated illusion and disillusion in infant life, neither can we be conscious of how objects in adult life will affect similar transformative self-experience. We just hope fervently that they can and they will. The moving image, as an 'environment-mother' provides illusions and disillusions literally and affectively, and while cinema and media might not directly mother us in such a way that occurs in early infant life, they certainly facilitate an environment wherein we are affected and respond experientially. The moving image offers its own idiomatic language of "gestures, gazes and intersubjective utterances" in the spaces it provides (via aesthetic experience including stillness, negotiation of experience, sound, image and temporality). The overall shared reality of the moving image is aimed at evoking ego memories that might lead to transformational experience of its audiences.

An aesthetic of being: *Westworld*

HBO's series *Westworld* (2016-present), created by Lisa Joy and Jonathan Nolan, garnered "an average of 12 million viewers across all platforms" making it "the most-watched first season of an HBO original series ever" (Andreeva, 2016). In line with Bainbridge's assertion that television is increasingly a barometer of "the emotional and psychological investments we make in our media consumption" (Bainbridge 2012: 154), *Westworld's* success across multiple media platforms highlights the popularity of themes that examine significantly emotionally turbulent experience and also reflect our desire to grow from such difficult emotional experience. Further, these two main themes of 'emotional turbulence' and 'desire to grow from it' are the narrative threads that occupy *Westworld* Season One, demonstrating that television fuels a therapy culture or in Bollasian terms works as a transformational object.

Set in the future, Westworld is an embodied immersive amusement park that offers 'omnipotence-without-cost' for its wealthy visitors in the American Wild West. Artificially intelligent (A.I.) 'hosts' play out interconnecting narratives for these guests who seek to live out their fantasies without legal retribution or moral penalty. Over the course of the first season, the relationships between the A.I. hosts are developed significantly more than the guests (except for the Man in Black (Ed Harris)), and we follow the evolution and growth in their consciousness. Despite it being a far cry from the analyst's room, the impetus for Westworld (both the televisual story world and the HBO program) is indeed transformative self-experience, as guests come to Westworld in order to live out their most 'violent delights', believing that such immersive and hedonistic experience will facilitate their truest self. Beyond this premise however, the show adopts an overt therapeutic structure, evident in its recursive storylines and mimetic therapy encounters between the A.I. hosts and their industry programmers and developers. It is possible to read the function of the A.I. hosts as what Arne Jemstadt (2011) has referred to as 'evocative objects', which include people, places, music, art or "something else that we encounter significantly in our everyday lives" (2011: xx). Jemstadt writes that the evocative object is sought out, often intuitively and that they "come from our inner world, a memory or feeling that surfaces deep inside us" (2011: xx) and in doing so, their evocativeness "release the self into being ... and facilitate the articulation of our idiom" (2011: xx). There are echoes here of Winnicott's use of an object as well as Bion's theory of containment and his concept of O precisely because the A.I. host object is seen to enable a 'becoming' of the guest's self. We are left with a sensorial evocation when we encounter the A.I. hosts. They are not human and in the same moment more human due to their evocative status. The hosts transcend the 'uncanny valley' because we witness them in relation to the human visitors. Somewhat ironically, it is the humans that betray the normative values of society – they are too cruel, too selfish, too driven by immoral egos. Perhaps the ultimate evocative object that transcends both A.I. and human is to be found in the final episode when Hector (Rodrigo Santoro) and Armistice (Ingrid Bolsø Berdal) show care, compassion and sacrifice for each other, all the while demonstrating the superhuman attributes of A.I.

An example of *Westworld's* recurrent therapeutic narratives is seen in its first episode where the A.I. hosts are experiencing faults in their recent upgrade. The hosts are brought into the Westworld programming facility and examined – not as one might expect via a wired, computational or technological sense – but more as an analytic encounter, being asked a series of questions. Dolores (Evan Rachel Wood), the oldest host in Westworld, is asked three questions: "Have you ever questioned the nature of your reality?", "Have you ever lied to us?" and "Would you ever harm a living thing?" Even further, Dolores is asked to tell a programmer what she thinks of 'her world'. Such questioning offers a mimesis of the psychoanalytic setting, although in *Westworld* there is a stronger concentration on the interrogation and expression of the A.I. hosts' idiom, that is, their specific perspective and relationship to their reality in Westworld. The show focuses on the intimacy of revealing one's innermost thoughts and 'true self' rather than on the fantasy of 'erotic transference' (Bainbridge 2012: 161). The mirroring of the analytic encounter is not limited to the interaction between hosts and their programmers. The director of Westworld, Robert Ford (Anthony Hopkins), is also shown as having many 'therapeutic encounters' with both his A.I. hosts and his staff. His therapeutic encounters adopt a nostalgic form, and in doing so Ford manages to construct a narrative basis in memory, underlining the essential feature of such encounters as being ultimately about how the past shapes and influences the present and the future. In this manner, Ford's exchanges harken back to Freud's conception of the mystic writing pad and repressed memories.

Bainbridge extends Roger Silverstone's (1994) premise that television works as a transitional object, arguing that audiences use television programs as objects in order to negotiate difficult emotional experience in everyday life. In Winnicott's (1999) original paper, the transitional object is both a material object (blanket, teddy bear) and (more importantly) the emergence of a capacity to use (that is think) the object. The object is a symptom for establishing a foundation and future capacity to think emotional experience in adult life, "It is not the object, of course, that is transitional" (Winnicott 1999: 14). Bollas refers to the transitional phase as the "heir to the transformational period" (2011: 2) as it represents the evolution of sensed, lived emotional experience to the expression of it. In this capacity the transitional object itself is an invariant – the object itself does not change but rather through the infant's capacity to use it creatively does transformative self-experience occur.

In this way, Bainbridge's consideration of television as transitional object improves on Silverstone's original argument as she begins to identify the idiomatic capacity of television programs as objects, observing the mimetic offering of creative use of space through the number of 'therapy shows' in the US, such as *The Sopranos*, also noting the socio-political context for the popularization of such shows. "We need to heed the cultural context in which a programme emerges, to see it as symptomatic of the popular cultural mode of any given moment" (Bainbridge 2012: 161; Bainbridge and Yates 2005). It is with respect to the latter aspect of Bainbridge's argument where Bion's concept of O, as an evolution of lived experience is crucial. Bion is concerned with how an analysand realizes emotional experiences, that is, how a capacity to use objects leads to a capacity to link inner and outer worlds. For Bion this the 'becoming of O' rather than the 'knowing of O' (the transformation of O to K). Inasmuch as the moving image cannot work as the analyst or indeed replicate the analytic situation, Bion's concept of O does enable us to speak to the affective experience that evolves from the potential space available through our encounters with moving images. This may give us a clue as to why the A.I. hosts in *Westworld* seem 'more' human or evocative of affect in a way that the human characters do not. In what can be identified as 'therapeutic stumblings', the A.I. hosts reveal a Bionian becoming of O, rather than the knowing of O. In doing so they are the aesthetic of being – transformational objects becoming (or struggling to become) subjects.

I identify the 'idiomatic capacity of television' here to highlight the very inexpressibility of what happens with our use of with moving images. This draws on Bollas's notion of idiom which is an extension of Winnicott's true self, where "the true self is an idiom of organization that seeks its personal world through the use of an object" (1989: 110), put another way, the idiom is "the defining essence of each subject, and, although all of us have some acute sense of the other's idiom, this knowledge is virtually unthinkable" (Bollas 1989: 212). Both Silverstone and Bainbridge write of the potential space of television and describe its promise as a psychological object; however, by only using Winnicott's notion of the transitional object little can be developed about the affective experience as Winnicott himself did not develop this line of thought (Bollas 1989: 9).[3] Central to Bollas's idea of the idiom is the "need to know and the force to become" (1989: 25), two compulsions (knowing and becoming) which are resonant of Bion's theory of transformation and the concept of O (which as noted above, is the primary narrative of the A.I. hosts in *Westworld*). Bollas clarifies that our idioms are not 'hidden scripts' of our unconscious (1989: 9), rather he specifies that each person has a unique set of possibilities that are able to be expressed via "lived experience in the actual world" (1989: 9). As such the evolution of our idiom depends precisely on the *specific* objects that we use, and extending this to use of the moving image, 'idiomatic capacity' or the 'idiomatic encounter', we can more accurately unpick the consequences and outcome of the "choices and uses of objects that are available" (1989: 10). Winnicott's true self, Bollas's idiom and Bion's concept of O, therefore, are all differing contemporary psychoanalytic models that designate the experience of object use rather than object-relating, and they offer powerful frameworks for future research on our capacity to use moving image objects, particularly in terms of the differences between types of moving images (such as television genres as well as the difference between cinematic or social media images). The 'idiomatic capacity' of the moving image is indicative of the affective character of Bion's concept of O as it too attends to the 'psychic movement' (Bollas 1989: 8) in transformative self-experience.

Notes

1 See Chapter 5 for a more depth discussion of Teresa Brennan's *The Transmission of Affect* (2004).
2 See Silvan Tomkins's discussion on 'affect-object reciprocity' in *Affect, Identity, Consciousness* volume 1 1962: 133) where he writes on the "freedom of object of the affect system" (133). He notes that more time has been spent on identifying stimuli of affect and not as much on the "mechanisms that determine affect". Tomkins also refers to Euclidean and non-Euclidean geometry as a metaphor of form for and feeling. As discussed in Chapter 2,

there are many points of connection between Bion and Tomkins on the question of affect and emotional experience. Here I wish to note that for both authors, the freedom of affect and its impact on the object embodies the potential for transformation (Bion) and motivation (Tomkins).

3 In later work, Bainbridge (2014) incorporates the Kleinian notion of projective identification and Bion's theory of container-contained in her analysis of the films of Lars von Trier.

References

Ahmed, S. (2014). *Willful Subjects*. Durham: Duke University Press.
Ambrósio Garcia, C. (2017). *Bion in Film Theory: The Retreat in Film*. Abingdon, UK: Routledge.
Andreeva, N. (2016). 'Westworld' Finale Hits Season High, Caps Most Watched First Season of HBO Series. *Deadline.com*. 5th December 2016. Web. 7th November 2017.
Arnheim, R. (1974). *Art and Visual Perception: A Psychology of the Creative Eye*. Berkeley: University of California Press.
Aumont, J., Berala, A., Marie, M. and Vernet, M. (2009). *Aesthetics of Film*. Translated by R. Neupert. Austin: University of Texas Press.
Bainbridge, C. (2012). Psychotherapy on the Couch: Exploring the Fantasies of in Treatment. *Psychoanalysis, Culture and Society*, 17, pp. 153–168.
Bainbridge, C. (2014). 'Cinematic Screaming' or 'All about my mother': Lars von Trier's Cinematic Extremism as Therapeutic Encounter. In Bainbridge, C. and Yates, C. (eds.) *Media and the Inner World: Psycho-Cultural Approaches to Emotion, Media and Popular Culture*. Basingstoke: Palgrave Macmillan.
Bainbridge, C., Ward, I. and Yates, C. (2014). *Television and Psychoanalysis: Psycho-Cultural Perspectives*. London: Karnac.
Bainbridge, C. and Yates, C. (2005). Cinematic Symptoms of Masculinity in Transition: Memory, History and Mythology in Contemporary Film. *Psychoanalysis, Culture and Society*, 10 (3), pp. 299–318.
Bainbridge, C. and Yates, C. (eds.) (2011). Therapy Culture/Culture as Therapy: A Media and the Inner World Special Edition. *Free Associations*, 62.
Bainbridge, C. and Yates, C. (eds.) (2012). Media and the Inner World: New Psycho-Cultural Perspectives on Psychoanalysis and Popular Culture. *Psychoanalysis, Culture and Society*, 17 (2), pp. 113–119.
Bainbridge, C. and Yates, C. (eds.) (2014). *Media and the Inner World: Psycho-Cultural Approaches to Emotion, Media and Popular Culture*. Basingstoke: Palgrave Macmillan.
Barthes, R. (1972). *Mythologies*. Translated by A. Lavers. New York: Hill and Wang.
Berlant, L. (2011). *Cruel Optimism*. Durham: Duke University Press.
Bion, W.R. (1962). *Learning From Experience*. London: Tavistock.
Bion, W.R. (1965). *Transformations: Change From Learning to Growth*. London: William Heinemann Medical Books.
Bion, W.R. (1967). Notes on Memory and Desire. In Spills, E.B. (ed.) *Melanie Klein Today: Developments in Theory and Practice, Vol. 1*. London: Routledge, 1988.
Bion, W.R. (1970). *Attention and Interpretation. A Scientific Approach to Insight in Psycho-Analysis and Groups*. London: Karnac Books.
Bléandonu, G. (1994). *Wilfred Bion: His Life and Works, 1897–1979*. Translated by C. Pajaczkowska. New York: Other Press.
Bollas, C. (1989). *Forces of Destiny: Psychoanalysis and Human Idiom*. London: Free Association Books.

Bollas, C. (2010). *Being a Character: Psychoanalysis and Self-Experience*. Hove, East Sussex: Routledge.
Bollas, C. (2011). The Transformational Object. In *The Christopher Bollas Reader*. Hove, East Sussex: Routledge.
Brennan, T. (2004). *The Transmission of Affect*. Ithaca and London: Cornell University Press.
Caldwell, L. (2013). Foreword. In Kuhn, A. (ed.) *Little Madnesses: Winnicott, Transitional Phenomena and Cultural Experience*. London: I.B. Tauris.
Cartwright, L. (2015). Affect. In Adams, R., Reiss, B. and Serlin, D. (eds.) *Keywords for Disability Studies*. New York: New York University Press.
Chatman, S. (1985). *Antonioni, or, the Surface of the World*. Berkeley: University of California Press.
Civitarese, G. (2016). Transformations in Hallucinosis and the Receptivity of the Analyst. *International Journal of Psycho-analysis*, 96, pp. 1091–1116.
Clough, P. and Halley, J. (eds.) (2007). *The Affective Turn, Theorizing the Social*. Durham: Duke University Press.
Elsaesser, T. and Hagener, M. (2015). *Film Theory: An Introduction Through the Senses*. 2nd edition. London and New York: Routledge.
Gregg, M. and Seigworth, G.J. (eds.) (2010). *The Affect Theory Reader*. Durham: Duke University Press.
Grotstein, J. (2007). *A Beam of Intense Darkness: Wilfred Bion's Legacy to Psychoanalysis*. London: Karnac Books.
Gunning, T. (1986). The Cinema of Attraction: Early Film, Its Spectator and the Avant-Garde. *Wide Angle*, 8 (3 and 4).
Hardt, M. (1999). Affective Labour. *boundary 2*, 26 (2), pp. 89–100.
Jemstadt, A. (2011). Introduction. In *The Christopher Bollas Reader*. Hove, East Sussex: Routledge.
Jones, A. (2008). Seeing Differently: From Antonioni's Blow Up (1966) to Shezad Dawood's Make It Big (2005). *Journal of Visual Culture*, 7 (2), pp. 181–203.
Kaplan, E.A. (ed.) (1990). *Psychoanalysis and Cinema*. London and New York: Routledge.
Kuhn, A. (ed.) (2013). *Little Madnesses: Winnicott, Transitional Phenomena and Cultural Experience*. London: I.B. Tauris.
López-Corvo, R.E. (2005). *The Dictionary of the Work of W.R. Bion*. London: Karnac.
Massumi, B. (2002). *Parables for the Virtual: Movement, Affect, Sensation*. Durham: Duke University Press.
Mayne, J. (1993). *Cinema and Spectatorship*. London and New York: Routledge.
Ogden, T. (2004a). On Holding and Containing, Being and Dreaming. *International Journal of Psychoanalysis*, 85 (6), pp. 1349–1364.
Ogden, T. (2004b). An Introduction to the Reading of Bion. *International Journal of Psychoanalysis*, 85, pp. 285–300.
Sandler, P.C. (2009). *A Clinical Application of Bion's Concepts: Dreaming Transformation Containment and Change, Vol. 1*. London: Karnac Books.
Sedgwick, E.K. and Frank, A. (1995). Shame in the Cybernetic Fold: Reading Silvan Tomkins. In *Shame and Its Sisters: A Silvan Tomkins Reader*. Durham: Duke University Press.
Shouse, E. (2005). Feeling, Emotion, Affect. *M/C Journal*, 8 (6). http://journal.media-culture.org.au/0512/03-shouse.php.
Silverstone, R. (1994). *Television and Everyday Life*. Abingdon, UK: Routledge.
Symington, N. (2007). *Becoming a Person Through Psychoanalysis*. London: Karnac Books.
Symington, N. and Symington, J. (2008). *The Clinical Work of Wilfred Bion*. London and New York: Routledge.

Tomkins, S. (1962). *Affect, Imagery, Consciousness, Volume 1, The Positive Affects*. New York: Springer.
Williams, L. (ed.) (1995). *Viewing Positions: Ways of Seeing Film*. New Brunswick, NJ: Rutgers University Press.
Winnicott, D.W. (1965). *The Maturational Processes and the Facilitating Environment*. New York: International Universities Press.
Winnicott, D.W. (1999). *Playing and Reality*. London and New York: Routledge.
Yates, C. (2010). *Emotion: New Psychosocial Perspectives*. Basingstoke: Palgrave Macmillan.
Zittoun, T. (2013). On the Use of a Film: Cultural Experience as Symbolic Resource. In Kuhn, A. (ed.) *Little Madnesses: Winnicott, Transitional Phenomena and Cultural Experience*. London: I.B. Tauris.

Filmography

Blow-Up (1966). Directed by Michelangelo Antonioni.
The Sopranos (TV Series: 1999–2007). Created by David Chase.
Westworld (TV Series: 2016–). Created by Lisa Joy and Jonathan Nolan.

8
BEING EMBEDDED
Rhizome, decalcomania and containment

Throughout this book, Bion's theory of thinking has been presented as an alternative psychoanalytic model for the study of moving image experience, more specifically looking at emotional experience with moving images. Each chapter has explored key elements of this theory, highlighting the divergence a Bionian approach presents to the consideration of cinematic experience, repeatedly presented as an alternative to the dominance of classical psychoanalytic frameworks employed in film and media studies. Laura Marks writes: "It can be argued that psychoanalytic explanations ultimately found meaning linguistically, rather than in the body, thus translating sensuous meaning into verbal meaning" (2000: 1), and at the time, this was an accurate assessment of how psychoanalysis was applied within cinema and media studies scholarship. With the growth in attention of Bion's work and all its revolutionary ideas in the clinical world, the time has come in cinema and media studies to view psychoanalysis in plural terms, noting the significant amount of material that not only attends to sensory, emotional experience but also foregrounds it as a core concern. Psychosocial and object relations approaches (Bainbridge and Yates 2005; Bainbridge, Ward and Yates, 2014; Bainbridge 2012; Yates 2010, 2015; Kuhn 2013; Ambrósio Garcia 2017; Piotrowska 2015) have paved the way for a stronger relational turn in psychoanalytic theory for the study of the moving image, making new forays into the development of a more visible psychoanalysis that addresses affective emotional experience with moving images.

By bringing Bion into dialogue with other thinkers on the topics of sensory experience, affect, memory and phenomenology, the aim has been to create a series of scholarly associations that may lead to future interpretations and further applications of Bionian psychoanalysis in film and media studies. This project is in part driven by the similarities between Bion and the other thinkers discussed throughout the book that extended beyond shared theoretical emphases. There were similarities in their philosophies of conceiving and presenting ideas, in writing style, and in their respective overall resistant positions to specific disciplinary parameters. Most significantly, when the classical model of psychoanalysis was recontextualized with Bion's more contemporary version, many themes between the various authors did not seem so very different in agenda. In this final chapter and in continuance of this spirit, a line can be drawn to Gilles Deleuze's and Felix Guattari's *A Thousand Plateaus: Capitalism and Schizophrenia* (2014). Brian Massumi notes in his introduction to their work that Deleuze and Guattari hoped "elements of [their book would] stay with a certain number of its readers and will weave into the melody of their everyday lives" (2014: xiv). Here we can see the similar intention in Bion's work discussed in the previous chapter, regarding his concept of O where he suggested readers 'disregard' all that he said until the experience (O) of reading had evolved. The intention has been therefore, to not only highlight points of convergence between such areas of thought that are concerned with similar themes, but to also acknowledge similar techniques and perspectives regarding processes involving the linking and transmission of affect, which further my conceptualization of 'being embedded' within moving image experience.

The question posed at the start of this book was to see if Bion's theory of thinking could be used as a fruitful model to further thinking on the intersubjective 'spectator-moving image' experience. I have shown the different emphasis Bion places on emotional experience as offering a way to think about our use of moving images as an embedding, dreaming practice, which in many ways is used here to address the intention and the experience, as well as the consequence of object use of the moving image. This final chapter continues this project by bringing Bionian ideas in dialogue with other thinkers to highlight the rhizomatic potential of the concepts constitutive of his theory of thinking and for exploring sensory spectatorship experience. In light of this, Deleuze's and Guattari's concept of rhizome and its specific principle of decalcomania is used to further Bion's theory of containment as a model to consider moving images as rhizomatic reverie experience. Whilst much of this chapter focuses on the theoretical similarities between rhizome, decalcomania and Bion's theory of thinking within the context of moving image experience, toward the end of the chapter I discuss Richard Linklater's *Boyhood* (2014) as an example of rhizomatic film form and content, and consider how Bion's theory of containment offers a psychoanalytic theory of affect regarding spectatorship.

Reverie as space and rhizome

In the previous chapter, Bion's metaphor of geometric form was discussed within the context of transformation and the concept of O, the sensory experience (thing-in-itself) he termed 'becoming'.[1] In the second chapter of *Attention and Interpretation*, Bion continues to use the metaphor of geometric form to outline the problems within the act of interpretation (specifically the analyst's interpretation) which he discusses in terms of space. He writes (1970: 8):

> [a patient's statement] can be considered as a statement or as a transformation; as multi-dimensional or multi-faceted; it could be represented by a visual image of a figure in which many planes meet or lines pass through a common point. I can represent it to myself by a visual image of a geometric solid with an infinite number of surfaces. It depends on a realization, derived from space, of sensuous experience. The attempt to externalize the visual image is restricted as if the representation by points and lines was itself a 'space' too restricted to 'contain' the visual image; thus, has breadth whereas the mental visual image of a line or a point has not.

On first reading, it seems as though Bion is outlining the specific physical space that exists in the analytic situation through lines, points and space. Later he clarifies that this metaphor is better understood as representing emotional mental life, more specifically the relation between thought and emotional experience. Mental space, for Bion, was a thing-in-itself and unknowable (1970: 11), and it is here we begin to see space as possessing more processural rather than limiting physical qualities within a Bionian frame.

This focus on interpretation within the context of spatial aesthetic processes was crucial for the formation of Bion's container-contained model as the attention on three-dimensional space was the foundation for conceiving of relationships between objects, people and therefore emotional experience (1970: 5). This emphasis on three-dimensional space was Bion's way of indicating how experience, sensuous and emotional, is put or rather projected into people as though they have the 'space' to contain it. The penumbra of the term space is problematic in that its connotation of space-as-physical-vessel supersedes the intended 'space-as-process' character Bion assigns to containment. He writes that projective identification has

> been formulated in terms derived from a realization of the ordinary man's (or woman's) idea of three-dimensional space. The usual Kleinian formulations depend on a visual image of a space containing all its objects. Into these objects in this space it is supposed that the patient project parts of their personality that they have split off.
>
> *(Bion 1970: 8)*

As I have mentioned, Bion uses Klein's theory of projective identification as a foundation for his own theoretical evolution, the container-contained model, yet diversifies the function of projective identification by seeing it as a more positive connection through which he developed his notion of reverie, more specifically the mother's capacity for reverie (1962). I return here to the notion of reverie to further argue its potential as a crucial concept that rethinks our relationship and use of the moving image object and therefore of moving image experience. Reverie, as is argued here, illuminates the strong rhizomatic activity of emotions within moving image experience, which is essential to transformative self-experience and containment that I equate with 'being embedded' within affective, moving image experience.

Ambrósio Garcia has also made the case that projective and introjective identification are the psychical mechanisms that facilitate strong emotional links in cinema between subject and screen. She writes,

> [l]inks are destroyed when the emotions they carry are too powerful to be contained, but if the working of reverie allows the subject to contain, investigate and assimilate these emotions, cinema could be seen as thoughts searching, and finding, a thinker.
>
> *(2017: 44)*

Her claim is that by viewing cinema as a retreat, we are effecting the primary, originary retreat (between infant and mother) into our internal worlds. Cinematic experience transcends the auditorium, referring much more to the spatialization of our experience with moving images. Such moving image experience can be viewed as a rhizomatic and containment process, particularly if containment is understood as providing the mental space and capacity to think and feel turbulent thoughts-in-themselves which are unknowable. As a psychoanalytic model, the container-contained reorients the previous motivation placed on spectatorship, moving it away from immediate gratification and pleasure, and more toward an affective "motivation that lies in the possibility of emotional growth" (Symington and Symington 2008: 55). Additionally, the container-contained model, as will be discussed later, speaks to the importance of providing spectators with the physical and psychical space to experience challenging affective aesthetics so that emotional growth may occur.

Bionian psychoanalysis, being much more concerned with affective and sensuous experience, speaks to Tomkins's freedom of affects. He writes, "any affect may have an 'object'. This is the basic source of complexity of human motivation and behavior" (1962: 7). The freedom of affect that Tomkins notes is resonant of the freedom of reverie in Bion's notion of containment. Eve Kosofsky Sedgwick, following Tomkins, writes that affects "can be, and are attached to things, people, ideas sensations, relations, activities, ambitions, institutions, and by any number of other things, including other affects" (2003: 19), noting that there is no rule to the linking of affect to experience – positive or negative – or even over time. Bion's theory of thinking similarly extends a freedom to sensory lived experience – his beta-elements – which like Tomkins's affects, preexist us. It is not that affects stick to people, but rather that objects incite affective responses. In Chapter 2 I noted Cartwright has argued a "nuanced model of affect" (2008: 46) and speaks more effectively to the intersubjectivity and transience of affect; on the freedom of affect-object reciprocity, she elaborates, "[t]he object to which I impute a characteristic may evoke affect, but the evocation of affect may in turn restructure the object within the terms that I seek" (2008: 46). Whilst Cartwright reads this restructuring in terms of desire and pleasure, I view it more within a Bionian desire of a 'need to know', that is knowing as emotional experience. Within film and media theory, the image may cause and be a condition of desire for the spectator (as Cartwright sees it) but it also offers the spectator space to enact the containing function through a capacity *to reverie*. Bion's notion of reverie as a facilitator of containment offers a particular emphasis on the motivation within spectatorship experience, as it suggests that when we watch moving images we are in search of transformation that develops our capacity for tolerating frustrating emotional experience, unconsciously of course.

Ferro writes that within the analytic field, both analyst and patient engage "in an ongoing *baseline activity of reverie* . . . and *baseline projective identification*, which is the indispensable engine of any reverie activity" (Ferro 2009: 1), referring to the constant processing of sensoria in lived experience. Reverie, framed as a capacity that enables and facilitates dreaming, "is the cornerstone of our mental life" (Ferro 2009: 1), and evoked as an intersubjective field of three-dimensional space, one that identifies an interpersonal receptivity not unlike Marks's ambivalent 'sense knowledges' (2000: 238) that occur in audiences of intercultural cinema. As P.C. Sandler notes, Bion verbalizes the term reverie in its first theoretical introduction "*in the psychotic we find no capacity to reverie*" (Bion 1959 in Sandler 2005: 643, italics original), noting its processural quality. Further, Sandler notes that reverie is also a mitigating factor in the "transformation from material to immaterial" (2005: 643), locating reverie as a core function for dreaming in the processing of lived experience. It is an action that is never complete and whose efficacy is entirely dependent on linking affective sensory experience.

Later I view Bion's theory of containment (made possible by reverie) as an evocation of space that works as a process, specifically a rhizomatic process within moving image experience. This is to interpret 'being embedded' as a process, that is never completed and which is argued to be rhizomatic in character. The embedding that occurs with our use of moving images is argued to replicate the containment made possible through baseline activities of reverie and projective identification that originally occurred between the mother and infant. I will argue that the capacity to think and dream made possible by the mother's reverie is simulated in cinematic experience, explored via Bion's theory of containment and Deleuze's and Guattari's concepts of tracing and rhizome which are governed by the interrelated field (spatial) concepts of time, territory and surface. In this sense, we can connect Bion's conception of reverie with Deleuze's and Guattari's notion of rhizome, which function as both noun and verb. As a noun, reverie denotes the capacity to think and dream, identifying the co-constructed open, intuitive and intersubjective relationship between mother and infant; as a verb, it speaks to the psychic movement of projective identifications (through sharings and splittings) that engineer the activity of reverie.

'Being embedded' with moving images illuminates the potential of Bion's theory of thinking for the study of spectatorship experience as it relates to and engages with cinematic affective, aesthetic experience. In coining the phrase 'being embedded', the goal was to foreground the physical and psychical sensations present in the O of moving image experience and to clarify the predominant attention Bion gives to the sensory affective experience in 'theory of thinking' – not easily ascertained in its phrasing. A 'theory of thinking' does not readily imply the vital role of relationships in determining emotional experience, nor does it immediately suggest strong attention on sensory lived experience. As scholarly attention continues to explore the relationships between body, image and affect, Bion's ideas on thinking as a proto-mental experience are also about our wider relationships (conscious and unconscious) to psychic pain, suffering, frustration, tolerance and satisfaction. In *The Senses and the Intellect* (1864: 198) Alexander Bain described sensation as being embedded in movement, underlining 'embeddedness' as something that is in-between, or at the very least relational and engaged in an action and feeling that links one object to another. As I have explored throughout this book, thinking (for Bion) works affectively as an apparatus that can be said to permit the experience of 'being embedded', particularly if we are reminded of his theory where sensual lived experience (beta elements) precedes thoughts (alpha elements) as felt sensation and the thinking process (alpha function) as the psychic movement of sensation.

Bion's theory of thinking is significantly more than the identification of inner mental activity as a negotiator of everyday life and our external worlds. It is also a way to position and talk about the intersectional and embodied experience of psychic tension as emotional experience, and what role such tension plays in mental and emotional growth. If we are able to think/feel thoughts in the Bionian sense, then we are able to tolerate frustrations and (hopefully) diffuse them. Bléandonu writes that the "capacity to think facilitates deferment and the toleration of the waiting time between the moment at which a desire is experienced and the moment when appropriate action can bring satisfaction" (1994: 146). Such negotiation of inner desires and external worlds reflects a rhizomatic approach to how we connect affect, thought, and body. Civitarese has argued that Bion's psychoanalytic theory of reverie has restored "the body to the mind, [overcoming] the mind-body dualism, and frames a convincing model of how emotions record almost like the sensitive tips of a seismograph, the slightest vibration of the body immersed in its natural medium" (2014: 145). Bionian psychoanalysis, whilst attendant to the importance of emotional turbulence for psychic growth, can also be considered as a series of primary and secondary affective tracings that sometimes become known in order for a thought to be realized, and which are sometimes not known but necessary for emotional experience (beta elements). These 'thought tracings' place pressure on the psyche "to think because [the psyche] comes across thoughts that pre-exist it" (Bléandonu 1994: 146). Bion's use of geometrical forms was equally invested in identifying space as a physical experience and an emotional experience, that is, to theorize the interrelationship between space and form as a way to think differently about the spaces that emotional experiences leave within us. Consequently, such thinking on the interrelationships between material, emotional and experiential space echoes the distinction Deleuze and Guattari make between cartography and decalcomania regarding their concept of the rhizome.

Rhizome

Deleuze and Guattari assign six criteria to the configuration and mechanics of the rhizome. These include principles of 'connection and heterogeneity'; 'multiplicity'; 'asignifying rupture'; and 'cartography and decalcomania' (2014: 7–12). Claire Colebrook writes that the rhizomatic method necessarily involves chaos and also repeats Deleuze's and Guattari's use of geometry to characterize the nature of the rhizome, "any point can form a beginning or a point of connection for any other" (Colebrook 2002: xxviii). She goes on to specify that the paradox or 'opposition in their thought' is essential to the diversity and plurality particular to both rhizomes and a rhizomatic method. Ian Buchanan, in his correlation of the rhizome with the structure of the internet, views the rhizome as "not manifest in things, but [is] rather a latent potential that has to be realized by experimentation" (2007: n.p.), that is the rhizome – wherever and whatever space, time, territory or surface it finds itself – must be constructed, or, put in Bionian terms, linked as emotional experience. "The rhizome is the subterranean pathway connecting all our actions, invisibly determining our decision to do this rather than that . . . [it is] in this sense a therapeutic tool" (2007: n.p.). In such definitions of the rhizome, what becomes most apparent are the qualities of paradox (frustration), linking, intersubjectivity and growth – very similar to the concepts that underpin Bion's theory of thinking and of Ferro's baseline activity of reverie. The rhizome, like reverie, is non-linear and intuitive in its linking of time, territory and surface.

Regarding the final principles of the rhizome, Deleuze and Guattari introduce the metaphors of tracing and map (termed decalcomania and cartography respectively), which they then liken to the classical structure of psychoanalysis – Freud's unconscious-conscious model. As Symington and Symington have noted, Bion rejected this unconscious-conscious schema (2008: 9), electing to develop his theory of thinking that privileged transformational processes, that permit "translation, rotation or projection" (Bléandonu 1994: 196) of emotional experience over unconscious-conscious in order to achieve awareness (or self-consciousness) of the ultimate reality, O. This transformation is indicative of mental growth and the use of thought in an aware, self-reflexive manner wherein we are able to know 'truth'. Bion's move away from unconscious-conscious is not a rejection of the Classical Freudian model, rather it shifts the emphasis of psychoanalysis to the importance of self-consciousness in the reflection of emotional experience in order to facilitate transformation, which Chapter 7 discussed as altered self-experience. In choosing to move beyond the unconscious-conscious dynamic, Bion highlights a process of exchange that "allows conscious lived experience to be altered in such a way that it becomes available to the unconscious for psychological work (dreaming)" (Ogden 2004: 1356). Therefore Bionian psychoanalysis did not tie "its fate to that of linguistics" (Deleuze and Guattari 2014: 13), but much more to the sensoria of affect in lived experience. Bion's divergent conception does not specifically refute the principles of tracing and map in Deleuze's and Guattari's rhizome – instead it affirms Colebrook's observation of the necessity of the paradox to the rhizomatic method. However, it does challenge the location of 'psychoanalysis' (as a homogenous field and method) as a tracing and suggests a reconsideration of its rhizomatic potential.

Deleuze and Guattari argue that the rhizome is "a map and not a tracing", which they distinguish by viewing the map as "entirely oriented toward an experimentation in contact with the real" (2014: 12). Their view of the map, it must be pointed out, is used equally as a tangible object and conceptual device to privilege creative engagement and interactive thinking over the copying and limitations found in the act of tracing; a map links you to other places but you must determine the pathway of getting there, whereas traceable images do not offer such creativity. The map "does not reproduce an unconscious closed in upon itself; it constructs the unconscious"; further they state that "*the tracing should always be put back on the map*" (2014: 12–13, italics original) which parallels Bion's theory of thinking, wherein he argues that thoughts (as transfers or tracings of sensory lived experience – beta elements) need to be "put back into" the psyche for thinking and dreaming (alpha elements into alpha function).

The rhizome has been a popular trope in academic discussion for some time, particularly within media studies, perhaps not surprisingly because the rhizome trope offers a deterritorialized method for the development and bringing together of different areas of thought (what Deleuze and Guattari would call an 'assemblage' (2014: 333–34)), but possibly too because much of academic craft is the assembly of arguments using relevant scholarship within related disciplinary fields. Deleuze's and Guattari's rhizome is as much about how we link things together – space, time, territory, affect, thought, emotion, – as it is about being a tangible, subterranean system. Bionian psychoanalysis can be read as rhizomatic and fractal, as his theory of thinking, attacks on linking (inability to think thoughts) and his theory of container-contained employ similar cartographic and tracing principles in outlining the process of linking sensory, lived experience to the activity of thinking and dreaming.

Decalcomania

Deleuze and Guattari begin *A Thousand Plateaus* with a mission statement that rejects totalizing linearities and emphasizes the necessity of thinking as "lines of flight, movements of deterritorialization and destratification" (2014: 3), another similarity to Bion's vertex that an emotional experience cannot exist outside of a relationship. In spite of their critique of classical psychoanalysis, there are a number of resonances within their rhizomatic technique with Bion's theory of thinking. Their notion of the rhizome as a 'line of flight' can be thought of as tracing-as-linking with the specific aim of locating rhizomes as a practice of 'embedding' in both inner and outer environments, as well as linking relationships with others. In the context of moving image experience, both rhizome and containment offer a framework for considering the intersubjective and affective relationships that might emerge between audience and image, moving beyond textual analysis and looking more to how affective psychical and physical responses are indicators of capacity to tolerate emotional growth.

The appeal of using Deleuze and Guattari's concept of rhizome as a discussion on the function, assembly, and affect of thoughts and thinking in the Bionian sense, is that two conceptualizations are presented within the same frame: decalcomania (to trace, to follow) and cartography (to map, to create). Decalcomania is defined in the *Oxford English Dictionary* as "a process or art of transferring pictures from a specially prepared paper to surfaces of glass, porcelain, etc." As a tracing process, it also identifies and brings together – via either attachment or impression – two surfaces, two territories, in order to produce a third. When connected together, these surfaces support the aim of decalcomania, which is to create a new 'fractal' image that could not be determined or reproduced again in exactitude. Deleuze and Guattari use decalcomania and cartography as separate qualities of the same principle in order to foreground the phenomena of thought and form within rhizomatic nature, present in experiences of thinking and becoming.

Decalcomania, as a rhizomatic action and process that involves tracing, transference and iteration (repetition of effects), allows us to think about the transfer or tracing of affective aesthetic experience with moving images. As a formal artistic technique, it is concerned with the interrelationships between space and time, and the transferences that occur in-between. On a more interpretative level, decalcomania is one way to identify the affect present and operative in and through the intersubjective connections that are formed and sustained between objects (of time, of territories and of surfaces), and between physical bodies and psychical selves. When we use moving images, we respond by making meaning of the narrative of their story-worlds, but we also observe and are affected by the unspoken, ineffable tracings that occur between characters, scenes, sounds, scores, dialogue and lightings. Our bodies become tense, warmer and more alert in watching horror films; they become looser, more relaxed when we laugh (see Soler (2014) who discusses the function of laughter as release from the search for meaning). We cry when we watch melodrama; or difficult films can put us in difficult moods. Such emotional responses, I argue, are examples of (or abstractions of) decalcomania, that is the transference that occurs between such spaces which affect our bodies and minds.

There is something additional to be gained by linking Deleuze's and Guattari's conceptualization of decalcomania within the context of affective emotional experience, particularly in terms of how affect is relative and fractal to embodiment and containment, in the experience of becoming (O). Decalcomania looks at the place and significance of surfaces, transferences and attachment, implying that 'being embedded', or the experience of becoming (O), involves iterable affects, "there are very diverse map-tracing, rhizome-root assemblages, with variable coefficients of deterritorialization" (Deleuze and Guattari 2014: 15). Sedgwick and Frank write of such affect tracing in their experience of reading Tomkins's work, "*Affect Imagery Consciousness* isn't least affecting for the traces it bears of an intensively problematized verbal process" (2003: 95). They write of their own affected, embodied response to learning Tomkins's work as 'becoming addicted', and which is tiring but full of growth (2003: 95). Their learning and experience of Tomkins's affect theory is written as a rigorous account of falling in love with an author's work, "[w]hat does it mean to fall in love with a writer?" (2003: 117), a literary decalcomania that transfers the abstract pursuit of learning to the affective aesthetic experiencing of enjoying the material.

There are similarities to be drawn in the decalcomania of moving image experience, which can be noted in the scholarship discussing cinephilia – the love for cinema and falling in love with the image (de Valck and Hagener 2005; Rosenbaum 2010; Balcerzak and Sperb 2012). Sedgwick and Frank state "[a]ny theory, to be a theory – to at least partially or temporarily specify a domain – requires or produces figure ground relations, the function of which Tomkins calls the "cognitive antenna" of a theory" (2003: 116). The 'working with' moving images is what I am regarding as a type of decalcomania, where such images and the emotions they portray are able to be seen as transferable and traced affective objects. 'Being embedded' is a theory that aims to 'partially or temporarily' specify the affective domain of working with moving images within a particularly Bionian psychoanalytic frame – not to the exclusion of other approaches – but to offer a 'cognitive antenna' for a psychoanalytic affect model for moving image experience. The acts of observing and looking are real, often immaterial, linking of surfaces that engender affect and as Gibbs notes the "power of the image lies in part in its speed of reach" (2013: 252). The rhizomatic, reverie gaze of the moving image operates as both a deterritorializing and reterritorializing of sense knowledges in aesthetic experience. Whilst Deleuze's and Guattari's rhizome offers external visual cartographic examples, Bion's theory of thinking and Tomkins's affect theory (there is still much work to be done on the associations between these thinkers) introduce an internal decalcomania (tracing) of mental and embodied space and experience.

Sara Ahmed has stated:

> Thinking of affects as contagious does help us to challenge an "inside out" model of affect by showing how affects pass between bodies, affecting bodily surfaces or even how bodies surface . . . to be affected by another does not mean that an affect simply passes or "leaps" from one body to another. The affect becomes an object only given the contingency of how we are affected, or only as an effect of how objects are given.
>
> *(Ahmed in Gregg and Seigworth 2010: 36)*

Whilst Ahmed does not specifically use the term 'decalcomania', her position on 'contagious affects' (see also Gibbs 2001) similarly acknowledges the inherent characteristics of tracing and transference. As a practice and as a purpose, decalcomania helps to address how affective experience is to be found in the pulling apart (as much as the coming together) of the surfaces that create new images (experiences) or patterns. Decalcomania identifies the central aspects of transfer from one surface, time or territory to another, so that whatever has been transferred might be experienced differently, or invite a different vertex (point of view). Cartography differs because it is fixed (or attempts to fix); possessing a certitude that both articulates and claims space. This is why Deleuze's and Guattari's rhizome must include both elements of tracing and mapping in order to effect its 'antigenealogy', "without an organizing memory or central automaton" (2014: 21). Moving image experience puts us in the in-between of our figurative and literal environments; our dreaming with moving images links the traces and contours of our thoughts with our affective lived experience.

Negative capability

An active appropriator of other's concepts, Bion often implicitly practiced rhizomatic thinking in the development of his affect-focused theory of thinking. In addition to the appropriation of geometric forms, Bion also used John Keats's notion of 'negative capability' (1970: 25) to suggest one of his more controversial revisions of psychoanalytic practice, which was for the analyst to divorce expectation and control in the interpretation of analysis. Being the last chapter in *Attention and Interpretation*, it is safe to see this as Bion throwing down a gauntlet for psychoanalytic practice. Bion believed that interpretation, more specifically a belief in one's own capacity to interpret (to understand) was symptomatic of control and interfering with any possibility of becoming (O) in analysis. He used Keats's term 'negative capability' – "when a man is capable of being in uncertainties, mysteries, doubts, without any irritable reaching after fact and reason" (Keats in Bion 1970: 125) – to continue his practice of defamiliarizing the reader, which I argue can also be viewed as a practice of decalcomania – the transference from one (conceptual) territory to another; but also to introduce a new modality of psychoanalytic life and practice. Negative capability, for Bion, was to remove any sense of expectation from the circumstance and event of the analytic situation, and attend more specifically to open, intuitive observation and be reflexive about the significance of observation. This included paying attention to any wandering of mind that occurred within analysis – what we can locate as rhizomatic reverie – as this is what Bion perceived to be one of the most attentive and productive elements of psychoanalysis. Furthermore, it removed the 'arborescent' infrastructure of the subject who is supposed to know, and placed psychoanalysis more in line with dreaming and the concept of O. This is because, for Bion, memory and desire belong to sensuous experience that cannot be known, only felt. The desire to interpret is seen as an inhibition on any potential for psychic growth in the analytic situation. Bion's negative capability echoes Deleuze's and Guattari's rhizomatic 'antigenealogy' as it also argues that becoming (O) can only occur "in the state where there is NO memory, desire, understanding" (1970: 129).

Using Bion's notion of negative capability, Ambrósio Garcia asks what might such a state of cinema be, arguing that an experience might be possible if a spectator encounters a film without "deliberate attempts at remembering . . . but is still open to thoughts unbidden, that is evolutions" (2017: 61). For Bion, this would mean being attentive to all the reveries that occur within the experience of the film and reflecting on their significance in the moment of their emergence. Such intuitive receptivity with moving images would mean that the "emotional experience of the present [would] lead to contact with the ultimately real" (2017: 61), returning us to the conjoining of corporeal and psychical affective, sensuous experience.

Time, territory and surface

The usual example given for the rhizome is the literal grass rooting, prostrate structure. The botanical definition being "an elongated, usually horizontal, subterranean stem which sends out roots and leafy shoots at intervals along its length" (*OED*). The analogy of grass as rhizome acknowledges the tangible aspect of rhizomatic life – that is, how things appear to fit and grow together in the world. Grass also demonstrates what rhizomes do; namely, they reach, link, blend and grow together. It does not matter if different blends are sown together, or grow at different rates, as rhizomes they will still attach, weave and claim surface and territory over time – echoing the very principles Deleuze and Guattari imbue in their own conceptualization of rhizome. Yet this literal interpretation and exemplification of rhizome only flirts with what Deleuze and Guattari are offering in their thinking. To take up their invitation, as repeated by Massumi, and weave their theory of the rhizome into another melody, I want to consider use of moving images and moving image experience within the context of Bion's containment a little further.

If we include Bion's theory of thinking within the remit of the rhizome, it is possible to introduce a series of challenges and reversals; an awareness grows on the importance of tension across time, territory and surface. In terms of time, rhizomes work in a circular motion, they are anachronistic, non-hierarchical and repetitive, yet not replicative – a "rhizome has no beginning or end; it is always in the middle, between things, interbeing, *intermezzo*" (Deleuze and Guattari 2014: 25). Rhizomes therefore may not always be productive in terms of emotional experience, but they may speak to the recursive affect that circulates within traumatic experience. Memories from long ago can have incredible impact on our current state of being, yet affect us just as strongly as when first experienced. We can repeat bodily responses to anxious or traumatic memories even if we are no longer in those moments. We can watch films and be aware of intertextual references without being disoriented and which contribute to the meaningfulness of the experience. In terms of territory, rhizomes facilitate links that are "detachable, connectable, reversible, modifiable, and [have] multiple entryways and exits and its own lines of flight" (2014: 21). As surfaces, rhizomes are a way for us to think about the gaps and the in-between aspects of our moving image experience. Deleuze and Guattari further view the rhizome as a plateau, "any multiplicity connected to other multiplicities by superficial underground stems in such a way as to form or extend a rhizome" (2014: 22). These rhizomatic presentations parallel Bion's theory of thinking as creative, dreaming and adaptive – particularly with regard to the necessity of being able to tolerate frustration. To recall, if we can bear frustrating emotional experience, and are (unconsciously) willing to think elements that are frustrating (time), we can begin to think them, contain them (territory); such mental activity establishing an internal map from which we then build our apparatus for thinking (surface).

There is no certitude attached to the rhizome or the idea of rhizomatic action. Embedded within the list of principles that Deleuze and Guattari offer is the paradoxical invitation that to embrace the idea of the rhizome, you must break with the offered principles. In addition to rhizomes working as a series of linked possibilities, without a beginning or end and with no linearity or hierarchy, there is the quality of 'decentered cohesion', meaning that in order to posit what might work as a rhizome requires a displacement – to put it another context in order for it to be examined or thought of differently. This makes the actuality of the rhizome elusive and resistant to prescription. Nevertheless, let us persist.

Containment

What is it to be contained within moving image experience? In addition, how might a concept specifically designed for psychoanalytic practice offer fresh perspective for moving image experience? Bion's container-contained model and container function, like Deleuze's and Guattari's rhizome, are not to be interpreted as concrete terms or prescriptive theories. We cannot let ourselves fall into the trap of thinking we know what they mean definitively, or think that they work as concrete methods across all affective, sensuous experience. As discussed in Chapter 6, Bion used symbols ♂ and ♀ to address the difficulty of using words to describe an affective and ineffable process. He believed that symbols would avoid the sticky connotations already associated with 'container' and 'contained' (curious then that he chooses two gender symbols that have arguably the *stickiest* connotations, save perhaps in Western culture the crucifix and swastika). That said, the symbols convey the intention of his theory of containment and the container function, which is to link emotion to thought, sensory data to felt experience.

Within Bion's model, the term container is said to allow thoughts to be processed so that they can be dreamed and in the process of dreaming, the painful elements can be thought/felt in a non-threatening, productive environment. Duncan Cartwright has differentiated the container-contained model from the container function, which he sees as representing "an area of mind or mental connection that attempts to find ways of tolerating underdeveloped psychic content and emotions so that they can be understood" (2009: 5), to which I add 'dreamed'. Bion offers little in the way of describing how containment works in analysis; he spends more time outlining types of containment instead (1970: 95).[2] In part, Bion's lack of description on how to effect containment fits into his reticence to prescribe or author any psychoanalytic concept. All of his ideas and notions were to be tools that helped with clinical technique, and on this note we can appropriate the model of container-contained and the container function within the agenda Bion intended – using it as a tool to study experience with moving images.

On the one hand, viewing moving images as a container can help to think about how some cinematic experience works specifically to avoid confronting difficult thoughts and emotions, what Cartwright calls 'idealizing the container' (2010: 6). In essence, these moving images require very little from its audience in the way of participation, avoiding any confrontation with overt difficult emotions or psychic pain. On the other hand, the container function is a linking experience, the mating of thoughts to a thinking structure through affective experience and therefore transcends the very literal or specific psychic link between two people (or indeed between spectator and the immersive film world). Instead it offers a sense of capacity and receptivity that may eventuate over time; where images that are continuously projecting and being introjected, form a 'fragile mental connection' (Cartwright 2010: 8), a 'becoming'. This specific action of linking is a further nodal point where Bion ideas merge with Deleuze and Guattari's rhizome. Whilst linking is often viewed as a way to connect and relate objects, for these authors, the notion of linking embedded within containment and rhizome respectively, is also about the activity and affect-object reciprocity (Tomkins 1962) of thinking. How well we do this (or not) is what Bion referred to as 'learning from experience' which was discussed at length at the start of this book. In a sense, this 'learning from experience' is misleading, as it seems to suggest that we avoid pain or mistakes made in the past. However, Bion's 'learning from experience' was aimed at the recognition of a thinking pattern, much like how Deleuze and Guattari's rhizome is argued to work as a map that must be produced.

Containment, as a model viewed in terms of moving image experience, permits us to consider our working with moving images as a technique of processing everyday life into bearable experience. It is a model that works best when regarded as tool to address the relationship between audience and moving image, that is, it abstracts the overall experience with moving images within affective and sensuous terms. Regarding the container function, the receptivity within spectatorship is foregrounded, offering a purpose to our watching of films and a (psychoanalytic) rationale for affective response. Very literally, the spectator receives the projection of images and introjects them, but more broadly, this application of Bion's model helps to think about Tomkins's freedom of affect mentioned earlier, that is the motivation within spectatorship. Third, containment is best conceived as a way of thinking about the overall interaction within moving images, where only after the 'use' can we reflect and dream the experience to psychically grow. Containment is a theoretical model that identifies the cinematic field and the intersubjective receptivity relevant to the experience of moving images (the object use of moving images) but it must be noted that within Bion's theory, the container is unconscious material that can never be represented or known.

Ferro's view that the baseline of projective identification act as the engineer of reverie, is a key element within Bion's container-contained model; it being an activity that attempts to manage anxiety (in the best scenarios), but also as a management of appetite and expectation. In infant experience, the container-contained is observed through breastfeeding (or bottle equivalent) and the infant's mouth. In terms of affect, containment is a way for us to understand object use in terms of relationships between tolerance, satisfaction, frustration and growth. In the psychoanalytic experience, containment is said to happen through the transference. These emotional links, between a container and what is contained, cannot always be made or be sufficient, or perhaps even thought. In terms of containment as a rhizomatic activity, the trace cannot always be formed between analyst and analysand; or for film and media – between spectator and moving image. Let us turn to *Boyhood*, discussed below as an example of both a cinematic rhizome in form, content and container function regarding moving image experience.

Boyhood

The production of *Boyhood* took place over 11 years, lending itself on purely technical merit to the idea of rhizomatic filmmaking, being formed of embodied time, territory and surface in ways that differ from almost all other practices of filmmaking. Filmed between May 2002 and October 2013, *Boyhood* comes together as a film through a series of ruptures of time and lived experience. The seamless editing between ages and stages of Mason Jr.'s (Ellar Coltrane) childhood emphasize the evolution of time in Linklater's film as experience that is both felt and thought. Deleuze and Guattari write that a "rhizome may be broken, shattered at a given spot, but it will start up again on one of its old lines, or on new lines" (2014: 9), and *Boyhood* reflects this rhizomatic quality with respect to its treatment of age and time through each of its characters.

Boyhood follows the life of Mason, his sister Samantha (Lorelei Linklater), and mother Olivia (Patricia Arquette) – a low income, split Texan family with shared emphasis given to Mason's experience of childhood and Olivia's experience of motherhood. Linklater uses time in a highly segmented, territorializing and deterritorializing manner, as time is split into stages and specific sections of Mason's and Olivia's lives, which feel mnemonic and nostalgic in tone. The events within each specific age appears secondary to the characters' own respective aging and the traces of their experiences shown in each stage of Mason's childhood. *Boyhood* asks the audience to hold both the ages of Mason and Olivia in their minds, and equally let them go at the same time. As witnesses to Mason's childhood, we view his ages embedded within each stage that develops. We see the 6-year-old Mason in the 10- and 11-year-old Mason that experiences difficulties and trauma, such as the alcoholic abuse from his step-father Bill (Marco Perella) and the traumatic haircut he enforces on Mason; we witness Mason's disappointment in his parents, particularly his feeling let down by her choice(s) to remarry: "Why'd you have to marry him? He's such a jerk". It becomes inevitable that we view the later 15-, 16-, 17-, 18-year-old Mason as affected by such lived experience, all his past ages embedded within him to determine each evolving present. This is Linklater's territorializing and deterritorializing of time as a narrative component and affective resonance. It is through Mason Jr. where we see the relativity of age as time and age as space between the film's cast, also resonating within the audience, and their own lived experiences as potential resonances of their own childhood experiences.

Olivia seems to articulate this at the end of the film when she says:

> You know what I'm realizing? My life is just gonna go, like that! This series of milestones. Getting married, having kids, getting divorced, the time that we thought you were dyslexic, when I taught you how to ride a bike, getting divorced AGAIN, getting my masters degree, finally getting the job I wanted, sending Samantha off to college, sending YOU off to college. . . . You know what's next? Huh? It's my fuckin' funeral! . . . I just thought there would be more.

This is one of the ways that Linklater's film demonstrates an abstract rhizome of decalcomania, by evoking a transference of memory of time, experience and reflection within the film's story to the personal and individual memory of the cinematic spectator. Linklater uses the growing up of both Mason Jr. and Olivia (biologically and experientially) to deterritorialize time. Each progression of either Mason Jr. or Olivia contain traces of their former selves, appearing affected by the transfer from ages 6, 7, 8 etc. to 10, 11, 12, 13 etc. Another example of the deterritorialization of time is event in the traces of Mason Jr.'s former selves present, and indicative in the sadness, hopefulness, disillusion and creativity of the 18-year-old Mason at college that we are finally shown (there is poetry in his choosing to study photography).

Linklater suggests that we do not leave our childhood, just as our childhood never leaves us (the unfinished business of childhood, as Freud put it). This is summed up in Mason's final conversation with his new friend, Nicole (Jessie Mechler), where she reflects that in order to seize the moment, 'the moment seizes us'. In this reflection, viewers are presented with the message that time itself, even in its passing and in the marks that it leaves as it passes, is rhizomatic. There is no imitating or reproducing of former selves, as Deleuze and Guattari (2014: 10) write:

> something else entirely is going on: not imitation at all but a capture of code, surplus value of code, an increase of valence, a veritable becoming. . . . Each of these becomings brings about the deterritorialization of one term and the reterritorialization of the other; the two becomings interlink and form relays in a circulation of intensities.

No character in the film exemplifies Mason's boyhood specifically, rather all members of the family and their experiences go into the construction of what can be recognized as the 'collective assemblage of enunciation' (2014: 7) with regard to childhood in general. If any one of the character's experiences had changed, then the rhizome of the film's narrative changed with it. Linklater's film understatedly emphasizes the critical importance of interlinked lived experience in the relationships between parents and children, and the negotiations of their inner and external environments.

How does the film effect containment? At a very basic level *Boyhood* offers a revisiting to childhood; and containment, as argued by Bion, involves a return to the difficult, and often painful experiences (not known but felt) in our lives. Containment, when successful, shows us that there is (at least) a relational two-step process between lived experience and thoughts that can be dreamed, which may evolve as psychic growth. The notion of 'being embedded' with moving images is a linking of intersubjective experience, where our interactive spectatorship takes place within the 'cinematic' field, making the object use of the moving image possible material for new emotional growth. A potential of cinema, television and other moving image experience is to offer its audiences story-worlds which make the impossible possible, put in Bionian terms, the unthinkable thinkable. The projective identification that occurs within moving image experience permits the thinking of thoughts that are not able to be thought by the spectator or audience on their own. The containing function of moving image experience therefore, exists within the intersubjective cinematic field that requires participation between two or more minds. The significance of the *moving* image regarding the container function is its recursive and shared characteristics – the images must be watched (and are often watched) by more than one person, and rely on the repeated form of filmmaking, in genre and narrative, to be meaningful. For example, in the time it takes to watch a film, a television program, or play a video game, the spectator may be able to bear unthinkable experience whilst at the same time, use the containing function to process (dream) difficult, painful thoughts. 'Being embedded' then, is a term that might speak to the containment that occurs within moving image experience.

Emphasizing the study of experience *with* moving images throughout the book has been intentional, as I have aimed to think of cinema and media as dynamic systems that involve encounters between minds and bodies (Cartwright 2010: 12). A core concern of the book has been to consider how our working with moving images occurs at multiple levels of experience, (unconscious and conscious), and this chapter has discussed how such affective experience often incurs the rhizomatic principle of decalcomania, that is, traceable and transferential affect which is non-linear and projective. Sensoria within moving image experience creates new 'fractal' surfaces that, over time, might lead to the development and growth of new psychic territory.

Notes

1 'Becoming' is another key term that Deleuze and Guattari have in common with Bion, particularly in terms of their shared interest and intention with 'becoming' being about affect (that is, intensities), described via 'lines' once again appropriating metaphors of geometric form to describe relationships. Most significantly for this chapter, 'becoming' is a concept for all three authors that is non-representational and beyond experience. There are many interesting points of commonality between the immanence of Deleuzian and Guattarian 'becoming' and Bion's concept of O.
2 For a discussion on the three types of containment – commensal, symbolic and parasitic see Bion (1970); for clinical commentary see Symington and Symington (2008: 56–7); and as applied to film theory, see Ambrósio Garcia (2017: 45).

References

Ahmed, S. (2010). Happy Objects. In Gregg, M. and Seigworth, G.J. (eds.) *The Affect Theory Reader*. Durham: Duke University Press.
Ambrósio Garcia, C. (2017). *Bion in Film Theory: The Retreat in Film*. Abingdon, UK: Routledge.
Bain, A. (1864). *The Senses and the Intellect*. London: Longman and Co.
Bainbridge, C. (2012). Psychotherapy on the Couch: Exploring the Fantasies of in Treatment. *Psychoanalysis, Culture and Society*, 17, pp. 153–168.
Bainbridge, C., Ward, I. and Yates, C. (2014). *Television and Psychoanalysis: Psycho-Cultural Perspectives*. London: Karnac.
Bainbridge, C. and Yates, C. (2005). Cinematic Symptoms of Masculinity in Transition: Memory, History and Mythology in Contemporary Dilm. *Psychoanalysis, Culture and Society*, 10 (3), pp. 299–318.
Balcerzak, S. and Sperb, J. (eds.) (2012). *Cinephilia in the Age of Digital Reproduction*. New York: Columbia University Press.
Bion, W.R. (1959). Attacks on Linking. *International Journal of Psycho-Analysis*, 40, pp. 308–315.
Bion, W.R. (1962). *Learning From Experience*. London: Tavistock.
Bion, W.R. (1970). *Attention and Interpretation. A Scientific Approach to Insight in Psycho-Analysis and Groups*. London: Karnac Books.
Bléandonu, G. (1994). *Wilfred Bion: His Life and Works, 1897–1979*. Translated by C. Pajaczkowska. New York: Other Press.
Buchanan, I. (2007). Deleuze and the Internet. *Australian Humanities Review*, 43. www.australianhumanitiesreview.org/archive/Issue-December-2007/Buchanan.html (Accessed 19 January 2016).
Cartwright, D. (2010). *Containing States of Mind: Exploring Bion's Container Model in Psychoanalytic Psychotherapy*. Hove, East Sussex: Routledge.
Cartwright, L. (2008). *Moral Spectatorship: Technologies of Voice and Affect in Postwar Representations of the Child*. Durham: Duke University Press.
Civitarese, G. (2014). *The Necessary Dream: New Theories and Techniques of Interpretation in Psychoanalysis*. Translated by Ian Harvey. London: Karnac Books.
Colebrook, C. (2002). *Understanding Deleuze*. Crows Nest: Allen and Unwin.
De Valck, M. and Hagener, M. (2005). *Cinephilia: Movies, Love and Memory*. Amsterdam: Amsterdam University Press.
Deleuze, G. and Guattari, F. (2014). *A Thousand Plateaus: Capitalism and Schizophrenia*. Translated by B. Massumi. Minneapolis: University of Minnesota Press, 1987.
Ferro, A. (2009). *Mind Works: Technique and Creativity in Psychoanalysis*. Translated by P. Slotkin. London and New York: Routledge.
Gibbs, A. (2001). Contagious Feelings: Pauline Hanson and the Epidemiology of Affect. *Australian Humanities Review*, pp. xxx
Gibbs, A. (2013). Affect Theory and Audience. In Nightgale, V. (ed.) *The Handbook of Media Audiences*. Hoboken, NJ: Wiley-Blackwell.
Kuhn, A. (ed.) (2013). *Little Madnesses: Winnicott, Transitional Phenomena and Cultural Experience*. London: I.B. Tauris.
Marks, L. (2000). *The Skin of the Film: Intercultural Cinema, Embodiment, and the Senses*. Durham: Duke University Press.
Massumi, B. (2014). Introduction. In Deleuze, G. and Guattari, F. (eds.) *A Thousand Plateaus: Capitalism and Schizophrenia*. Translated by B. Massumi. Minneapolis: University of Minnesota Press.
Ogden, T. (2004). On Holding and Containing, Being and Dreaming. *International Journal of Psychoanalysis*, 85 (6), pp. 1349–1364.

Piotrowska, A. (2015). *Embodied Encounters: New Approaches to Psychoanalysis and Cinema*. London and New York: Routledge.
Rosenbaum, J. (2010). *Goodbye Cinema, Hello Cinephilia: Film Culture in Transition*. Chicago: The University of Chicago Press.
Sandler, P.C. (2005). *The Language of Bion: A Dictionary of Concepts*. London: Karnac Books.
Sedgwick, Eve Kosofsky and Frank, A. (2003). Shame in the Cybernetic Fold: Reading Silvan Tomkins. In *Touching Feeling: Affect, Pedagogy, Performativity*. Durham and London: Duke University Press.
Soler, C. (2014). *Lacan: The Unconscious Reinvented*. London: Karnac Books.
Symington, N. and Symington, J. (2008). *The Clinical Work of Wilfred Bion*. London and New York: Routledge.
Tomkins, S. (1962). *Affect, Imagery, Consciousness, Volume 1, The Positive Affects*. New York: Springer.
Yates, C. (2010). *Emotion: New Psychosocial Perspectives*. Basingstoke: Palgrave Macmillan.
Yates, C. (2015). *The Play of Political Culture, Emotion and Identity*. Basingstoke: Palgrave Macmillan.

Filmography

Boyhood (2014). Directed by Richard Linklater.

INDEX

Abraham, Karl 35
acousmatic sound 58–59, 61
aesthetic experience 16; affect and 49; function within cinema 63–64; irregular turning of 59–61
affect: compositional aspect of 26–29; emotional and aesthetic experience 49; theory about transmission of 29–30; Tomkins's theory 49, 162, 167–168
Affect, Imagery, Consciousness (Tomkins) 7, 27, 155n2, 167–168
Agutter, Jenny 57, 66n5
Ahmed, Sara 168
A.I. (artificially intelligent) 153–155
alpha elements 44
alpha function 3, 107; dream and 10; term 8; theory of functions and 128; transferential moment 41
Ambrósio Garcia, Carla 12
analytic field: metaphor for dreaming 69–70; metaphor within 79–83; within film and media studies 70–71
analytic field theory: Barangers' 80–81, 86n1; examining relations 72–73; and field theories of cinema 83–85; idea of shared journey 80; metaphor of 75; model of 72; transference in spectatorship 72
Antonioni, Michelangelo 19–20, 137, 145–149
Arendt, Hannah 13, 19, 115, 125–129
Armstrong, John 5–6
Arnheim, Rudolf 147

Arquette, Patricia 173
Art as Therapy (de Botton and Armstrong) 5–6
Attention and Interpretation (Bion) 137, 140, 160, 169
Australian outback, *Rabbit-Proof Fence* (film) 122–125

Bain, Alexander 164
Bainbridge, Caroline 137, 154–155
Baranger, Madeline 80
Baranger, Willy 80
Barthes, Roland 71, 145
basic assumption group mentality 29–30, 37–38
Baudry, Jean-Louis 71
Bazin, André 147
becoming: concept of 175n1; forming fragile mental connection 172; term 160
Being and Appearance 125
being embedded: aimless passing through dreaming 64–66; *Boyhood* (film) 173–175; container-contained model 130, 161–163; containment in moving image experience 171–173; decalcomania and 166–169; description of 128; experience of 44–45, 90; groups and memory 105–106; negative capability 169–170; rhizome and 165–166; term 4–7; theory of thinking and cinema spectatorship experience 163–164; time, territory and surface 170–171

Berdal, Ingrid Bolsø 153
Bergstein, Avner 49
binocular vision, Bion's concept of 32–33, 37–38, 45n7, 146
Bion, Wilfred: concept of binocular vision 32–33, 37–38, 45n7, 146; concept of O 19, 138–141, 148, 154–155; linking emotion and thought 125–129; theory of dreaming 64–66; theory of thinking 1–6, 8, 13–17, 20, 113
Bléandonu, Gérard 3, 41
Blow-Up (film) 19–20, 137, 145–149
Bollas, Christopher 6, 19
Boyhood (film) 160, 173–175
Brennan, Teresa 7
Brown, William 77, 79
Buchanan, Ian 165

Caldwell, Lesley 150
cartography 164, 165
Cartwright, Duncan 171
Cartwright, Lisa 12, 39, 139
Casebier, Allan 18, 112, 116–120
Casetti, Francesco 70–71
Chion, Michel 58
Christie, Julie 61
cinema: analytic field theory for 69–70; collective memory 92; as container-contained 129–130; field theories of 83–85; function of aesthetic experience 63–64; intuitive movement of reverie 51–53; life expressing life 127; viewing as retreat 162
cinema-machine, Metz's definition of 84
Citizen Kane (film) 10
Civitarese, Giuseppe 79–83
Coënarts, Maartin 73
cognitive film studies, psychoanalytic thinking and 7–14
Colebrook, Claire 165
collective memory: cinema playing 92; of family group 99–103; *Force Majeure* (film) 99–103; Halbwachs's theory on 91–92; *Prisons Memory Archive* (documentary) 103–105; social frameworks and 96, 109; *see also* dreaming; memory work
Coltrane, Ellar 173
concept of O 3, 31, 136–137; Bion's 19, 138–141, 148, 154–155; transformation and 139–140; transformation and sensory experience 160–161
connection-as-displacement 77
consciousness: act of 119; 'being-an-issue' 124, 125; lived reality and experiences 121–122; phenomenological film theory 114–116
container-contained 3, 42, 43; cinema as 129–130; model formation 161; projective identification as 161–162, 172–173; theory of 36; in *Unforgiven* (film) 130–133
containment: Bion's theory of 163; *Boyhood* (film) 175; idea of 78; moving image experience 171–173; types of 175n2
Cooper, Sarah 85

Dasein state-of-being 124
Dawood, Shezad 147
daydream/daydreaming 48–50, 110
de Botton, Alain 5–6
decalcomania 20, 164; abstract rhizome of 174; being embedded and 166–169; of moving image experience 168–169; *Oxford English Dictionary* definition 167; practice of 169
Deleuze, Gilles 13, 160
depressive position 35, 36–37
Derrida, Jacques 82
Dewell, Robert 78
displacement; condensation and 75–76, 107, 129; Freud's theory of 75, 107; of national identity 57, rhizome requiring 171; role of 74
Don't Look Now (film) 16, 48, 56, 61–64
dream: films 64; memories and 106–108; as process 16; recollection of 108
dreaming 16–17; being embedded through 64–66; Bion's theory of 54–55; container-contained model 129–130; founding principle of mental functioning 70; relevance of Bion's revision on 108–110; reverie and 53–55, 74–75; waking thoughts 41–42, 74–75; wandering as 53–55
dream work: conscious and unconscious thought in 110; dream metaphor and 74–75; Freud's notion of 18, 65, 75–76, 129; Freud's theory of 106–107; working of dream as 95
Dufrenne, Mikel 106

Eastwood, Clint 130
Eco, Umberto 82
Ego and the Id, The (Freud) 34–35
Elements of Psychoanalysis (Bion) 11
Elliot, R. K. 105
Elsaesser, Thomas 13

embed: definition 4; embedded experience 127–128; embedded *vs* embodied 14–20
embeddedness 4–5, 11, 17, 30; concept of 15; sensation of 50, 164; of dreaming 83
embedded spectator 71, 85–86
embedding: action of 4; atmosphere 139; collective memory and 94; concept of 10; dreaming as 85, 91, 97, 160; method of 30, 166; relating and 14, 51
Embodied Metaphors in Film, Television and Video Games (Fahlenbrach) 77
emotional experience 16, 18; affect and 49; basis for satisfaction 40; in film theory 7–14; group 91–92; links as 116; term 29, 46n8; transmission of affect and 29–30
epoché 115, 133n4
Eugeni, Ruggero 75–76
experience: phenomenological film theory 114–116; reversible intentionality 120–122; world of appearances 115, 126–127
experience of emotions 39
Experiences in Groups (Bion) 9, 17, 25, 32, 93–98

Fahlenbrach, Kathrin 73
fearful orientations to reality 29
Ferro, Antonino 2, 79–83
field theory/theories: analytic, and cinema 83–85; Baranger 80–81; conceptions of 69; concept of play 82–83
Film and Phenomenology (Casebier) 117
Film and the New Psychology (Merleau-Ponty) 123
Film Structure and the Emotion System (Smith) 11
film theory 12, 14; cognition and emotions 7–14; metaphor and 1970s theory and beyond 71–79; perception and expression 18; phenomenology in 112–114; use of metaphor 70
Film Theory (Elsaesser and Hagener) 13
Film Worlds (Yacavone) 14
Forbidden Planet (film) 58
Force Majeure (film) 17, 91–93; memory work and memory texts 99–103
Forces of Destiny (Bollas) 139
Foresti, Giovanni 2
Frank, Adam 7, 25
free association, reverie and 53, 66n3
Freud, Sigmund 2–3; dream work 64–65; revision of ego 39–40
Freudian-Lacanian methodology 11–12

frustration: capacity to tolerate 40–45; theory of thinking 39–40

gaze 13, 55; direction of 119, 121; film effects 146–149, 152; reverie and 168; theories of 80–81, 83
Gondry, Michel 66n7
Green, André 12
Grotstein, James 145
group: Bion's experiences in 93–98; experience 91–92; *Force Majeure* (film) 99–103; immersion and being embedded with 105–106; mentality 96–98, 110n4; *Prisons Memory Archive* (documentary) 103–105; task of the 98–99
Group Psychology and the Analysis of the Ego (Freud) 94
Guattari, Felix 13, 160
Gulpilil, David 57, 66n5

Hagener, Malte 13
Hagman, George 69
Halbwachs, Maurice 13, 17, 91
Hansen, Mark 84–85
Hate (H) 116, 119
Heath, Stephen 72
Hemmings, David 20, 146
hinge mechanism 28, 32, 34, 41
Hinshelwood, Robert 32
Hockley, Luke 15
hooks, bell 80
Hopkins, Anthony 154
Husserl, Edmund 19, 115, 116–120

Imaginary Signifier, The (Metz) 74, 81
immersion: in cinema 14, 82, 94; embedded spectator 85–86; groups and memory 105–106
Inception (film) 10, 11, 64
Ingarden, Roman 116
intentionality 119; concept of 18; phenomenological film theory 114–116; reversible 128; reversible, in *Rabbit-Proof Fence* (film) 120–122
Interpretation of Dreams, The (Freud) 75
intersubjective aesthetic experience 5, 16, 48, 69–73, 77, 82, 86
intersubjective field 16, 29, 34; being embedded and 26–29; Bionian model 77; of cinematic experience 15–16; concept of 86; definition 45n2; moving image experience 33, 35, 38; reverie and 163
intersubjectivity 3, 100, 162, 165; of analyst and analysand 45n2, 56; of emotion

86n6; notion of 12, 69–70; reverie and 83; term 73
invariants: definition 142; importance in transformation 141–145

Jakobson, Roman 75
James, Anthony 131
Jemstadt, Arne 153
Johnson, Mark 76
Jones, Amelia 146–149
Joy, Lisa 152

Katz, Wendy 72
Keats, John 169
Kickasola, Joe 77
Klein, Melanie 6, 12–14, 24–25, 34–39
Knowing (K) 31, 116, 119, 126, 137
Kravana, Peter 73
Kristeva, Julia 79
Kuhn, Annette 18
Kuhnke, Johannes 99
Kurosawa, Akira 64

Lacan, Jacques 128–129
Laine, Tarja 14
Lakoff, George 76
language 26, 36, 57, 104; cinema and media 141–142, 144; experience of being embedded 125–128; Indigenous 123; in moving images 150, 152; structure 12, 76, 133; term 133–134n6
learning from experience 24, 31–32, 45, 110, 113, 136, 172
Learning from Experience (Bion) 1, 2, 5, 30, 112
lebenswelt (lifeworld) 116, 118
Lebovici, Serge 74
Leys, Ruth 27
Life of the Mind, The (Arendt) 115
Linklater, Lorelei 173
Linklater, Richard 160, 173–174
Little Madnesses (Kuhn) 138, 150
López-Corvo, Rafael 32, 142
logic of emotionality 8
Love (L) 116, 119; love-hate conflict 35

magical thinking 33, 110n4; idea of 78; seduction of 137; spectator experiences encouraging 44; term 30–31
Make It Big (Dawood) 147
Marks, Laura 18, 159
masculinity 99, 101, 130–132
Mason, Hilary 61
Massumi, Brian 138

Matania, Clelia 61
materiality 19, 58, 120; of film 71, 73–74; of group 97; term 104
Mechler, Jessie 174
Meillon, John 57
Meltzer, Donald 64
memories: dreams and 106–108; *see also* collective memory
memory work: documentary of group interrelationships 103–105; family group 99–103; immersion and being embedded with group 105–106; Kuhn's concept of 18, 100
me-ness 97
mental functioning 4; binocular vision 32–33; dreaming 43–44, 70; experience of emotion 39; id in 35; infant's early 37, 41; need for truth 31; principles of 4, 5, 25–26, 33–35; reverie in 16, 48–50; thought development 33, 39, 41, 127
Merleau-Ponty, Maurice 19, 51, 81, 115
metaphors 25; analytic field as 69–71, 76, 79–86, 86n1, 91, 94; of archaeology 70; in cinematic encounter 76; concept of 70; of dead body 148; definition of 45n2; of digestion 75; as displacement 74, 77; of dream 74; of field 83–86, 86n1, 150; film theory 1970s and beyond 71–79; function of 17, 70, 73–76, 78, 82; geometric figures as 139, 142–144, 160–161, 175n1; intermediary structure of 76; linking experiences 125–128; metonymy and 75–76; Picasso painting 142–143; of skin 73; space-as-a-physical-container 78–79; walkabout as 57
Metz, Christian 11
Momigliano, Luciana Nissim 82
Monaghan, Laura 122
Moral Spectatorship (Cartwright) 12
moving image: analytic field theory for 69–70; Antonioni's *Blow-Up* 145–149; being embedded in 163–164; being embedded within and between 14–15; Bion's concept of O 138–141; intersubjective aesthetic experience 73; invariance in transformation of 141–145; phrase 24; as time-based art 6; as transitional and transformational object 150–152; as wandering of mind 51–52; *Westworld* (HBO television) 152–155
moving image experience 45, 48, 136; affect within 33–34, 38–39; analytic field and 70–71, 74; being embedded and 127, 137, 140, 160–164; in cinema and media

90; concept of O and 140–141, 164; container-contained as model within 43; containment in 171–173; decalcomania of 166–169; dreaming and 64–65, 74–75, 109–110; entrainment within 28; intentionality and 121; memory and 93, 99; phenomenology to investigate 112–113, 133; phrase 24; in *Rabbit-Proof Fence* 124; reverie and 51–53, 55–57, 60, 70, 161; study of 1–7, 11, 15–16, 29–30, 42, 44, 94, 159; task of group 98–99; theory of thinking as psychoanalytic model for 159–160; thought and 126
Mulvey, Laura 11, 80
Münsterburg, Hugo 114
Mythologies (Barthes) 145

narratology 74, 75, 82
negative capability 169–170
Nolan, Christopher 10
Nolan, Jonathan 152
Northern Ireland, conflict of 103–104
Northfield Military Hospital 93, 94
Noyce, Philip 118; *Rabbit-Proof Fence* (film) 120–122

object: affect-object reciprocity 155n2, 162, 172; analytic 56, 58, 83, 114; of art 91; capacity to use 139; creative 63–64; cultural 104–105, 138; everyday 64, 116; evocative 153; external 20, 35, 64, 137, 149; good and bad 34–36; moving image as 150–152; object relations approach 12, 14, 145, 159; object-relations psychoanalysis 6–7, 14, 24–25, 34; object-relations theory 12, 15, 20, 36, 81; real 116, 118–119; term 19–20; transformational 6, 19, 137, 138, 145, 150–152, 153, 155; transitional 14, 49, 137, 138, 150–152, 154, 155
Ogden, Thomas 2–4
oneness 97
On the Theory of Anxiety and Guilt (Klein) 35

Pahl, Katrin 8
Parables for the Virtual (Massumi) 138
paranoid-schizoid position 35, 36, 37
Pasolini, Pier Paolo 33
Passionate Views (Plantinga and Smith) 7
Perella, Marco 173
phenomenology: Casebier's in-between qualities 116–120; experience, consciousness and intentionality 114–116; film and media studies 112–113; 'first generation' film- 112–113; Husserlian beginnings 116–120; investigating moving image experience 113–114; psychoanalysis and 128–129; seminal film- 112
Phillips, Adam 40
Picasso 141–142
Pigsty (film) 33, 45n7
Piotrowska, Agnieszka 6
Plantinga, Carl 7
play: children's 34–35, 62, 65; concept of, in field theory 82–83; culture and 45n8; free play 56, 58; of video games 141, 175
pleasure principle, Freud 3, 40–41
Porcile (Pasolini) 33
Prisons Memory Archive (documentary) 17, 92; collective memory 103–105
projection: Being and 124; conception within conscious 124–125; containment and 129, 172; of emotional experience 63, 76; linking 125; object use and relating 151; of reverie 51; unconscious 36; variation of transformation 144–145, 165
projective identification 9, 12; in affect theory 39; aggressive 38; baseline of 163, 172; being embedded and 20; concept of 38; excessive 41, 127; of container-contained model 130, 161–162, 172–173; Klein's 14, 34–39, 42, 80, 95, 129, 156n3, 161; positive 38; reverie and 54, 163; theory of 14, 37
psychoanalysis 1–2; Bionian 2, 5, 9, 26–27, 44, 53, 55, 72, 79, 86n1, 90, 108, 113, 118, 127, 133, 143, 159, 162, 164–166; classical 12, 25, 29, 44, 74, 79, 112, 147, 166; phenomenology and 128–129; relational 10, 12–13, 20; reorientation for film theory 24–25; wandering as reverie 53–55
psychoanalytic theory 1, 5, 7; of affect 39, 48, 160; of dreams/dreaming 44, 108, 129; of emotional experience 40, 69–72, 112–113, 159; in film and media studies 25–26, 29, 76, 86; of group experience 30; of instinct and drive 11; of object-relation 20, 34, 137; relational 13; of reverie 164
psychoanalytic thinking 2, 25; cognitive film studies and 7–14; object relations in 149
Psychosomatic (Wilson) 9, 27

Rabbit-Proof Fence (film) 118, 120–122, 122–125
Rashomon (film) 64
reality principle 3, 12, 40, 41
reverie 3; capacity to daydream 48–50; cinema in movement of 51–53; concept of 16, 74; definition of 163; psychoanalytic theory of 164; as space and rhizome 160–164; as spacings 59–61; term 48; in *Walkabout* (film) 55–57; wandering 49; wandering as 53–55
reversibility: of perception and expression 121, 132; term 120
rhizome 20; abstract, of decalcomania 174; concept of 160; configuration and mechanics of 165–166; reverie as space and 160–164; theory of thinking and 170–171; time, territory and surface 170–171
Richards, Angela 46n9
Rickman, John 93
Roeg, Nicolas 16, 56, 64
Rosen, Philip 71

Salter, Nicholas 61
Sampi, Everlyn 122
Sandler, P. C. 144–145, 163
Sansbury, Tianna 122
Santoro, Rodrigo 153
Sartre, Jean-Paul 124
satisfaction: frustration and 2, 6, 25, 31, 39–40, 134n8, 164, 173; thinking apparatus 39–40; tolerance and 164, 173; wandering 50–51
Saussure, Ferdinand de 71
Science of Sleep, The (film) 66n7
Second Thoughts (Bion) 25
Sedgwick, Eve Kosofsky 162
Senses and The Intellect, The (Bain) 164
Shadow of the Object, The (Bollas) 51
shock, Deleuze's notion of 84–85, 86n8
Silverstone, Roger 154–155
Smith, Greg M. 7
Sobchack, Vivian 13, 18
Sopranos, The (HBO television) 154
Sorfa, David 113
space: containment process 160–162; creative use of 154; groups and memory 96; mental 150, 161–162; metaphor of container 78–79; potential 150, 154–155; projected 145; of retreat 140; reverie as, and rhizome 160–164; space-field as process 79; time and 12, 51–52, 59–61, 63, 83, 120–121, 133, 142, 144, 167; unconscious space 106; wandering dreamed 55
spacings 17, 48, 50, 53; affect in *Don't Look Now* (film) 61–64; metaphor of 78–79; psychic 54–55; reverie as 59–61; term 59; in *Walkabout* 57
spectatorship 2–3; audience 104; cinematic 6, 13, 17, 18, 24, 27, 29, 175; containment and 162–163, 172; emotional experience of 140, 160; film 15, 17, 24, 70, 72, 117; intentionality of 121; motivation in 162–163; moving image 48; reverie and, in *Walkabout* 55–57; self-reflection in 132; theatre-going and film-going 114; theories of 25, 27, 29–30, 33, 76, 83, 86
Spitz, René 12
Stolen Generation 122
subjectivity 56–57, 60, 71, 73
Sutherland Donald 61
Symington, Joan 9
Symington, Neville 9

Taming Wild Thoughts (Bion) 49
television 175; as transitional object 154–155
Theories of Cinema 1945–1995 (Casetti) 70–71
theory of collective memory, Halbwachs's 17, 92, 106
theory of thinking: Bion's 1–6, 8, 13–17, 20, 113; capacity to tolerate frustration 40–45; capacity to use objects and 151; collective memory and 91; dreaming and 53, 74, 108; experience with moving images 15–16; Klein's projective identification and 34–39; linking to other minds 85, 93, 114; links as emotions 116; lived emotional experience and 69, 126, 162–164; metaphors and 70, 82; model for moving image experience 24–25, 159–160; rhizome and 165–166, 170–171; satisfaction and frustration 39–40; Tomkins' affect theory and 168; towards comprehensive meta-theory 25–34, 43, 98
'third way' of watching cinema 15
Thomson, Anna 131
Thousand Plateaus, A (Deleuze and Guatarri) 160, 166
Tomkins, Silvan 6, 12, 25, 26–27, 155n2
transcendental egological state 118
transferential poetics 26, 33, 34

transformation 128; concept of O and 139–140; importance of invariance in 141–145; moving image as object of 150–152; via concept of O 137
Transformations (Bion) 19, 77, 136, 141, 142–143
transitional object, television as 154–155; *see also* object
Turquet, Pierre 96

unconscious-conscious model 165
Unforgiven (film) 130–133

visual flashes 10

waking dream thought 10; Bion's 41–42, 44, 65; concept of 74–75; dreaming as 44; reverie as 66n3; unconscious 2, 16
Walkabout (film) 16, 48, 61, 64; reverie and spectatorship in 55–57; story of 57–59
wandering: definition 50; note on 50–53; as reverie 49, 53–55, 57; sequence of acousmatic sounds 58; VR technology 66n2; in *Walkabout* (film) 57–59
Webb, David Peoples 130
Western cinema, *Unforgiven* (film) 130–133
Westworld (HBO television program) 137, 151, 152–155
Wettegren, Clara 99
Wettegren, Vincent 99
Williams, Linda 75–76
Williams, Sharon 61
Wilson, Elizabeth 7, 26–28
Winnicott, D. W. 6, 13, 14, 34
Wood, Evan Rachel 153
Woolvett, Jaimz 131
work group mentality 29, 93–95, 97–98, 104
world of appearances 115, 126–127

Yacavone, Daniel 14, 92
Yates, Candida 137

Zittoun, Tania 150